THE RED BARON'S LAST FLIGHT

A MYSTERY INVESTIGATED

NORMAN FRANKS
&ALAN BENNETT

GRUB STREET • LONDON

This new updated edition paperback published in 2006 by
Grub Street
4 Rainham Close
London SW11 6SS

Copyright © Grub Street 2006
Text copyright © Norman Franks and Alan Bennett
Map artwork by Steve West

First published in hardback 1997

British Library Cataloguing in Publication Data
Franks, Norman L. R.
  The Red Baron's last flight: an in-depth investigation
  into what really happened on the day von Richthofen was
  shot down
  1. Richthofen, Manfred, Freiherr von, 1892-1918 – Death
  and burial 2. Fighter pilots – Germany – Death 3. World War,
  1914-1918 – Aerial operations, German
  I. Title II. Bennett, Alan, 1929-
  940.4'4943'092

ISBN 10: 1-904943-33-0

Printed and bound in Spain by Bookprint

CONTENTS

THIS BOOK IS DEDICATED
TO THE MEMORY OF

JOHN COLTMAN

SERGEANT BOMB AIMER, NO.115 SQUADRON RAF
KILLED IN ACTION 29 OCTOBER 1942

Acknowledgements

Canada. Dr Diane Bennett; Captain Frank R McGuire; the late Wing Commander Philip Markham; Theodore E Crayston (WW1 enthusiast); Dr J Segura MDCM McGill (pathologist); Dr D King MD (ballistic pathology); Gregory Loughton (RCMI, Toronto).

USA. Mrs D Page, (née Carisella); the late Pasquale J Carisella; the late Cole Palen (Old Rheinbeck WW1 Flying Museum); Dale M Titler; Dr J Moats MD (coroner).

England. Peter Franks LLB; Brad King BA (IWM, London); C Hunt (IWM, London); J McSherry (WW1 enthusiast); Mrs Hazel Orme (niece of the late John Coltman); Keith Rennles; Captain P Snook and Lt-Colonel D Storrie (Holts' Battlefield Tours); Mr A Twycross; Wing Commander P J Dye RAF.

Germany. Dr.-Ing Niedermeyer; Madame Niedermeyer.

France. Societé Les Amis des Moulins Picards.

Australia. Lambis Englezos; Russell Guest (aviation historian); Harold Edwards (centenarian, 3 AFC Squadron in 1918); S Denholm (ballistics section, Tasmanian Police); Bain P Simpson.

INTRODUCTION

Von Richthofen was far from a natural born pilot but he learned rapidly and became highly proficient. Over the years many people have tried to present him as a man who could not have achieved his 80 recorded victories without the support of his Jasta pilots, two of whom were supposedly detailed specifically to protect his tail while he made the kills. Also that he took credit for other pilots' claims or took a share in kills credited to the Jasta or Jagdgeschwader. This is far from the truth; such a man would not have been held in such high esteem by his men who would certainly have not celebrated his memory for many years after WW1 at the annual gathering of 'The Old Eagles'. Certainly he flew at the head of his unit and it was his job to make the first attack, but this was the German system, this is how the fighting units acted, it was nothing specially attributed to von Richthofen's personal way of doing things. He achieved his remarkable score in just 18 months of front line combat duty by pure ability and shooting expertise.

In the years between 1918 and 1997 there have been numerous attempts to resolve the contra–dictions, both apparent and real, concerning events that occurred on 21 April 1918: namely, the day that Rittmeister Manfred Freiherr von Richthofen was killed in action.

In the late 1920s, Floyd Gibbons, an American journalist, wrote what is still justly believed by many historians to be the best biography of the German air ace yet published, *The Red Knight of Germany*. To describe the events surrounding the death of the Baron he used information which was provided to him through 'official channels' (mostly Air Ministry in London) and which, by no fault of his own, he accepted in good faith.

He found that under the 50-year rule, records were sealed until 1969. The sealing had considerable justification for the files, which the present authors have examined, include personal character evaluations and so on. Air Ministry offered to arrange for someone to study the records and to provide Gibbons with a summary of the information requested. The information that he subsequently received unfortunately contained many serious errors. It is to be found at the Public Records Office, Kew, London, where it has been filed together with a resumé of an interview with Captain Roy Brown some years

later. (see Appendix D)

Prior to Gibbons' book being published it was serialised in the American magazine *Liberty*. His descriptions of the events of 21-22 April, in both the serial and the book, were, therefore, based upon flawed information. However, in some of the subsequent reprints of the book, a few of the errors were corrected, although one or two then introduced further errors. It appears that rather than consult the Air Ministry, Gibbons would have done much better to have travelled to Canada and interviewed Brown himself.

In short, Gibbons' honest, best efforts were seriously flawed from the outset and had a 'snowball effect' as a *Liberty* copywriter would later insert many of the flaws into his dramatisation of Brown's wartime service recollections which were published under the title *My Fight with Richthofen* in November 1927. By chance, an anonymous description of the air battle on 21 April 1918 was making the rounds at the time. It had more flaws in it than facts but read convincingly and phrases from it, which are recognisable, were also inserted. Doubtless this copywriter was doing his best to make the story interesting by filling in details which Brown had 'apparently' omitted. (See Appendix B)

The reader, furthermore, was led to believe that Brown himself had dictated every word. However, many years later the magazine editor admitted that the text had been 'heavily edited' prior to publication. (See Appendix E)

Following the diffusion around the world of the two stories, letters from participants and witnesses of the actual event began to reach magazines and newspapers. These called attention to serious omissions and alleged the inclusion of pure invention in both stories. Into the latter case fell the description, one given in great detail, of the roles played by two of 209 Squadron personnel, Major C H Butler (who did not lead his unit in the air that day), and Lieutenant F W J Mellersh, who had landed and was at Bertangles aerodrome at the time he was supposed to have been seen at the crash site.

People in many countries took an interest in the matter but unfortunately some newspapers, even as far away as Australia (who in any event knew some of their Anzac readers would have a vested interest), saw that the creation of a 'controversy' would increase circulation. In one known case, a key letter which would have settled one aspect once and for all, was, for that very reason, not published! On a private level, some people began corresponding with surviving participants and eye-witnesses. However, with the coming of WW2 interest understandably declined. The letters disappeared into filing cabinets and in many cases were later thrown away upon the death of the correspondent.

In recent years one such collection from the 1930s came to light in England and by a chain of lucky circumstances it was sent to the present authors for study. The collection has great importance as memories at that period had only to go back some 20 years and personal recollections were less likely to have unintentionally been influenced by the statements and writings of others post WW2. In addition the collection of information gathered over several decades by the late Bill Evans, who lived in Cleveland, Ohio until his death in 1996, also had interesting items in it.

The first collection, circa 1937-39, was assembled by a young man, John Coltman, who as an RAF navigator in WW2 was to die in action over Germany in 1942. His approach was to advertise in newspapers asking for people to write to him. One of those who replied, provided a definite location for Brown's aerial attack on the Baron. What was interesting about this collection was that the majority of contributors were not the same as those contacted by later authors such as Carisella and Titler.

Some time after WW2 three Americans took a similar interest and approach. After years of research, the late Pasquale (Pat) Carisella published *Who Killed the Red Baron* in 1969 and Dale Titler published *The Day the Red Baron Died* in 1970. The third author, Charles Donald, published several articles but no book. All three managed to contact participants and witnesses. The copious correspondence which followed filled filing cabinets with letters, and boxes with audio tapes. Donald and Carisella also achieved collections of artefacts ranging from the silk scarf, goggles and belt worn by von Richthofen at the time of his death, to pieces of Fokker Dr.I Triplane 425/17, factory serial number 2009, which he was flying. Pat Carisella's efforts included a journey to the field where the Baron's life ended and to the cemetery where he was first buried. He was even invited to the 50th Anniversary of 'The Old Eagles'; the surviving members of Jagdgeschwader Nr.I, known to the British by the nickname –'The Flying Circus'.

The origin of the name Flying Circus was that the unit's function was one of being able to move en-masse to various sectors behind the front in order to bring a large number of aeroplanes to support offensive or defensive actions. Reference has also been made to the aircraft colour schemes, but this is secondary to the main reason for the name.

To the present authors a most interesting point is the large number of witnesses who came forward or who were located and agreed to participate. Combining the five above-cited cases, the total is around 250, and the overlap, especially of Coltman's 1930s people, is quite small. The size of the various units of the British Fourth Army, commanded by General Sir Henry Rawlinson, which were stationed along the Morlancourt Ridge, on the Somme, is a matter of record. From this it can be adduced that the English and Australian soldiers, from private to general, who witnessed either some or the greater part of the action which culminated in the fall of the Baron, numbered approximately 1,000. This means that close to one quarter of the witnesses can be shown to have testified in private enquiries of which a record still remains.

For any one person standing on the ground to have followed the entire sequence of events without a gap of some sort was impossible. Wherever any observer stood, some part of the action was hidden from his particular view by cloud, mist or some geographical feature such as a forest and the Ridge itself. Probably the best overall view was obtained by one of Captain Brown's colleague flight commanders who watched the entire aerial action from above. A full account is provided in Dale Titler's book.

From the German side, three artillery observers and two fighter pilots from von Richthofen's staffel also saw significant parts of the fight. The new information obtained by the present authors confirms a statement made by one of the pilots which until now had not been given much credence.

The four private enquiries mentioned above concentrated on testimony from England, Germany, Australia and the USA. Another source, Canada, although occasionally mentioned, was not explored. The Canadian evidence was brought to our attention by Frank McGuire, a former historian at the Canadian War Museum in Ottawa. He kindly provided a number of Canadian newspaper clippings on Captain Brown. These revealed that about one year after Roy Brown had returned to Canada he officially inaugurated a

Richthofen exhibition in a military club in Toronto (which is still on display), and that for some time afterwards wherever he travelled on business he was greeted by the local press which rarely failed to enquire about his celebrated victory over Germany's top ranking air ace. Roy Brown's words were thereby recorded for posterity many times over and, when taken together with the text of the plaque which graced the exhibition, provide evidence which is 'old' by the calendar, but 'new' to most of the public, and of enlightening content.

An unintended off-shoot of checking the new information against old documents was the revelation of what appears to be the key to the puzzle as to why Roy Brown wrote TWO Combats in the Air reports, both dated 21 April 1918.

Using 1918 army maps and the new information, the present authors, one of whom has fifty years experience as an aircraft pilot, made a high level and a low level flight following the path down the River Somme taken by Lieutenant W R May as he was being chased by the Baron. The ground speed of the low level flight was the same as that of its 1918 predecessor. From this exercise the authors believe that they may have stumbled across the explanation of how the Baron came to violate his own strict rules against flying low down over enemy territory. During low level flying a pilot can easily lose track of his exact position and confuse one spot with another, or in the case of von Richthofen on the day in question, one partly demolished village and bend in a river with another.

The author-pilot also held long conversations with two people who have built and flown replica

Fokker Dr.I Triplanes. One of them was exact to the point of having a 110 hp LeRhône rotary engine and was flown about thirty times each year for several years by the late Cole Palen of New York. The flight characteristics of these aircraft, he learned, are considerably different from those which both he and the general public had been led to believe. The differences contribute to the misrepresentation of some of the eye-witness evidence. By design intent the Fokker Triplane did not have inherent stability. This made it extremely manoeuvrable in combat as it did not resist sudden changes of attitude desired by the pilot. The most obvious indication of this feature is the complete absence of wing dihedral. The disadvantage was that the Triplane would not automatically recover from any upset caused by strong wind or turbulence; the pilot had to restore it to level flight. This made the aircraft appear to be *unsteady* when flying through zones of turbulence. However, it was not a difficult aeroplane to fly, or land, provided that it was landed directly into the wind.

The following photographs serve to demonstrate how old information may not necessarily be well-known or even believed. The subjects are still in place today and may be seen by anyone who cares to do so. Two of them have been there for over 70 years and their condition bears heavily upon a correct understanding of the manner of the Baron's death. The reader is recommended to make a most careful examination of the photographs of the seat and the engine.

Right: The aluminium seat from von Richthofen's Fokker Triplane, on display at the RCMI, Toronto.

Below: The rear view of the line of 'bullet holes' in the seat – in reality the rivet holes which held the seat in place.

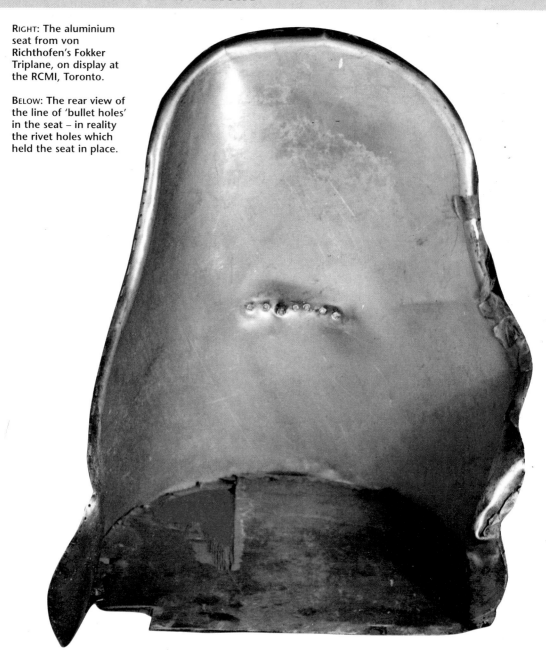

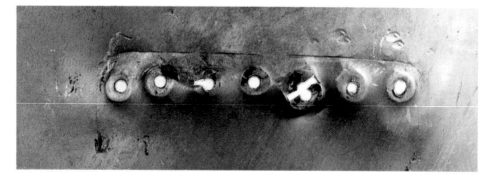

ABOVE: The Le Rhône engine from von Richthofen's Triplane 425/17. It was obviously not rotating at the time of impact.

RIGHT: Despite several references to the contrary, Manfred von Richthofen is buried in Wiesbaden Municipal Cemetery, in a family plot together with his brother Bolko, his sister Elisabeth and her husband. There is also a memoriam plaque to brother Lothar, who is buried at Schweidnitz together with their father. In the photo Madame Niedermeyer places a flower on Manfred's headstone.

FOREWORD

This framed plaque was displayed in 1920 at the Canadian Military Institute (now the Royal CMI) in Toronto, Canada on the occasion that Captain Roy Brown ceremonially inaugurated an exhibition which included his personal trophies from Fokker Dr.I 425/17. This was the aircraft in which Rittmeister Manfred Freiherr von Richthofen met his death on 21 April 1918 over the Somme Valley. The principal item exhibited was the aluminium seat from the Baron's Triplane.

On 10 November 1977, the Librarian and Curator of the Institute, Lieutenant-Colonel W G Heard, in reply to an enquiry from Captain Frank McGuire, a historian at the Canadian War Museum in Ottawa, exlained the origin of the plaque exactly as follows:

The caption [that] you have, was used when A R Brown donated the 'seat' to the R.C.M.I. It in turn was taken from an Ontario Board of Education grade 8 History of Canada textbook published by Coppe, Clarke and Company. The caption was dictated by Roy Brown.

> *This case contains the seat of the Fokker triplane of Baron M. Von Richthofen regarded as the most distinguished of the German airmen in the Great War, having 82 Allied planes to his credit. He was shot through the heart by Captain A. Roy Brown, D.S.C., and bar, Royal Air Force, of Carleton Place, Ont., in an air engagement over the Somme Valley, 21st April 1918. Captain Brown was flying after Richthofen, and while slightly above and behind him on his left rear brought him down by the shot mentioned.*
>
> *When the German triplane reached the earth, a claim was made by the crew of a machine gun, and also by an anti-aircraft battery, that they had fired the shot which ended the career of Richthofen. These claims, and the statement of Captain Brown were enquired into by a Board, and the evidence adduced by those firing being somewhat conflicting, the evidence of the surgeon who examined the dead and gallant airman, proved that the course of the bullet through the body showed that it could only have been fired from an aeroplane in the position of Captain Brown, and a finding was made accordingly.*
>
> *Captain Brown having been given this trophy and memento, has kindly deposited it in the Museum of The Canadian Military Institute .*

ABOVE: The Plaque in the Royal Canadian Military Institute, Toronto.
OPPOSITE PAGE: Rittmeister Baron Manfred Fr von Richthofen.

The clear and concise description of the position of Captain Brown's own Sopwith Camel aeroplane given on the plaque was confirmed in Brown's own statements during interviews when he visited various cities and towns throughout Canada on business in the 1920s. His words were reported in the local newspapers and are to be found later in this work.

The altitude and the map location at which the engagement took place are also described later, using information provided by Captain Brown and by some of the very few people who actually saw where this happened.

The total number of Allied aircraft officially credited to the Baron by the German High Command is now known to be 80, not the 82 as recorded on the plaque. Additional information on the composition of the 'board' is to be found in this book and appendices.

The Plaque is currently (1997) on display in the private museum of the Royal Canadian Military Institute in Toronto.

The authors will have cause to return to the wording of this plaque during their analysis of events.

PREFACE

The subject of the Red Baron's last flight is not a new one, we know that. Argument and discussion have taken place since the flight on the day in question. That we have something to say on the matter is obvious because of this book, but we are not just jumping on a band-wagon which people may believe had long ago lost most of its wheels.

In trying to look subjectively at the events of 21 April 1918 we have been mindful that many writers in the past have begun from the wrong premise and with already flawed information. Journalistic hypberbole (*hype* in present parlance) over the years did not help either. Therefore we have tried to be objective as well as subjective.

The two main authors who have already written excellent books on the subject, Dale Titler and the late Pat Carisella put everything they discovered into their well-read studies, but one problem in reading their books is that the sheer volume of the evidence presented can confuse a reader who is not deeply familiar with the subject. In other works people have gone into such great detail by putting in argument and counter-argument, claim and counter-claim, that one becomes almost punch-drunk and it is easy to lose the thread of whence such-and-such an argument started or whither it is leading.

Our approach was to start with a clean slate, put down what we believe are the salient facts and features of the occurrences and try, with common sense, to trace what either happened in fact, or where there is doubt, to apply a logical approach to suggest the most plausible answer. Where we are dealing with the trained, instinctive reactions of an aircraft pilot, the simplest answer is most likely to be the correct one.

Readers of this book may wonder why we have not mentioned many of the witnesses who have been approached over the years for their stories. In not mentioning them we do not imply that we discount their recollections, although it must be said that a number were quite obviously remembering an event, which while similar, was quite divorced from the one under review. Some, for instance, who insist the Baron was shot down soon after dawn or that his aeroplane had two wings, not three, must be confused about this incident or actually recalling another. Had it not been for the name of von Richthofen, most people on the ground would have had little reason even to remember the event at all, but it is quite natural for another, similar event, to be placed in the forefront of the memory so that they believe they must have seen the Baron's fall.

The Carisella and Titler books are so well known, and most serious WW1 air historians will have them on their book-shelves, that it will be easy to cross-reference these other participants' stories. We have had to mention several of the main characters in the drama as their statements are exceptionally important, or the events cannot be recorded faithfully without them. However, we mean no disrespect to those we have left out; we simply wish to refer the reader to these other books if they wish to read about them.

What we hope we have achieved is to portray as simple an overview of the 21 April 1918 as can be written down in order for the reader to follow easily and clearly the events of that day.

We believe that this new account will clear rather than further muddy the waters and earnestly feel that some interesting facts, especially concerning the pathology, and the logic we have applied to the story, will clarify much and at the same time put other things into proper perspective.

Norman Franks, Surrey, England
Alan Bennett, Grimsby, Ontario, Canada.

CHAPTER ONE
The Military Situation

Towards the end of March 1918 the Ludendorff Offensive (Operation Michael), Germany's final effort to end WWI favourably before the weight of American arms could be felt, had ceased to make progress after a successful start. The last assault made had attempted to capture the city of Amiens but on 30 March the Australian Imperial Force had halted the German advance ten miles short of its objective. By the next morning the Australian infantry was starting to run short of ammunition and might soon have been forced to withdraw. 3 AFC Squadron came to the rescue. Its RE8s flew over the Australian positions at an extremely low height and the observers tossed out small containers of ammunition from the rear cockpits to the troops. With pieces of old blankets tied with rope around the containers, sufficient ammunition survived the drop unscattered to save the situation.

Private Vincent Emery was one of the recipients of this largesse. According to his later testimony, he was down to the last two panniers of ammunition for his Lewis gun as the re-supply came from the skies. His helpers were able to gather enough undamaged drums for their gun to remain in action. This was the first known air-to-ground ammunition supply drop.

In early April the German High Command decided to renew the attempt to take Amiens. Troops and supplies were being concentrated in the area of the town of Le Hamel, situated just south of the Somme, 18 kilometres due east of Amiens. Although Le Hamel itself was protected from an Allied counter-attack by trenches, there was no continuous front line. The German forward defences were merely a series of strong points where their advance had been halted. The gaps between the strong points were linked by barbed wire and covered by machine-gun positions and trench mortars.

In the first fortnight of April the Allied forces had constructed a similar series of strong points. The gaps between them, from Corbie to Sailly-le-Sec, had mainly been filled by Vickers machine-gun crews who had dug their weapons into camouflaged and sheltered positions along the north bank of the Somme. This tall bank forms part of the south edge of the Morlancourt Ridge.

The Ridge itself, from a geographical point of view, is composed of the high ground between the River Ancre to its north and the Somme to the south.

In this Sector the main weapon, both for the Germans and the Allies, was artillery. It was one of the rare occasions in the First World War that the Allies enjoyed the strategic advantage of holding the high ground. Two Australian Field Artillery Batteries, the 53rd and the 55th, each equipped with six 18-pounder guns, were situated in a field just below the top of the Morlancourt Ridge on the Ancre (north) side of the crest, with the town of Bonnay behind them, just across the river. They were therefore completely hidden from the German artillery observers on the south side of the Somme, beyond Le Hamel.

The eyes of the two Australian Field Artillery Batteries were several carefully sited Forward Observation Posts (FOPs) whose crews were equipped with binoculars, a telescope and a field telephone. The best of the German observation positions was located in the church tower in the town of Le Hamel. The German observers enjoyed a panorama of Allied territory to their north and north-west which included an excellent view of the ruins of an old windmill silhouetted against the skyline some five kilometres away. This excellent German view of Allied territory was countered by the 53rd Battery FOP located in three short trenches near the ruined stone windmill. Being dug a little below the crest of a section of Ridge which jutted out to the south, the three trenches gave an overview of Le Hamel and German-held territory around it. The clearest and most easily recognised object was the Hamel church tower. The continued existence after the war of both the ruins and the tower, suggests a tacit *modus vivendi* between the opposing observers.

To the left of the windmill FOP trenches sat a small forest known as Welcome Wood, which blocked the view to the north-east but in that direction lay Allied-held territory. In a large field just behind the windmill (to the north of it) lay an Advanced Landing Ground (ALG) used recently by aircraft of 3 Squadron, Australian Flying Corps, whose main base was at Poulainville five miles

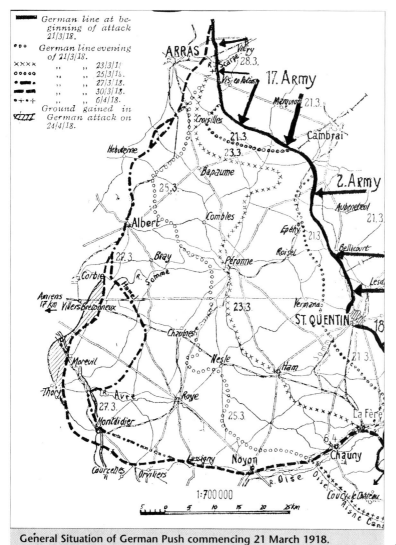

German line at beginning of attack 21/3/18.
German line evening of 21/3/18.
×××× ,, ,, 23/3/18.
○○○○○ ,, ,, 25/3/18.
•▬•▬ ,, ,, 27/3/18.
▬▬▬ ,, ,, 30/3/18.
•+•+ ,, ,, 6/4/18.
Ground gained in German attack on 24/4/18.

General Situation of German Push commencing 21 March 1918.

(8 km) north of Amiens. However, now that the German lines were so close, this had been abandoned. The German attack was planned for 24 April and would be repulsed by the Australians at Villers Bretonneux, to the south-west of Le Hamel.

Two mobile 18-pounder guns of the Royal Garrison Artillery were operating along the Corbie to Bray road, which ran along the top of the Morlancourt Ridge, in a more or less west to east direction. Their FOP was dug into a field just to the south of the road. The field sloped away gently towards the Somme, then suddenly the incline became quite steep. The observers, who were near the Sainte Colette brickworks, at the high end of the gentle slope, had a clear view of the German-held territory west of Le Hamel from

one half to five miles away (0.8 – 8 km). They were very well positioned to deal with a German attempt to move forces or supplies towards the river or the town of Corbie. Although the skyline created by the change from a gentle slope to a steep gradient blocked the River Somme below from view, this was of no great consequence as an observation trench was being prepared near the edge of the slope by the 51st Battalion. The FOP observers could move forwards to join them if required. The surface of the gently sloping field going back as far as the road was clearly visible in the German telescopes. Prudent men avoided forming groups there in daylight. Vehicular traffic used the road only at night.

From the Sainte Colette FOP the view to the east was blocked 1½ miles (2.5 km) away by Welcome Wood. The village of Sailly-le-Sec, in the distance behind the wood, could not be seen. Similarly, the brow of the Ridge in front (south) of the post completely hid the nearby village of Vaux-sur-Somme and the river itself from view.

The opposing armies stayed far enough apart for one to be relatively safe from rifle or machine-gun fire from the other. However, it was wise to avoid bunching-up in groups large enough to provoke an ever-watchful artillery observer into picking up his telephone. German shells continually cut the telephone wires between the various levels of headquarters and their outposts. Daily repair work was required, especially alongside the Corbie to Bray road which was shelled nightly (nicknamed 'The Evening Hate') by pre-ranged guns in attempts to disturb and disrupt the supply vehicles on their way to the forward defence positions. A 'wag' with a theatrical background claimed that the Germans staged a

The two RE8's of 3 AFC Squadron were photographing the German assembly area around Le Hamel.

The air battle between 209 RAF Squadron and Jasta 11 began in square Q8. The wind carried the combatants into squares Q7, Q1 & Q2.

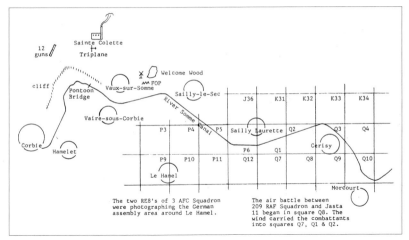

Top left: Corbie to Laurette-Cerisy showing major points and where the day's air battles would be fought.

Top right: Manfred von Richthofen and his father Major Albrecht von Richthofen.

Left: Troops walking along the Somme Canal, looking east.

show called 'The Evening Hate' twice nightly with a matinée on Saturdays.

The opposing air forces were primarily concerned in discovering the dispositions of the others' ground forces. The presence of any photographic reconnaissance RE8 aeroplane near Le Hamel or of a German Rumpler CV near Bonnay was a serious matter. In early April, both sides took steps. 209 Squadron RAF (formally 9 Naval Squadron RNAS until the RFC and RNAS merged into the RAF on 1 April 1918), commanded by Major C H Butler DSO & Bar, DSC, and equipped with Sopwith Camel fighters of the latest type, was ordered to Bertangles aerodrome on 7 April, as reinforcement for 22 Wing RAF. Butler had received his DSO & Bar fighting against German Gotha bombers raiding England in the summer of 1917, both awarded within a fortnight.

At the same time, the German High Command ordered von Richthofen's Jagdgeschwader Nr.I to Cappy aerodrome on 12 April. Abbreviated to JGI it was better known to the Allies as Richthofen's Flying Circus, and comprised four Jastas, Nos 4, 6, 10 and 11. All were equipped with Fokker Triplanes, although they also had a few Albatros DVa machines. For some time Richthofen had been awaiting the arrival of the new Fokker DVII biplane, which he had test flown in Germany, but he was destined never to fly one in front line service.

On the same day that von Richthofen was killed the British captured a document which explained his presence on that part of the front. It read as follows:

'From Kofl (Kommandeur de Flieger) HQ, 2nd Army, to Commander JGI. Strong enemy opposition is preventing flights west of the River Ancre. I request that this air barrier be pushed back to permit reconnaissance flights as far as a line between Marceux and Puchevilliers.'

(The line mentioned was about 20 kilometres behind the front line.)

Von Richthofen, despite being Germany's premier

Australian machine gunners take up positions near Vaux-sur-Somme, 30 March 1918.

fighter ace, having downed his 79th and 80th opponents on 20 April, was still only a Rittmeister, ie: cavalry captain. This was because his father, a former army officer now brought out of retirement for service during the present war, held the rank of major. In Germany a son could not hold a rank higher than a father on active service.

On the morning of 21 April, the two rostered anti-aircraft machine gunners of the 53rd Battery, Gunner Robert Buie and Gunner William James 'Snowy' Evans, had prepared their Lewis machine guns. Their position was just beyond the top on the north-western slope of the Morlancourt Ridge, at the north end of the line of the Battery guns; they were passing time by playing poker nearby.

The duty officer at the windmill FOP site was Lieutenant J J R Punch; his telegraphist was Gunner Fred Rhodes. The Sainte Colette FOP was occupied by Lieutenant Turner and his signaller Gunner Ernest Twycross RGA. Five other signallers, Privates Dalton, Elix, Harvey, Newell and Ridgway, were at work on the telephone lines in the Sainte Colette area.

In a short trench near the brickworks, an expert anti-aircraft machine-gun crew, Private Vincent Emery, a trained anti-aircraft gunner, and his helper Private Jack Jeffrey, had their Lewis gun prepared in case a daring German flyer tried a 'strafe and run' attack on the Corbie-Bray road. Private Jeffrey was also a well experienced infantry support machine gunner who had been decorated with the Distinguished Conduct Medal for bravery.

Lieutenant-Colonel J L Whitham was in charge of the 52nd Battalion stationed in the village of Vaux-sur-Somme from which position

he could easily see the Le Hamel church tower to the south-east and the ruins of the windmill to the north-east. The 51st Battalion, also under Whitham, was manning defences on the slope of the Morlancourt Ridge between Vaux and Sainte Colette. A platoon of this Battalion, under Lieutenant R A Wood, was working near the lip of the Ridge restoring an old trench, said to have been dug much earlier by the French, so as to have it ready for action when the renewed German attack came. This trench held a commanding view of Vaux below. It would be perfect for directing the fire of the Battalion's machine gunners who were dug-in on the slope ahead.

Sergeant Gavin Darbyshire was supervising a party of soldiers repairing pontoon bridges across the Somme canal. That morning they were repairing one situated behind a large farmhouse on the south bank, half a mile before the canal makes a sharp turn from west to south prior to reaching the town of Corbie. If Lieutenant Wood were to direct his binoculars down the slope to the south-west (his right) he would be able to watch them at work.

That morning too, at Bertangles airfield, north of Amiens, Captain Roy Brown's mechanics attached two long coloured streamers to the elevators of his Sopwith Camel, B7270. He had been designated by the CO, Major Charles Henry Butler, to lead 209 Squadron on patrol that day. 209's other flight commanders this morning, Captain Oliver LeBoutillier, an American, and Lieutenant Oliver Redgate, from Nottingham, England, a deputy flight leader, had a single streamer attached to the rear interplane strut on both sides of their machines. (The Squadron's senior flight commander, Captain S T Edwards DSC, a Canadian, was on leave in England.)

Some 35 kilometres due east of Bertangles, on the German airfield at Cappy, JGI's commander, Manfred von Richthofen, elected to lead Jagdstaffel (Jasta) 11 that morning. The displaced Staffelführer, Leutnant Hans Weiss, (himself standing in for the brother of the Baron, Lothar von Richthofen, wounded on 13 March), would accompany him on the extreme right of the formation. A German account disagrees with the arrangement of the pilots between the two flights. This is explained in Appendix G.

With the exception of Major Butler, all the above-mentioned persons would become involved in a chain reaction provoked when the morning cloud, mist and drizzle cleared sufficiently for both sides to send photographic reconnaissance aircraft aloft.

CHAPTER TWO
Lieutenant 'Wop' May's Adventure

Shortly before 11 am Allied time (German time was one hour ahead of Allied time at this period, ie: 1200 hours), on 21 April 1918, a field telephone rang in the HQ of the 53rd Australian Battery; Sergeant H E Hart answered. Gunner Fred Rhodes was on the line from the windmill FOP, watching the activity in and around Le Hamel. The duty officer, Lieutenant Punch, wished to advise the battery commander, Major Leslie Beavis, that two aeroplanes, a British one pursued by a German, had just passed his observation post and were heading west along the River Somme towards the 53rd Battery's gun positions. The aircraft were flying low-down in the thin mist and were just above the surface of the water.

As Oliver LeBoutillier later described it, even in perfect weather there were times when the Camel pilots flew home and kept themselves hidden from the Germans as they crossed the lines in the hilly Somme area, by simply flying low and using the mist as cover.

The distance between the FOP and the Battery being about 1½ miles (2 km), Major Beavis expected the aircraft to arrive in less than a minute. There was not much time to alert the Battery's air defences which were two post-mounted Lewis guns under the orders of

Looking south to Welcome Wood and the windmill from the Morlancourt Ridge; German shells exploding 12 April 1918. The 53rd Battery OP comprised three short trenches in front of the ruined base of the windmill.

Bombardier J S Secull. On this morning the company cook and assistant cook, Gunners Buie and Evans respectively, had been rostered for gun duty.

From the descriptions provided by three people, each one from a different location, it is possible to piece together what most probably occurred.

The two aeroplanes had approached the FOP from the direction of the village of Sailly-le-Sec and had been hidden from view until then by the trees of Welcome Wood and a bend in the river. Lieutenant Punch and the crew of the FOP, being on high ground and out of the mist, suddenly had a front seat view of the chase. The two aeroplanes resolved into a Sopwith Camel followed by a red Fokker Triplane. The observers watched them pass by and saw them enter the mist over Vaux-sur-Somme, re-appear and then continue westwards towards the two Field Artillery Battery emplacements. Lieutenant Punch later said that the two aeroplanes had actually flown by him

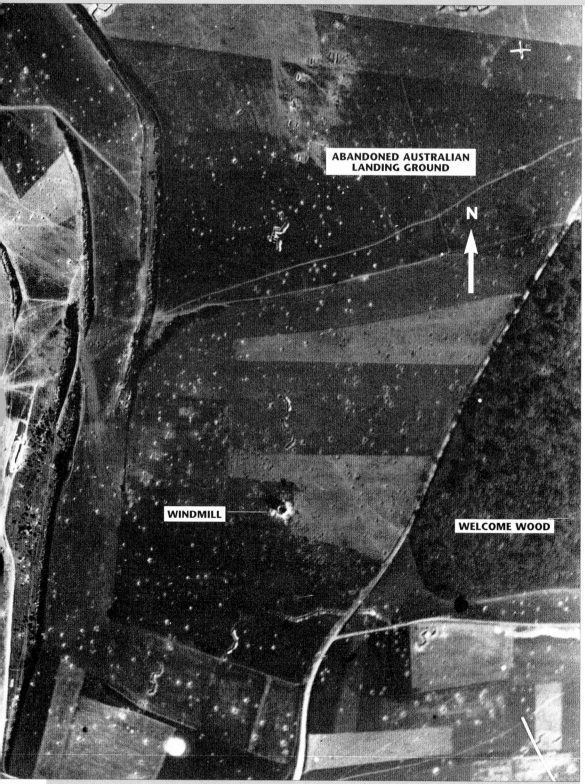

ABANDONED AUSTRALIAN
LANDING GROUND

N

WINDMILL

WELCOME WOOD

Aerial shot of the windmill, with Welcome Wood just off to the right; the FOP trenches are clearly shown in front of the windmill.

TOP: Looking south-east over the Somme River and canal, on 29 March 1918, with Sailly-le-Sec on the far left. Picture taken from approximately the spot of the FOP position in front of the windmill by Welcome Wood.

ABOVE: View to the south-east from the windmill FOP trenches taken in July 1996 (as would be seen through binoculars). Coming towards them from the background to the foreground the observers saw a Camel being chased by a German Triplane. Even in 1918 the foliage was plentiful alongside the river.

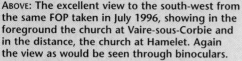

ABOVE: The excellent view to the south-west from the same FOP taken in July 1996, showing in the foreground the church at Vaire-sous-Corbie and in the distance, the church at Hamelet. Again the view as would be seen through binoculars.

ABOVE RIGHT: Australian 18-pounder gun in action. JGI was brought into the area to help locate several batteries of these guns shelling the Hamel area prior to a new German offensive.

RIGHT: Looking south today from in front of the Sainte Colette brickworks. Welcome Wood is off to the left and Vaux-sur-Somme is below the slope, out of sight. The lone tree, and scrub to the right, show the beginning of the slope down to the canal.

within pistol range. However, the mist over Vaux prevented Punch from seeing a third Camel – Captain Brown – pass on the far side of that village on its way to intercept the red Triplane. The actual interception also took place outside their view, as did the turn made by May and von Richthofen by Vaux church. [Author's note: the authors have stood where Lieutenant Punch's FOP used to be and looked west along the Ridge face. The view both to the left and the right of the canal is obstructed by trees and natural obstacles. It is only along a narrow path, straight ahead (and down), that the end of the valley can be seen in the distance. Any aeroplane that was not following that path would disappear from view from time to time. It is acknowledged that today the trees have grown, but in 1918 this area was not a devastated lunar-type landscape and the early spring foliage had started on nearby trees and saplings.]

Lieutenant-Colonel J L Whitham, in Vaux itself, had heard the noise of the air battle over Cerisy. Although he could not see any aeroplanes through the blanket of mist overhead,

confirmation of their presence had been coming for some time in the form of spent bullets fired in the fight dropping near him; in itself a dangerous situation, which did not lend itself to standing around gaping at the sky. Suddenly the loud engine noises typical of low-flying aircraft caught his attention and distracted some soldiers of his Battalion from their mid-day meal.

Those who did step outdoors to look up saw two aircraft approaching below the mist just above the surface of the mud flats beside the canal. To avoid hitting the houses at the eastern edge of the village, the Camel took avoiding action and a wingtip came very close to grazing the tiles at the top of an ornamental gateway in front of one of them. Behind the Camel came a red Triplane equally low down and the two aeroplanes skimmed over the rooftops heading straight for the village church; from a distance its tower blended into the background. Just in time, May saw it and made a steep banking turn to the right, changing direction from west to north. The second aeroplane, the Fokker, which was not yet

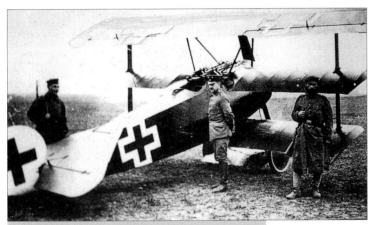

Top left: Lieutenant Wilfred 'Wop' May, 209 Squadron RAF.

Top right: Sopwith Camel.

Above: Von Richthofen's red Triplane 425/17. (This photo has in the past been captioned as under guard after capture. Unfortunately the soldiers are obviously German.)

Above right: Leutnant Wolfram von Richthofen, Jasta 11.

close enough for effective shooting and whose pilot, doubtless, had just had an equally unpleasant surprise, did likewise. Some soldiers who had their rifles handy fired a few rounds at it.

The Camel continued north for a few moments, its pilot seeing the Morlancourt Ridge ahead of him. He would not want to start a climb over the Ridge, thereby presenting his pursuer a good shot as he came onto the skyline. Therefore he turned left, towards Corbie, keeping the slope of the Ridge to his right, the canal to his left. The Camel pilot would then begin to see the bend in the canal, the Ridge curving round with

it. The Triplane followed the manoeuvre.

Although those on the ground obviously would have no idea as to the identity of the airmen, some of the more experienced might have hazarded a guess seeing an all red Triplane. The Camel was piloted by Second Lieutenant Wilfred May and the Triplane by Baron Manfred von Richthofen. Lieutenant-Colonel Whitham did not see the third Sopwith Camel either, as it flew at high speed and gradually curved round above the mist behind him to his south on its way to intercept the German machine. In following the line of flight of the two aircraft that flew over Vaux, he would, of course, be looking north.

From his newly-prepared trench on the brow of Morlancourt Ridge at Sainte Colette, Lieutenant Wood had been watching the air battle high up over Cerisy and Sailly Laurette. One aeroplane had dived down to the river somewhere between Sailly-le-Sec and Vaux. A second aeroplane had followed it. Both had now passed Vaux and were skimming the lakes and mud flats on the north side of the canal. He had

Manfred von Richthofen – the Red Baron.

unfortunately prevented him from seeing Brown's attempt to rescue him. Even if he had heard any firing, he would most probably have taken it to be from the Triplane behind. Therefore, instead of using his superior speed to escape whilst von Richthofen was distracted, he continued to zig-zag. At ground level a Fokker Triplane was about 10 to 15 mph slower than a new Bentley-engined Camel. This Triplane pilot was obviously well aware of that for he expertly followed the basic direction of the faster Camel and thereby gradually shortened the distance between them.

On their way down the valley, the two aeroplanes had to pass in front of the defensive positions which various machine-gun companies had dug into the sloping (south-facing) face of the Morlancourt Ridge. The surprise of the Vickers machine gunners was such that there is no record of any having gone into action. One Vickers crew opened fire with their personal rifles as there was not enough time to fit a belt into the machine gun.

What appeared to be just another normal bend in the canal, suddenly developed into the sharp 90° turn of the river from due west to due south. Trees on this bend would mislead a pilot not expecting anything other than a 'kink' in the canal. Only as he entered it would he see the 'kink' as a much sharper turn. May was now suddenly confronted by the towering, steep slope of the Ridge face as it curved south with the river. He was faced in those split seconds with three options: turn sharply left (south, which led to German-held territory); climb over the crest directly in front of him; or misjudge either one and die in the crash. The strong tailwind made a short 45° straight climb safer than a steeply banked 90° turn to the left. The powerful Bentley engine could handle such a climb but the guns of the Triplane behind him were another factor not to be overlooked. Pilots who have flown a replica Bentley-engined Camel in recent years testify to the power of the aeroplane and its climbing ability at full throttle. May made his choice and hauled up over the Ridge.

The windmill FOP observers, who were by this time looking from behind (most probably through binoculars at this stage) and thus had little sense of forward motion, saw the Camel re-appear beyond the mist and then seem to stand on its tail and climb. The Triplane followed suit some way behind. The observers were surprised that the Triplane pilot did not shoot down this easy target. One later opined that at the time he had taken the German pilot as being a sporting fellow who

also seen a third aeroplane, now known to have been that flown by Brown, dive out of the air fight high up over Cerisy disappear behind the mist over Vaux and then re-appear from the south-east heading towards the second aeroplane. There had been some machine-gun fire and the third one had continued flying west down the valley towards the 53rd and 55th Batteries. The details of Wood's testimony are given later in this work.

Lieutenant May, who had his hands full with the difficult and dangerous task of 'hedge-hopping' with a tail wind, and a gusty, strong one at that, had to maintain a sharp look-out ahead. That he did not crash by touching the water with his wheels or brushing a tree with a wingtip is a tribute to his Advanced Training instructors. May's intense concentration on things ahead had given his adversary a chance. The truth was revealed later that day once the Triplane's guns were examined by a weapons expert from 3 AFC Squadron.

It would appear that during the skirmish with the RE8s a short time earlier a cartridge with a faulty primer and a flimsy case had been fed into the breech block of the left-hand gun. The pilot's efforts with the extractor mechanism to eject the cartridge had caused its case to split thus creating a jam that could not be cleared in the air. In armourer's terminology it was a 'number three stoppage'. At another time during that morning's combat, a further disaster had occurred; the firing pin of the right-hand gun had fractured. (One of the authors has seen and held the lock from this actual breech block [see colour photo], and if one shakes it one can hear the bit of the broken pin rattle.) This fault would still permit the gun to fire but only two or three rounds at a time. Automatic action would then cease and the firing mechanism would need to be re-cocked manually. With an expert marksman behind the gun, two or three shots would be sufficient, provided that he could get close enough to his quarry to make them tell. At the moment when such an easy target appeared in front of him, Richthofen probably had his mind occupied trying to handle an unexpected, dangerous, steep climb, avoid a mid-air collision and check that no-one was on his own tail - and all at the same time! (See Appendix I)

The machine gunners on the slope saw the Camel barely clear the tree-tops and half-turn to the right (north-west). It was still followed by the Triplane which, although slower, could climb much better.

The activities of the two aircraft had, one by one, attracted the attention of two German artillery observers, Leutnant Fabian and Leutnant Schönemann, and of a German infantry officer, Hauptmann A Koster. When the two aircraft crested the Ridge they came into clearer view and the German officers, quite independently, focused their telescopes on the scene.

Von Richthofen was also being watched from the air. Leutnant Hans Joachim Wolff (usually referred to as just Joachim Wolff) had been watching the chase from well above until the all-too familiar rak-ak-ak sound caused him to turn and defend himself. During the time that he had spent in wondering what his commander, whom he had seen chasing the Camel, was up to, he had forgotten to pay regular attention to his own rear. Twenty bullet holes ripped through a wing as a penalty.[1]

Now that the two aircraft had crested the Ridge, the soldiers of the 14th Field Artillery Brigade, which was part of the 5th Divisional Artillery, had the best view of all. Soldiers from other units were also stationed in that area. Their purpose was to man the Heilly Sector strong point in the event of a German attempt to clear the path to the river by launching an attack on the forward defences. The strong point was actually a network of trenches which formed a reserve position about two miles behind the advanced positions where the fighting would begin. It had been carefully sited on the higher ground to the north-east of Sainte Colette where nature had provided a good natural defensive position against an attack from the south.

The Allied ground forces in that area totalled around 1,000 men, and most of them, from private to general, now had a grandstand view of the events as they unfolded. Not a single one of the several reports submitted that morning by members of the 5th Division mentioned the presence of a third aeroplane within their immediate limits of visibility. The next day, or even later, in response to specific questions, a few witnesses stated that they had seen another aeroplane (one even said aeroplanes), one mile or further away but had not mentioned it in their reports because it had not been involved in the action. By that is meant the part of the action which they had seen. From various locations specified for that aircraft, it is obvious that more than one had passed by in the distance around that time. It is quite likely that the aeroplane seen by some to the south and then later, by others, to the west over Corbie church was not the same one. Captain Brown does not seem likely to have been the pilot of the west-flying Camel as when he approached von Richthofen he was well below the line of sight. The probable occupant was Captain 'Boots' LeBoutillier.

When not actually firing, the 18-pounder guns of the 53rd Artillery Battery were hidden beneath camouflage nets. This procedure had been successful for, although the Germans knew that there was artillery on the far side of the Morlancourt Ridge, they did not know exactly where the guns were sited. A lucky chance view

(1) Wolff in fact was credited with a Camel shot down at 1150 am (German time) south of Hamelet, which was over the Allied side of the lines. It was the seventh of ten victories he would score before being killed in action on 16 May in combat with SE5s of 24 Squadron.

from a German observation aeroplane could alter that situation and the gunners were taking great care for their guns not to be seen. As the Camel and the Triplane made their half turns to the right and flew along the top of the Ridge towards the hidden gun positions down the slope beyond, Lieutenant-Colonel Fitzgerald and some members of the gun crews noticed the unusual shortness of the bursts of fire from the chasing German aircraft. More than two witnesses claim to have observed the German pilot moving forwards and backwards in his cockpit immediately before he fired each short burst. This body movement conforms to that required to cock a firing mechanism manually.

Hollywood film-makers would have us believe that guns on WW1 fighter aircraft needed always to be cocked before they could be fired. It looked dramatic but was not true to life. The only need to cock a machine gun manually was to fire the first bullet. The recoil action of the breech automatically re-cocked the gun for further firing. Von Richthofen was only doing it now because he had a gun problem and was not getting automatic re-cocking.

Adding to von Richthofen's problems was the strong east wind blowing that morning which was causing a gusty up draught along the face of the Ridge. This created heavy turbulence at the crest which made it difficult for him to hold the Camel in his gun sights long enough for effective shooting at anything other than the point-blank range which the Baron was obviously seeking.

With the Fokker once more behind him and hearing the occasional Rak-ak-ak sound of bullets passing close by or even striking the fabric of his wings, Wop May must have expected the apparently inevitable shots to hit his back at any moment. Suddenly things became quiet and stayed quiet. It appears that a cartridge with a defective primer had this time been fed into the breech of the right-hand gun and it was now completely out of action. Von Richthofen at this point must have decided to desist and head for home. May later stated that after things had been quiet for a while he risked a look behind. It was a big risk, for to do so he had to turn his aircraft at least 30° to one side or the other. This would slow his speed down and at the same time increase the size of the target which he presented to his attacker. To his surprise and no doubt relief, the sky was clear. He could find no-one behind him or even near him.

For May to establish to his own satisfaction that there was indeed no Triplane on his tail,

higher, lower, to his right or to his left, took at least ten seconds. To find an aeroplane in flight is not so easy as widely believed by armchair-pilots, even when it is known to be in the vicinity. Lieutenant May mentioned this in one of his articles on this day's events. In *Canadian Aviation*, April 1944, he wrote: 'My experience was that it was very difficult to see an aircraft in the air.' Human eyes have to focus on the distance before an object in line with them can be seen. If the sought aeroplane blends in with the landscape, many seconds may elapse before a relative motion against the background indicates its presence. (The reader who wishes proof of this is invited to study the dust jacket of this book from close up and then from a distance. May's Camel blends into the background. This effect was not intentional. The first version of the painting had the Camel in its correct colour but it could hardly be seen against the vegetation – even by the authors who knew where to look. They had to request the artist to lighten its colour.)

May finally located the Triplane. It was far away to his right (east) near Sainte Colette and appeared to be out of control. Several interviews with May have been published over the years and in two he includes the detail that he saw the Fokker spin for one and a half turns followed by a cloud of dust when it slammed into the ground. Witnesses on the ground say that the Fokker made a quarter turn or a half turn as it slid along the rough surface of the field where the Sainte Colette artillery FOP was located. When seen from a distance in a slanting view, the height and the exact position of a low-flying aircraft are very difficult to judge, even for an expert. Analysing what happened, it appears that May caught sight of the Triplane as it spun around to the left at the end of its slide along the ground. Remember too, he was just getting used to the idea that he was no longer facing imminent death. From his position above and some way off he would have had the best view of the amount of turning to the left. One and a half turns are quite normal for a 'ground loop' and would indeed have raised a cloud of dust. May's story matches reality.

One of May's other accounts of this day's actions includes more detail. He said that being hardly able to believe his own eyes, he flew over to Sainte Colette and confirmed that the Triplane had indeed crashed. He then turned and headed towards Bertangles looking around on his way for some explanation. As he neared Bonnay he spotted Captain Brown's Camel above him. This has the ring of truth for he would not immediately have caught sight of an aircraft he did not know was around, but once spotted, the two streamers at the tail immediately identified it and its pilot.

The rotations (ground loop) of the Triplane on the ground and the formation of the cloud of dust took time too. Somewhere between 30 to 50 seconds total time must have elapsed between the beginning of the quiet period and the identification of Brown's Camel above him. By then May was about a mile to the west of the Triplane's crash-landing site. With most of those on the ground looking to the east or to the south, where, relative to their position, the Triplane had come to grief, it is not surprising that only two or three men reported seeing a Camel over Corbie church about one mile away to the west.

The experienced Captain Brown had a well-deserved reputation for looking after his men and Lieutenant May instantly concluded that, not very long ago and quite unseen by himself, his flight commander had been his saviour. A grateful May followed him back to their base at Bertangles aerodrome. Brown, May, Lieutenant Francis Mellersh and Lieutenant W J Mackenzie, were all logged as having landed at 1105 hours.

Historians were reminded (1995) by the late Ed Ferko in his booklet *Richthofen*, (Albatros Publications Ltd) that a German balloon observer, Joachim Matthias serving with Bullonzug 50, wrote an account in 1928 of the chase as he interpreted it from his lofty perch abut 15 kilometres away. In all essentials, it agrees with the foregoing.

Lieutenant May told his story several times with varying amounts of detail. It, logically, included pieces of the action which he had not personally witnessed but which had become familiar to him over the years. Considering his state of panic at the time, he did quite well in remembering as much as he did of his own part in the drama unfolding around him.

Although Captain Brown clearly stated in his second Combats in the Air report that the location of his attack on the red Triplane was Vaux-sur-Somme, it has been assumed that this meant east of it; that is in the direction of German-held territory. This may also have been assumed due to the suggestion in many paintings that there was a chase along the canal, with Brown following the Triplane, which was following May. It also explains why some people say they saw the second Camel while others say there wasn't one, due to the fact that everyone assumes they are all talking about the second Camel being to the rear of the other two machines heading down the canal.

Because the observers in the FOP near the old stone windmill east of Vaux did not see Brown's attack, it has traditionally been believed as having occurred even further east – closer to Sailly-le-Sec than to Vaux, whereas it was further west.

With the traditional belief in mind, a comparison of May's basic story with the terrain over which he flew and with the time factor involved has, until now, produced a puzzle. There seemed to be a gap in the narrative about a mile long and one minute wide between Captain Brown's rescue attempt and von Richthofen's cloud of dust.

John Coltman's collection of replies to his enquiries produced the answer. Captain Brown did not err; he did indeed make his attack in the locality of Vaux-sur-Somme, but it was to the west of it, low down, round the bend and out of sight of the machine gunners on the slope before the sharp southwards turn of the river by Corbie. There were several witnesses, and their stories will be told in a later chapter. The time factor correction has a positive effect on several other aspects of the story which until now have been a little cloudy, and will be revealed in due course.

CHAPTER THREE
3 AFC – THE FIRST CLAIM

By 1000 hours that morning the drizzle had stopped and, except down in the valley and over Vaux-sur-Somme, the morning mist had cleared enough for each side to send out their recce machines. Vertical visibility was quite good; it was not too bad over the river for even though there was a layer of mist, it was not dense and only about 200 feet thick. Horizontal visibility was about one mile through the mist except to the south where the effect of the sun reduced it to half a mile. Above the mist visibility was somewhat limited by the haze. Vertically, the haze was within the limits of the haze filters fitted to aircraft cameras but horizontally it was quite noticeable, especially when looking upwards to the south-east where the sun was behind it. When asked about the visibility

that morning, as many ground witnesses said that is was good as said the contrary. Speaking many years later, an airman said: 'On that morning visibility was layered.' In truth, the witnesses' impressions depended upon where they had been positioned and in which direction they had been looking.

As the weather improved and the sky began to clear, 3 AFC Squadron despatched two of their RE8 observation two-seaters off to the Front from their base at Poulainville. Their target area was the German supply dump and troops assembly area around Le Hamel. Both machines were crewed by

One of the aerial photos taken by the 3 AFC RE8s just prior to Von Richthofen and Weiss's attack upon them. Note Le Hamel at the bottom of the picture.

highly experienced airmen who were well-practised in the art of working together. Their progress was noted by German observers who very quickly made a telephone call to JGI at Cappy.

The observer in the leading RE8 (A3661) was Lieutenant E C Banks, from Mosman, New South Wales, his pilot being Lieutenant T L Simpson, from Hamilton, Victoria. In 1965, Banks wrote a long description of what occurred on this sortie. After taking six photographs (the other crew of Lieutenants S G Garrett, from Box Hill, near Melbourne, and A V Barrow, from Harrowgate, England, also took six), Barrow caught sight of about eight aircraft (there were actually nine) approaching them from the east. Suspecting they would be German, the two observers alerted their pilots and all four men prepared for action. The time was noted as 1045.

The nine hostile aircraft were soon identified as Fokker Triplanes, two of which separated from the formation and headed towards them. The colour of the leading Fokker was noted as red and its pilot selected Garrett and Barrow's RE8 for attention. The second Dr.I which had come from the outer edge of the German formation, attacked Simpson and Banks. The first shots of the day's action were about to be fired.

A duel between experts without surprise being a factor is rarely resolved rapidly. After some minutes of manoeuvring for position and some close-range exchanges of fire, the red Triplane suddenly rolled over and dived away; it did not return to the fray. This left the second Triplane alone to face two well-handled RE8s. Working together, Simpson and Garrett turned their machines so that their observers could concentrate their fire on the German fighter each time it came within range. The manoeuvre was successful and splinters were seen to fly off the Triplane's wings. Then its pilot abandoned hostilities, made a diving turn to the east and quickly disappeared into the distance.

The two REs, not wishing to push their luck with the other Triplanes that must still be around, or even other Germans who may have been attracted by the scrap, took shelter inside a nearby cloud. When they emerged a short while later, the sky was empty and so they resumed their photographic work.

From the description of the formation of Triplanes it has to be assumed that the red Triplane, the formation leader, was flown by von Richthofen and the supernumerary position on the outside edge would probably have been taken by Leutnant Hans Weiss (but see also the end of Appendix G). Weiss had scored his 15th victory the previous day and in fact 21 April saw the award for him of the Knight's Cross of the Royal Hohenzollern House Order. The part taken by von Richthofen has not been confirmed, but it is in keeping with the tactics used, that the senior pilots would attack while being covered by the rest of the Staffel. It is known, however, that Weiss returned home alone and early, to Cappy, with his rudder controls half shot away. In a letter to his friend Oberleutnant Heinz Schmauser, about the events of the 21st, Weiss wrote the next day:

> Unfortunately I was not there at the time he made his emergency landing. Shortly before, I had attacked a flight of enemy reconnaissance aircraft and a bullet cut a rudder cable. I had to return home because I was unable to turn properly.

Manfred von Richthofen was not famous for abandoning a fight without proper cause. There is a good possibility that the poor ammunition quality problems which were to plague him this day had started to appear and that, being temporarily disarmed, he sought some quiet airspace where he could try to un-jam his guns. By the time he managed to clear one, or both of them, the RE8s had vanished so he rejoined Jasta 11 on patrol.

Experienced pilots in WWI would often spend time in selecting the ammunition and helping to fill their own machine-gun belts, or fill a drum for a Lewis gun. This did not eliminate rounds with a defective primer. Each pilot might also select his own mix of cartridges; tracer, incendiary, explosive, armour piercing, or jacketted lead. For balloon attacks special ammunition was generally used – Buckingham in the case of the British. (see Appendix I)

The events which followed give the impression that it was during his efforts to clear the stoppage(s) that the firing pin of the right-hand gun fractured. That he rejoined the patrol indicates that he had at least one gun working. What is certain is that a short time later, von Richthofen, who was renowned for his marksmanship and accurate deflection shooting, and who several times had Lieutenant W R May in a *could not miss* position, failed to dispatch him.

The RE8 crews recorded their height when the fight began as 7,500 feet, and although neither crew claimed a Triplane shot down, later events made it seem to 3 AFC's CO, Major David V J Blake, that his men had downed von Richthofen. He anotated their combat report accordingly with

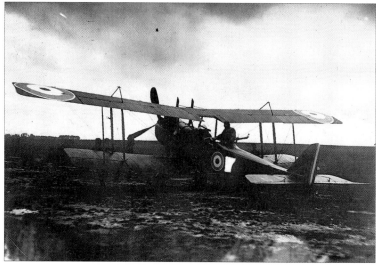

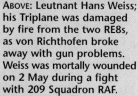

ABOVE: Leutnant Hans Weiss; his Triplane was damaged by fire from the two RE8s, as von Richthofen broke away with gun problems. Weiss was mortally wounded on 2 May during a fight with 209 Squadron RAF.

ABOVE RIGHT: RE8 reconnaissance machine of 3 Squadron, AFC. It was an aircraft from this unit that started the day's action.

RIGHT: While the RE8s were photographing Le Hamel, JGI's main task was to clear the air in order for German Rumpler CV photo-recce aircraft to locate the Australian batteries beyond the Morlancourt Ridge.

the word 'Decisive' and entered it as such in the Squadron Record Book. However, the fight having been fought between about 1040-50, this is too early to have been von Richthofen's final action. Oddly enough, when Banks later wrote the story of this fight, he noted the time as being even earlier – 1020, although this is clearly an error of memory.

The waters were further muddied by later events as far as 3 AFC were concerned, for when Major Blake was asked to provide a salvage crew to bring in the wreckage of a downed Fokker Triplane later that day (after lunch), which had crashed near Vaux-sur-Somme, included was the news that the pilot, who had been killed, was none other than von Richthofen. Blake may well have added two-and-two together even if it had not been the Baron, and assumed at this stage the Triplane had been that engaged by his crews that

morning, but as it was the Baron, he would have been even more keen to do so.

Later interest in the day's events brought forth the story that Captain Roy Brown had dived down several thousand feet to rescue two 3 AFC RE8s which were being attacked by two Fokker Triplanes. Records show that this is incorrect. In his combat report, Brown does not mention any RE8s, neither does his flying log-book entry, and nor do any of his companion's reports. And neither of the two RE8 crews mention any such rescue by Sopwith Camels. In fact, post war, the four RE8 men denied indignantly that Camels had come anywhere near them, let alone rescue them. Their saviour was good shooting coupled with teamwork and a nice fluffy cloud in which to hide.

All becomes clear when one discovers the 'rescue' occurred not on the 21st but on the 22nd! One of the RE8s (C2270) was crewed by

(3 50 25) W4130—773   20,000 9/16 HWV(P1484/1)   Forms/W3318/2   Army Form W. 3348.
10432—M1075 30,000 11/16

Combats in the Air.

Squadron :   **3rd Aust. Sqdn.**

Type and No. of Aeroplane :   **RE8 A3661**

Armament :   **1 Lewis. 1 Vickers**

Pilot :   **Lieut.S.G.Garrett**

Observer :   **Lieut.A.V.Barrow**

Date :   **21.4.18.**

Time :   **10.45 a.m.**

Duty :   **Photography**

Height :   **7500 feet**

Locality :   **near HAMEL, Sheet 62d.P.11**

Remarks on Hostile machine :—Type, armament, speed, etc.

Two Fokker Triplanes painted dark with red noses.

—— Narrative. ——

At 10.45 a.m. while engaged on photography we were attacked
by two triplanes as above. One triplane dived on us and the
Observer fired 120 rounds in bursts. One E.A. appeared to separate
from the others and might have gone down but the Pilot and
Observer were too busily engaged with the other E.A. to watch
him down. The other E.A. finally withdrew.

Signed   S.G.GARRETT,   Lieut.   Pilot.
              A.V.BARROW.   Lieut.   Observer.

Lieut. T.L.Simpson, Pilot and Lieut. E.C.Banks. Observer
state —
At 10.40 a.m. while proceeding over the lines on photography
we were attacked near HAMEL at 7000 feet by 4 E.A. triplanes. T
dived on us and the Observer fired 200 rounds. Two of the E.A.
appeared to attack Lieut. Garrett and Lieut. Barrow in another
RE8 but we were too busily engaged in the fight to see what
actually happened.

Signed   T.L.SIMPSON,   Lieut.   Pilot.
              E.C.BANKS.   Lieut.   Observer.

3rd Aust.Divisional Artillery report —
At about 10.40 a.m. several red-nosed triplanes were seen
to attack two RE8's in the neighbourhood of HAMEL. One of these
triplanes came down and crashed at J.19b.4.4. Pilot killed.
Papers on the Pilot's body show him to be Captain von RICHTOFEN.

Decisive.

David Blake   Major,
Commanding 3rd Squadron, Aust.Flyin

Combat Report: Made out by Lieutenants Garrett and Simpson of 3 AFC after the action with von Richthofen and Jasta 11.

(409.) W.10442/M1083. 200m. 11/16. G.P., Ltd.   Form....343/2.

Army Form W. 3343

Pilots available ____17____

Aeroplanes { S — 16
{ U 1 — — — —

SQUADRON RECORD BOOK.

No. _____209_____ Squadron.

Date __22nd April, 1918__

Type and Number	Pilot and Observer	Duty	Hour of— Start	Hour of— Return	Remarks	
Sopwith B.R.1			21:4:18 p.m	4:18 p.m	hrs mins	
B 6257	Lieut Wilson	Practice	5.15	5.45	30	
D 3328	Captn Boutillier	I.O.P	5.40	7.40	2.00	Decisive Combat with Albatross 2.seater
B 7273	Lieut Taylor	"	5.40	7.40	2.00	at 6.10.a.m over Albert, which crashed
D 3328	Lieut Brock	"	5.40	7.40	2.00	at 62D,J 23,D. Pilot and observer killed
B 3635	Lieut Foster	"	5.40	7.40	2.00	(See combat report)
B 7272	Lieut Barker	"	5.40	7.40	2.00	
B 7270	Captn Brown	I.O.P	8.20	10.30	2.10	
D 3326	Lieut May	"	8.20	10.30	2.10	Three Albatross observed attacking an
D 3340	Lieut Lomas	"	8.20	10.30	2.10	R.E.8's which were driven off. No decisive
D 3329	Lieut Mellersh	"	8.20	8.25	5	Returned owing to ignition result. trouble.
B 7250	Lieut Redgate	I.O.P	8.30	10.25	1.55	
D 3345	Lieut Drake	"	8.30	10.25	1.55	
D 3327	Lieut Siddall	"	8.30	10.25	1.55	Nothing to report.
B 6311	Lieut Stovin	"	8.30	10.25	1.55	
D 6331	Lieut Edwards	"	8.30	10.25	1.55	

Total war flying time = 26 hours 10 mins
"   Test   "   "   "   = 30 mins
Total flying time   = 26 hours 40 mins

W.M. Butler.

Major
Commanding 209th Squadron
Royal Air Force

In the Field
22/4/18

Record Book of 209 Squadron's final entries for 21April and initial entries for 22 April. Carbon copies of this page do not show the …'2' in the 21. The '22' in the "22.4.18" is completely missing. This has confused people in the past but the original clearly shows the correct dates. Note that the remarks concerning Captain Brown's patrol refer to Albatros machines and not Triplanes.

Lieutenants F L Baillieu and E R Rowntree, who reported '… three EA scouts attempted to attack this machine at 3,000 feet over Bois de Vaire but three Camels came up from the west and drove the EA back over their own lines. One EA is thought to have been brought down by Camels.' This action was timed at 0910 hours.

The Squadron Recording Officer of 3 AFC (the Adjutant) later sent the day's page(s) and Combats in the Air reports to RAF 22 Wing HQ, whence they would progress to 5th Brigade HQ. There, if considered to be of sufficient importance, a mention would be included in that day's Summary of Work, submitted that evening to higher authority, which included the HQ of the British Fourth Army, commanded by General Sir Henry Rawlinson. The Simpson/Banks/Garrett/

Barrow claim, although not listed in the Combats annex to the 5th Brigade Summary for 21 April, was shortly to be brought to the General's attention.

While 3 AFC had been skirmishing with the Fokkers near Le Hamel, 209 Squadron had been patrolling the Front. Half an hour into their patrol, Lieutenant Mellersh had dropped out with engine trouble and returned to Bertangles. Here he changed to a spare machine (B6257) and took off to rejoin the others, which he succeeded in doing, at about 1020.

At 1025, Oliver LeBoutillier, spotted and engaged what he believed to be two Albatros two-seaters over Le Quesnel, about ten kilometres south of the Amiens-St Quentin road. Together with Robert Foster and Merril Taylor, an Englishman and a Canadian respectively, they downed one of the two-seaters in flames and drove the other off .

This action took place at the southern end of the Squadron's assigned patrol line near Beaucourt, so once re-formed, they turned and headed north again. C Flight (Lieutenant Redgate) now became separated from A and B and saw no further action in the events that were about to unfold.

WL. W2637/M2210 200,000 6/17 McA & W Ltd. (X. 1336) Forms/W3343/3.

Army Form W 3343.

No. __3rd__ Squadron.

Pilots available _____

Aeroplanes { S_____ U_____ }

SQUADRON RECORD BOOK.

Date __22nd April 1918.__

Type and Number	Pilot and Observer	Duty	Hour of Start	Return	Time in Air	Remarks
RE8 B2271.	Captain J. M. Daigan. (P) Lt. A.S.Patterson. (O)	Artillery Patrol	5.20a	8.30a		Flash Locations. 6.45a 1 very large flash at approx.Sheet 62D.E.15 probably on railway there. Bombs Two 20 1b bombs dropped on E. 10b. Weather very misty, visib. poor.
RE8 C2270.	Lt. F.L.Baillieu " E.R.Rowntree (P) (O)	Counter attack Patrol	5.55a	9.45a		No movement observed in forward areas. E.A. 8.10a 3 EA scouts attempted to attack this machine at 3000' over BOIS DE VAIRE but 3 Camels came up from W. and drove the EA back over their own lines.1 EA is thought to have been brought down by CAMELS. Bombs and Machine Gun Fire Two 20 1b bombs dropped on MORLANCOURT. Heavy MG fire encountered from P.14b.2.5 evidently strong emplacement. Observer fired 200 rds Lewis at the position. The MG ceased fire. Weather misty visib bad.
RE8 C5079.	Lt. H.S. Foals Cpl. Hay (P) (Fitter)	Test Flight. Rigging.	10.35a	10.55a		Satisfactory.
RE8 B6576.	Lt. T.L.Simpson " E.C. Banks (P) (O)	Artillery Patrol	8.05a	10.55a		S: Flashes and Zone Call. 10.21a. NF KB I.4d.o.3.(Acc B) 1 flash. one call sent. 1 burst observed but no correction owing to poor visib. Bombs 8.30a Two 20 1b bombs dropped at E.21a.2.4 Weather cloudy visib poor.

04) Wt. W2637/M2210 200,000 6/17 McA & W Ltd. (X. 1336) · Forms/W3343/3.

Army Form W. 3343.

No. __3rd__ Squadron.

Pilots available _____

Aeroplanes { S_____ U_____ }

SQUADRON RECORD BOOK.

Date __23rd April 1918.__

Type and Number	Pilot and Observer	Duty	Hour of Start	Return	Time in Air	Remarks
RE8 A3662.	22.4.18. Lt. S.G. Garrett. (P) " A.V. Barrow (O)	After 4.pm. Artillery Patrol	4.15p.	6.15p.		S: Flashes and Zone Calls. 5.34p. AANF QA.Q.14b.52. 1 flash) Zone call sent, no fire observed. Fire. 5.00p. fire in ALBERT CAUSED by our shelling. E.A. 6.00p. 1 2-str EA over MORLANCOURT. Machine Gun Fire. Pilot fired 200 rds Vickers into ALBERT. Observer fired 100 rds into MORLANCOURT. Weather fine, visib good.
RE8 C2333.	Lt. N.Mulroney " W.P.Heslop (P) (O)	Artillery Patrol	5.15p.	6.20p.		Flash Location. 4.30p. 2 flashes from Sheet 57D.W.12b.cent (C Acc.) E.A. 4.00p. 4. EA (type not recognised) at 12000' flying E Machine Gun Fire. over MEAULT. Pilot fired 50 rds Vickers into ALBERT. weather fine, visib good.
RE8 A4404.	Captain H.D.E.Ralfe.(P) Lt. W.A.J.Buckland (O)	Dusk Reconn.	5.50p.	8.05p.		No movement observed in forward areas. Strong point at P.8d.5.4. seems to be strongly held. Enemy trenches betn MARRETT WOOD and J.6a6.6. appear to be in good order. Flashes and Zone Calls. 6.25p. NF PB P.10c.2.2.(Bacc. 4 yellow flashes) zone call sent, fire observed, corrections MC5. Battery neutralised.

Two pages of 3 AFC's Record Book for events of 22 April recording an action with EA scouts and Camels. The entry for RE8 C2270 has sometimes been misunderstood as Brown rescuing the RE8s on the 21st. Note that events after 4 pm are recorded on the sheet dated the 23rd.

CHAPTER FOUR
209 Squadron – The Second Claim

The pages of 209 Squadron's Record Book which were submitted to 22 Wing at the end of 21 April, showed that 15 pilots, divided into three flights, left Bertangles at 0935, 0940 and 0945 hours:

A FLIGHT
Captain A R Brown DSC B7270
Lieutenant W J Mackenzie B7245
Lieutenant W R May D3326
Lieutenant L F Lomas D3340
Lieutenant F J W Mellersh D3329

B FLIGHT
Captain O C LeBoutillier D3338
Lieutenant R M Foster B3858
Lieutenant M A Harker B7272
Lieutenant M S Taylor B7200
Lieutenant C G Brock B3328

C FLIGHT
Lieutenant O W Redgate B7250
Lieutenant A W Aird B6311
Lieutenant E B Drake D3345
Lieutenant C G Edwards D3331
Lieutenant J H Siddall D3327

As far as Wing HQ was concerned a squadron's day began at 1601 hours on one day and ended at 1599 hours the following day, not midnight to midnight. The pages of the various record books, depending on how busy a unit had been, might cover one page one day, several days or merely a few hours. In the case of 209 Squadron at this period, their Record Book page covers both the 20th and 21st, while the 21st also spills over onto a second page covering the 21st only, while the subsequent page covers later events of the 21st and then the 22nd (see page 33).

Upon reaching their assigned altitude, the three flights patrolled the front to discourage any German photographic reconnaissance aircraft from trying to cross the lines. Eventually Redgate's flight became separated from the others by cloud and a little later two of his pilots were forced to return to Bertangles due to engine problems. Redgate and his remaining two men patrolled until the end of the allotted time and then returned to base.

Around 1020 hours, LeBoutillier's flight saw a German two-seater recce machine over Beaucourt at 12,000 feet and Lieutenant Merril Taylor, a Canadian, shot it down. Before hitting the ground it caught fire. He identified it as an Albatros C-type but it was probably a Rumpler or LVG CV crewed by Leutnant Kurt Fischer and Leutnant Rudolf Robinius, of FAA203, who were both killed. They came down near Ignaucourt, just to the north-west of Beaucourt, the location given by Taylor for the combat. From a distance, Captain Brown saw the action, followed by an aircraft descending in flames. His testimony was used to confirm Taylor's claim.

Here fate took a hand and the path of Captain Brown's depleted Squadron crossed with that of Jasta 11. That morning, with von Richthofen leading, they had been joined by a few machines from Jasta 5, Triplanes and Albatros Scouts. At about 1040 hours British time battle was joined in the area of the town of Cerisy, map reference 62D.Q.3. (See map on page 15.)

Both Brown and von Richthofen had a similar habit which endeared them to their subordinates. After leading an attack, each would detach himself from any combat which followed, climb above it and be ready to go to the aid of any pilot who was in a tight spot. Von Richthofen even carried a pair of small binoculars on a cord around his neck for better identification of distant aircraft.

Having re-formed themselves after the engagement with the two RE8s, the Fokker Triplanes were once more patrolling behind the German lines looking for British aircraft. Von Richthofen had rejoined and was at the head of one Kette (Flight), flying with his cousin, Leutnant Wolfram von Richthofen, Oberleutnant Walther Karjus, Vizefeldwebel Edgar Scholz and Leutnant Joachim Wolff. It is not known for certain who was leading the second Kette following Weiss's departure, but one of the pilots was Leutnant Richard Wenzl, formally of Jasta 6. The Fokker pilots saw five Camels coming up from the south, approaching Le Hamel. These were Brown and his four companions. Wolff noted that the Jasta 5 machines were about four kilometres to the north-east, over Sailly-le-Sec, just the other side (north) of the Somme. Moments later Wenzl saw

Army Form W. 3343.

(6304) Wt. W2637/M2210 200,000 6/17 McA & W Ltd. (E. 1336) Forms/W3. 3/3.

No._____Squadron.

209th

Pilots available ___ 18

{ S ___ 18

Aeroplanes { U ___ 1

SQUADRON RECORD BOOK.

Date_____ 21st April, 1918

Type and Number	Pilot and Observer	Duty	Hour of		Time in Air	Remarks
			Start	Return		
Sopwith B.R.1			20:4:18		hrs mins	
D 3327	Lieut Siddall	Test	p.m 5.45	p.m 6.20	35	Gun test O.K
B 7200	Lieut Taylor	"	5.35	5.45	10	
B 7272	Lieut Harker	"	5.35	5.55	20	Gun test O.K
B 3858	Lieut Foster	"	5.35	5.55	20	Gun test O.K
B 7276	Capt Brown	I.O.P	5.45	7.30	1.45	
L 3328	Lieut May	"	5.45	7.30	1.45	
D 3329	Lieut Mellersh	"	5.45	8.10	25	No E.A seen, Nothing to report
D 3340	Lieut Lomas	"	5.45	7.30	1.45	
B 6297	Lieut Mackenzie	"	5.45	7.30	1.45	
			21:4:18			
			a.m	a.m		
B 7270	Capt Brown	H.O.P	9.35	11.05	1.30	Decisive combat with Red Triplane at 62D Q.2. (See Combat report)
S 7245	Lieut Mackenzie	"	9.35	11.05	1.30	Decisive combat with Fokker Triplane over Cerisy at 10.45 Pilot returned slightly wounded. (See report)
D 3329	Lieut Mellersh	"	9.35	10.00	25	Decisive combat with Fokker Triplane near Cerisy at 10.45.a.m. (See report)
B 6257	Lieut Mellersh	"	10.10	11.05	55	(See Combat report)
D 3326	Lieut May	"	9.35	11.05	1.30	
D 3340	Lieut Lomas	"	9.35	11.20	1.45	
B 7250	Lieut Redgate	H.O.P	9.40	10.40	1.00	Returned to Aerodrome owing to using all ammunition.
D 3345	Lieut Drake	"	9.40	10.30	50	
D 3327	Lieut Siddall	"	9.40	11.30	1.50	
B 6311	Lieut Aird	"	9.40	1.40	2.00	Engine cut out. Made forced landing at Camblain 1 hour
D 3331	Lieut Edwards	"	9.40	11.15	1.35	

W2637/M2210 200,000 6/17 McA & W Ltd. (E. 1336) Forms/W3343/3.

Army Form W. 3343.

Pilots available ___ 18

No._____Squadron.

209th

299

{ S ___ 18

Aeroplanes { U ___ 1

SQUADRON RECORD BOOK.

Date_____ 21st April, 1918

...nd Number	Pilot and Observer	Duty	Hour of		Time in Air	Remarks
			Start	Return		
B.R.			21:4:18		hrs mins	
			a.m	a.m		
B 7272	Lieut Harker	H.O.P	9.45	11.35	1.50	
B 7200	Lieut Taylor	"	9.45	11.35	1.50	Decisive combat with 2 seater Albatross over Beaucourt at 10.25.a.m (see report
B 3858	Lieut Foster	"	9.45	11.35	1.50	
D 3338	Captn Le Boutillier	"	9.45	11.35	1.50	Indecisive combat at 10.25 over Cerisy (See report)
D 3328	Lieut Brook		9.50	11.40	1.50	Made forced landing at Vert Galand Farm
D 3328	Lieut Brook	Return from forced landing	3.40	3.55	15	Return from Vert Galand Farm.

Total War flying time = 31 hours 25 mins

Total test,etc " " = 1 " 40 "

Total Flying time = 33 hours 5 mins.

(signature)

Major
Commanding 209th Squadron
Royal Air Force.

Two pages of 209 Squadron's Record Book dated 21 April, but also covering the events after 4pm on the 20th. All the entries for Captain Brown's Flight refer to area 62D Q.2 and Cerisy, which is 62D Q.3. The main fight took place above these locations.

another Flight of Camels – Le Boutillier's B Flight.

The formations met. Lieutenant Mackenzie, of Brown's flight, was taken by surprise and wounded early in the fight; perhaps this was Wolff's claim. Mackenzie turned to face his attacker and claimed to have shot him down. He then left the battle and headed back to Bertangles where he landed safely although in the Record Book his landing time is the same as Brown and Co. His copy of the combat report that went to Brigade is interesting because later that afternoon Major Butler's annotation in ink 'decisive' was amended in pencil either by 22 Wing or by 5th Brigade, with the prefix 'In-' so that the final decision on his claim became 'indecisive'.

Lieutenant Francis Mellersh, also in Brown's flight, was engaged by two Triplanes, possibly Joachim Wolff and Walther Karjus, who had him out-manoeuvred. Brown saw this and rescued him successfully. These are the two Triplanes Brown refers to both in his combat reports and log book, almost as an afterthought. Clear of immediate danger, Mellersh fired at a Fokker with a blue tail near Cerisy. He made his first mistake by following it down to be sure of his victory. Two other Triplane pilots saw this and, realising that the attacking Camel was following a predictable flight path (Mellersh's second mistake), angled down to intercept him. The blue-tailed Triplane, which could not have been from Jasta 11, but more likely from Jasta 5, force landed near Cerisy but as neither unit suffered any fatalities or men wounded, it is difficult to comment. Mellersh, having become unexpectedly otherwise engaged, claimed the Triplane as 'having crashed' in his combat report, and perhaps believed it had. Only Vfw Scholz is known to have been shot up but he returned safely.

In the action were pilots of varying degrees of experience, but two of them stood out, one a Canadian, the other a German. Lieutenant Wilfred Reid 'Wop' May, from Edmonton, Alberta, was a month past his 24th birthday. He had joined 209 Squadron this very month, so was still finding his feet, very much the novice. On the other side, Wolfram von Richthofen, aged 22, from Barzdorf, Silesia, and like his famous cousin, a former cavalry (Hussar) officer, had joined Jasta 11 on 4 April, so he too was very much a new boy. Both men had been warned to stay clear of any action and that if danger loomed, they were to break off and head for home – fast.

When the main fight erupted, Wop May, as instructed by his friend and flight commander, Roy Brown (they had known each other back in Canada), edged away but when he saw a Triplane tantilisingly close by, decided to take a crack at it. This turned out to be Wolfram von Richthofen, himself trying to stay out of trouble. However, the danger to the Fokker pilot had been spotted by the experienced eyes of the Red Baron, who came down from his 'guardian angel' position above the fight to help his young cousin. Those clear, experienced and now concentrating eyes latched onto the Camel. There can be little doubt that the Baron, while intent on saving his cousin, was also noting mentally his approaching 81st kill.

It was only May's third patrol into enemy territory and his second taste of combat. For such an inexperienced pilot to encounter the seasoned airmen of Jasta 11, supported by Jasta 5, was decidedly unlucky. Although May later stated that both his machine guns jammed in the fight, this is not mentioned in any documentation of the day. Such jamming is only mentioned in a report by May concerning another action one week later.

Brown had said to May: 'Keep out of any fight. Stay above it and watch. If an enemy begins to come towards you, head for home.'
Whatever had happened beforehand, May now lost altitude and decided to head for home. Unfortunately instead of climbing out of the battle as he should have done, he put the Camel's nose down a little for more speed and followed a predictable flight path. Two airmen saw this, Manfred von Richthofen and Roy Brown.

The Rittmeister's Attack on Lieutenant May

Von Richthofen saw an easy interception and dived to the attack; this required some rapid mental trigonometry. In order to finish his dive in a good firing position behind May's Camel, he had to aim for a point well ahead of it. Several ground witnesses, mainly those looking east rather than south-east and therefore not into the sun, saw one aircraft and then another dive out of the fight. Although there is no evidence whatsoever of this, it is safe, on the basis of combat airmanship alone, to assume that von Richthofen curved his dive around to the south so as to have the sun behind him in his approach to the Camel. An 'old hand', on either side, would not have done otherwise unless he had lost interest in surviving the war.

According to the Combat Reports and the squadron Record Book entries for Captain Brown's fight, map references 62D.Q.2 and 62D.Q.3 (Cerisy) appear. These locations are to the south-east of where Brown later attacked von Richthofen. Brown initially believed that May, whom he had last seen over the River Somme a short distance to his south, had successfully disengaged. A few seconds later, he noticed that a second aeroplane had also disengaged. It resolved into a Triplane which appeared to be taking an unhealthy interest in May's Camel.

For a reason which will never be known, von Richthofen failed to make a good interception; he came out of his dive too far behind May's Camel, which gave May the advantage as his machine was the faster of the two.

Taking May's later testimony as a basis, it may be concluded that von Richthofen came into maximum firing range of May somewhere between Sailly-le-Sec and Welcome Wood. From the Camel's flight path von Richthofen had probably suspected that its pilot was new to the game and decided to find out for certain. Even with the occasional defective round of ammunition in his belts that morning, he could safely tackle an inexperienced enemy. If the Camel pilot turned out to be otherwise, a Fokker Dr. I Triplane could out climb a Camel any day. He opened fire to see what would happen. An experienced pilot upon hearing the Rak-ak-ak sound of bullets passing close by or seeing the smoke of the tracer, would, without any hesitation whatsoever turn his machine to face his attacker. A novice would spend vital moments looking around to find his attacker who, if close by, was using those same vital moments to correct his aim! If the novice survived the second and more accurate burst of fire, he would probably begin to zig-zag. The urgency with which Brown regarded the situation may be deduced from the airmanship which he now displayed.

A third aeroplane was seen by ground witnesses to leave the 'dog fight' high up over Cerisy and start downwards heading south-west; it was Brown. An 'old hand' like him instinctively knew that in an attack from this direction – ie: into the sun with a layer of haze ahead of it – the dice would be loaded against himself. He would be heading into haze made opaque by the sun's rays, whereas his opponent's clearest view would be towards him. On the way down there would be time to remedy this and thereby gain the tactical advantage of surprise.

Having detached himself from the fight which was now down to 5,000 feet, Brown performed his own mental trigonometry. A dive from that altitude to ground level required that he start levelling out at 1,000 feet and then stabilise his

aeroplane on the final intercepting course. This required about 7,500 feet of forward motion and a lot of good judgement. To use the sun and haze to his advantage, he would need to attack the Triplane from above, behind and on its left. Brown stated in his Combat Report that he was fighting in 62D.Q.2 which would have placed him in a good position relative to the sun and the ground haze to observe the members of his Flight. Starting from 62D.Q.2 it would not be difficult to adjust his course on the way down so as to approach the aircraft from the south-east. Vincent Emery, in his trench at Sainte Colette, saw him do this. If he were then to pass to the south of Vaux-sur-Somme, the mist would help to hide him. After that, on his attack path, he would have the sun behind him. There was a good chance that the German pilot just might not see him…. Fundamental to any fighter pilot in any war, it has been estimated that 50% of pilots shot down, never saw the aircraft that attacked them. This is good tactics, giving the maximum result with the minimum risk.

Brown eased his Camel into a 45° dive, adjusted his engine power to obtain 180 mph, which was the maximum safe airspeed, so as not to separate his wings from the fuselage. LeBoutillier later confirmed this angle of dive by saying '… I saw him coming in from the right [of Boot's position] in a steep 45° dive.'

Von Richthofen's impression that the Camel pilot ahead of him might be a novice had been confirmed. Upon realising that someone was firing at him, May swerved his aeroplane and began to zig-zag. The aerodynamic drag of the turns reduced his speed. The Triplane, which was actually the slower aeroplane of the two, now held the advantage and the distance between them began to diminish. May descended lower and lower until he was, in his own words: 'Just skimming the surface of the water.'

Background and Circumstances

Due to the bad weather which had directly followed the arrival of JGI at Cappy on 12 April, von Richthofen had not made many flights over that part of the front from this base. He had, of course been fighting over this sector in early April when based at Léchelle, which is a little further north from Cappy. From studying maps, reinforced by those flights, he was certainly familiar with the river, the towns, the villages and the wooded areas.

All were easy to identify when seen from an altitude of 2,000 feet or more. However, from 50 feet above the ground things look very different. Virtually nothing has any quickly recognisable outline or form. The woods no longer have any shape; they are just trees seen from the side. The villages have no shape either, they are just a collection of houses, or ruins of houses. Worse yet, objects pass so quickly that there is no time for a second look just to make sure.

On 21 April there was an additional confusion factor. The wind, which normally blew from the west, was on this morning blowing strongly from the east. Lieutenant May, followed by the Baron, was heading west which means that the wind was hurrying them both along relative to the ground. A pilot who is mentally conditioned to the time taken for landmarks to pass by in a 110 mph aeroplane flying into a 25 mph headwind, can easily be a long way ahead of the place on earth where he believes himself to be when flying with a 25 mph tailwind. The distance over the ground that he would normally cover in three minutes now takes one minute, 44 seconds. With one village looking like another, no distinct forest outlines at this height and no front-line trenches within view on either side of the river (remember, there were only strong points at this stage, front-line trench systems had not been dug), it would be very easy to confuse Vaux-sur-Somme for Sailly-le-Sec. (Both of the present authors have flown over the area and were initially confused. This was around 400 feet and the Baron would have even less chance at around 50 feet.) Both villages are about the same size, both lie on the north side of the canal, and in both cases the canal has turned to flow north-west. Sherlock Holmes found the fact that the dog did not bark in the night to be of singular significance. Something similar was about to happen, or better, not to happen.

In April 1918 the important difference between the two villages was that Sailly-le-Sec was only half a mile inside Allied-held territory whereas Vaux-sur-Somme was two miles inside. The main night-time supply route to the Allied forces in the Sailly area was the Corbie-Bray road which runs past the Sainte Colette brickworks atop the Morlancourt Ridge. This road was a favourite target for German fighter pilots who regularly strafed it at dawn to catch breakdowns or stragglers, plus the odd attack during the day if cloud cover was favourable. The strong anti-aircraft defences along and nearby this road were very well known to the German Army Air Service. Von Richthofen's subsequent actions strongly suggest that he took a distant village on the north bank of the canal to be Sailly-le-Sec, whereas it was actually Vaux. On this hypothesis, von Richthofen, in quite unknowingly having proceeded beyond the genuine Sailly-le-Sec, was in absolute violation of his strictest precept: never to fly low down over enemy territory. He had never done so before and there was no reason for him to do so today. Moreover, in terms of anti-aircraft fire, he was fast approaching the most heavily defended sector for miles around.

In addition to the strong east wind and the badly manufactured ammunition in his guns, another adverse factor entered the situation for the Baron. Presumably because of the hazy air that morning, he was wearing flying goggles with special lenses. From their shape, they probably had been captured from an Allied airman. Their bright yellow double layer lenses considerably improved forward vision (one of the authors has inspected them) through haze, and by eliminating glare made moving objects stand out against a stationary background. But, being flat, they had the disadvantage of eliminating peripheral (side) vision. Like Lieutenant May and Captain LeBoutillier, to see either side von Richthofen had to turn his head considerably; to see directly behind he had to turn his aeroplane.

The later fanciful journalistic stories of Brown seeing the glint of von Richthofen's eyes as he glanced back at him are simply not true. Looking at someone wearing the goggles today from just a few feet away, the eyes are totally obscured.

It was at this point that Lieutenant Punch (windmill FOP) saw the two aircraft, both at tree-top height, approaching his position from the east. He spoke to Gunner Rhodes who cranked the handle of the field telephone and asked for the duty officer at the 53rd Battery.

The village of Vaux-sur-Somme now appeared right in front of May and the chasing Baron. This should have been the moment for the latter to turn back, but like the singular behaviour of the dog in the Sherlock Holmes story, he did not react to the situation. This tends to confirm that Richthofen had the erroneous impression that the village was Sailly-le-Sec and that he was in the relatively clear area which began a short distance behind the Allied forward defence positions.

From the testimony of the few people who saw the next part of the action, it appears that von Richthofen came within normal accurate firing distance of May's Camel at about this time. Judging by the events which followed, the most probable explanation why a man who was renowned for his accurate shooting failed to dispose of the easy target in front of him is that his left-hand gun was the only one in proper working order and it jammed the instant he opened fire. When the breech-block of the gun was later opened on the ground, it was found to contain a split cartridge case. This was a fault which could not be diagnosed accurately in the air and a pilot could easily expend useless effort in the hope of clearing it. It fits with the puzzlement of some of the ground witnesses as to why the Triplane's pilot did not take advantage of more than one instance when the Camel was at his apparent mercy. As to why von Richthofen continued the chase, the most plausible reason is that the right-hand machine gun was still operable. However, for the sole two or three rounds it would fire at a time to be effective, he needed to reduce the range considerably and, in the total absence of another hostile aircraft, he still had opportunity to do exactly that.

Lieutenant-Colonel J L Whitham (CO 52nd Battalion), in his command post in Vaux, could hear the noises of the air battle up above the patches of mist which lingered over the village and nearby canal. Spent bullets were dropping from the sky from time to time. He had a front seat in the Stalls and was about to receive a surprise such as occurs when the stage magician waves his magic wand. Suddenly before his eyes and those of the garrison of Vaux a British biplane followed by a German Triplane appeared at roof-top height. Until then they had been out of sight below the tree-tops along the river and canal banks to the east. The British aeroplane was so low down that it had to turn sharp right to miss the church tower. Some of the surprised soldiers took aim with their rifles and fired at the German machine. In early 1933, Whitham replied to his friend C E W Bean (a war correspondent), following an enquiry:

Iam very definite on the point that two
'planes only came down the valley. A heavy
fog or river mist, with a curtain of about
150 feet, had rested in the valley of the
Somme for several hours and prevented our
view of the air fight which we could hear
plainly...towards the east, ie: over Sailly-
le-Sec and Sailly Laurette. Both these
'planes came from the east and downwards,
and they flattened out as they passed over
Vaux-sur-Somme, less than 100 feet from the
valley level. It seemed certain that both
would crash into the spur immediately west
of the sharp bend of the Somme where it
turns southwards towards Corbie, but we saw

the leading 'plane rise at the spur, closely
followed by the triplane. The triplane
seemed definitely under control of its pilot
as it passed over Vaux-sur-Somme and it is
difficult to credit the assertion [1] that
the pilot was fatally wounded by a shot fired
from the air prior to his passing over Vaux.
I cannot say whether Richthofen was firing
at the Camel at this stage - the noise of
both engines was very great - but I heard
machine guns firing from the ground further
west down the valley.

After a short excursion heading north towards the Ridge, the British Camel turned west again just as though the pilot had realised that to make the steepish climb in front of his pursuer was tantamount to signing his own death warrant. The Triplane followed the manoeuvre, cutting corners as it went, and step by step reducing the distance between them. It was obvious that an 'old hand' was trying to catch a novice. The puzzle was why the 'old hand' had let pass two or three excellent opportunities to down the Camel. In those moments too, the usually cool and methodical Baron must have been feeling frustrated and quite busy in his cockpit, which must have reduced the amount of time to glance around and ascertain his exact position. Just moments earlier, the Camel pilot had almost led him into a church tower!

The chase at low-level through the wisps of mist along the south face of the Morlancourt Ridge had begun. One possible reason why von Richthofen made an exception to his normal operational limits and headed deeper into Allied territory is that he saw two Triplanes some distance away and at a higher altitude to his left (south) near Hamelet (not to be confused with Le Hamel) which would provide him with 'top cover'. Leutnant Joachim Wolff, the pilot of one of them reported having seen von Richthofen. There is no record whether Oberleutnant Walther Karjus, the pilot of the second Dr.I, also saw him.

The Witnesses to Captain Brown's Attack

Captain LeBoutillier had expended all his ammunition in the fight and was on his way back to Bertangles. Like most seasoned pilots who

[1] Whitham had read the historian, H A Jones's, words that Richthofen was probably hit as he chased May, by Brown who dived and attacked between Sailly le-Sec and Vaux-sur-Somme.

Australian field kitchen at Vaux-sur-Somme. May and von Richthofen flew towards this or a similar position.

survived the war, and the coincidence is not accidental, he kept a sharp look-out at all times and in all directions. Down to his right near Vaux, he saw three aeroplanes; a Camel, followed by a Triplane – both heading west; then a second Camel, higher up, diving at about a 45° angle to intercept the Triplane. Taking a good look round every few seconds and turning his own Camel as required to be sure that no enemy was sneaking up on him, he watched the show from a front row seat in the Gallery.

Lieutenant Wood, from his position on the brow of the Ridge, could see over and around the mist covering Vaux. He could also see downwards through the wisps over the Somme canal and the mud flats of the original river beside it. He had been watching the air battle above Cerisy and had seen an aeroplane drop out of the fight. He had seen a second aeroplane follow the first one, then, a little later, a third aeroplane start downwards after the other two. As they approached they resolved into a biplane followed by a triplane followed by another biplane; and they were all heading towards him. What they were, he could not yet tell, but the show was about to begin and he had a front row seat in the Dress Circle.

Lieutenant J A Wiltshire (on the Corbie-Mericourt road north of the Ridge, and near the 53rd Battery positions) saw the three machines

leave the far distant air fight and head downwards towards the Somme canal. He watched them until they disappeared below the Ridge to the south-east. If they kept their line of flight, he would probably see them again if forced to rise when they reached the western end of the Ridge where the Somme bends to the south.

Captain Brown's Considerations

To fire an air-cooled machine gun for longer than ten seconds was a direct invitation for trouble. The breech would overheat and cause a jam which the pilot must not attempt to clear until the machine gun had cooled down. Captain Brown would have mentally planned when to fire, when to cease fire, and his all-important escape route. Apart from not placing himself where he would be in danger from the Triplane's guns, he had to avoid a mid-air collision and to recover from his dive without losing his wings or touching the water with his wheels. From low-down, the escape route to the north involved an immediate climb over the Morlancourt Ridge. With a strong tail wind and controls stiff from speed, that was not an attractive proposition. To the south, the terrain was flat. An attack from the south-east, with the sun behind him, that is, towards the left side of the Triplane, could easily be developed into an escape to the south-west. To a professional airman, such a plan would be second nature.

At 180 mph, the maximum power-on forward speed of a Sopwith Camel, the dive down from 5,000 feet to 1,000 feet, would consume 28 seconds. From that point onwards the closing speed between the two aircraft became the important factor. Assuming 110 mph for the Triplane, the closure speed was 70 mph which corresponds almost exactly to 35 yards per second. Brown's objective being to rescue May from impending doom, it was logical for him not to wait until he was near enough to the Triplane to be sure of killing the pilot or destroying it. To distract the pilot of the red Triplane would be enough to save May. This could be achieved several seconds before accurate firing distance was reached. Two witnesses, one of whom was Private Emery, confirmed that the Camel pilot did exactly that.

Three hundred yards was the furthest range at which Brown could be sure that his bullets would pass close enough to the Triplane for its pilot to realise that he had company. Long-range fire might, by a fluke, hit the pilot or even the fuel tank. Such lucky shots had happened before, but not very often. Brown would have been distinctly aware that it had already taken several seconds to get into position, and every second had been one of mortal danger for May.

Brown's Attack

Making a montage of testimony of Captain Roy Brown, Oliver LeBoutillier, Lieutenants R A Wood, J M Prentice, J A Wiltshire and Sergeant Gavin Darbyshire, plus Gunner George Ridgway, it is reasonably certain that the following occurred.

Arthur Roy Brown had been in France since April 1917 and been awarded the DSC in October for having shot down four German aircraft. He was on leave over the winter but returned to 9 Naval as a flight commander in mid-February 1918. Since then he had raised his score of combat victories to nine. In short, he was an experienced fighter pilot.

Manfred von Richthofen had survived as a fighter pilot for eighteen months, approximately thirteen and a half of which had been on active duty at the front. Keeping a sharp look-out, having speedy reactions, keeping the dice loaded in his favour and a measure of good luck had kept him alive. On this day, the reduced side vision due to his special flying goggles would have forced him to turn his aeroplane in addition to his head to check his tail. During the elapsed time of Brown's dive and approach he would have done so several times. It is quite likely that Brown saw von Richthofen make a check to the left rear as, with an appropriate deflection angle, he aligned his gun-sights on the Triplane. Whatever happened Brown's strategy worked well. Von Richthofen, with his vision to the left impeded by the sun at 23° above the horizon, which would have blinded him through the haze, failed to see Brown diving on him. Brown later wrote: 'I got a long burst into him' – which by WW1 definition was five to seven seconds. In fact, Brown's strategy worked too well, for, during his low, high-speed pass from out of the haze, through the wisps of river mist and back into the haze again, he was not visible for very long to anybody who was looking upwards or horizontally to the south-east. Apart from a working party down in the valley, only those who were high enough up to see downwards over the Ridge at a steep angle through the mist, and who were looking that way at the right moment, saw the entire interception.

During such a burst of fire the Camel would have moved somewhere between 175 and 245 yards closer to the Triplane. Allowing distance for collision avoidance, it would appear by calculation that Brown was 300 to 350 yards away from his target when he pressed the triggers. To close the range to the normal 50 yards before firing would have taken seven or eight more vital seconds and could easily have cost Lieutenant May his life. From the tactics employed by Brown, it would appear that his plan was for May to use his superior speed to escape whilst von Richthofen was occupied countering the sudden new danger that Brown posed.

Up on the top of the Ridge just across the road from the Sainte Colette FOP, Private Emery, a trained and proficient anti-aircraft machine gunner, assisted by Private Jeffrey, was gazing upwards at the distant air battle now scattered between Cerisy and Sailly Laurette. Both were hoping that some 'trade' would come their way. They prepared their Lewis gun just in case. Together with Lieutenant Wood, in his trench on the brow of the Ridge overlooking Vaux-sur-Somme, they had a clear view to the south around the patches of mist. Gunner Ridgway, who was 20 feet up the Sainte Colette brickwork's chimney (which in 1918 was not in the present-day

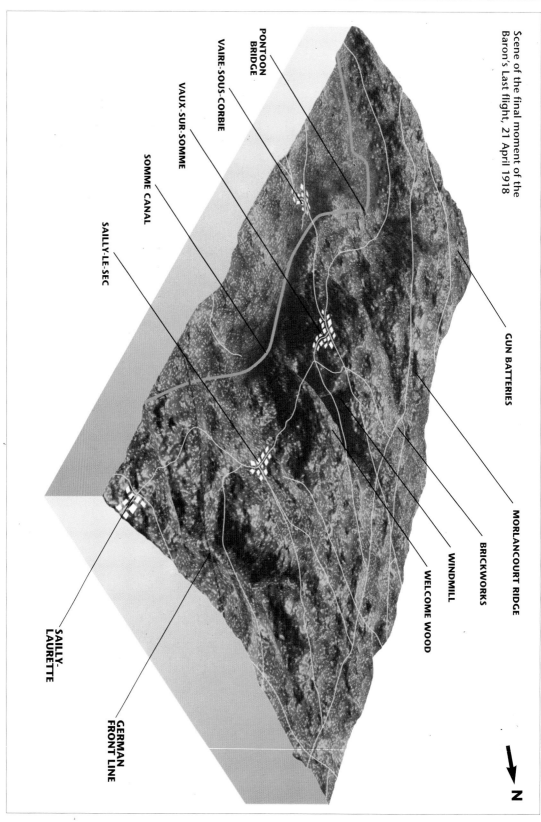

Scene of the final moment of the
Baron's Last flight, 21 April 1918

PONTOON
BRIDGE

VAIRE-SOUS-CORBIE

VAUX-SUR-SOMME

SOMME CANAL

SAILLY-LE-SEC

GUN BATTERIES

MORLANCOURT RIDGE

BRICKWORKS

WINDMILL

WELCOME WOOD

SAILLY-
LAURETTE

GERMAN
FRONT LINE

N

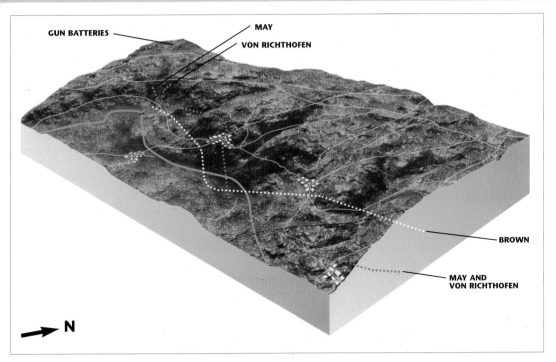

May, pursued by Von Richthofen, heads along the canal towards Vaux-Sur-Somme. Brown dives down and curves southwards to have the sun behind him as he makes his attack on the red Triplane west of Vaux.

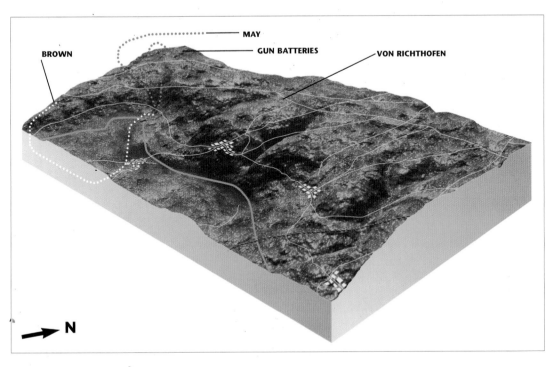

Roy Brown breaks away to the south and begins a climbing turn over the Ridge by Corbie. May pulls up over the Ridge as Von Richthofen continues the chase for a few moments but with both guns now inoperable, he turns east, by the Australian guns and, hit as he pulls back over the Ridge, attempts a crash landing by the Saint Colette Brickworks.

TOP LEFT: Captain A R Brown DSC, 209 Squadron RAF.

TOP RIGHT: Lieutenant W J Mackenzie, 209 Squadron RAF.

LEFT: Leutnant Joachim Wolff, Jasta 11.

ABOVE: Captain O Le Boutillier, 209 Squadron RAF.

position, but further forwards, closer to the road) was mending telephone wires. (Ridgway was not, as sometimes stated, on TOP of the chimney, nor half way up a telegraph pole.) He had the best view of all. He could not only see above and beyond Vaux but also down into the valley beside it. All four men watched the third aeroplane approach from the south-east in a 45° dive. Except for Privates Emery and Jeffrey, who were too low down, they saw the third aeroplane open fire on the German. Due to later reports that the leading aeroplane was an RE8 from 3 Squadron AFC, it was doubtful that all or any of the watchers identified the types or even the nationalities correctly in the early stages.

In late 1937 and early 1938 John Coltman was in touch with W J G Shankland, from Greenvale, Victoria, who was a gunner with the 27th Battery, AIF in 1918. In correspondence concerning whether or not there was a third aircraft in the vicinity, as he stood watching the scene facing south, he stated:

I say quite definitely that there was [a third aeroplane]... British and German machines [were] engaged in a dog-fight over the enemy lines and whilst manoeuvring for position they disappeared below the crest of the slope on which we had our battery position. In a few minutes a Sopwith Camel plane, flying very low, came into view a little to the right of the brickworks which were situated on the top of the slope and about 4-500 yards to our right and slightly in advance of our position. Sitting hard on the Camel's tail was Richthofen in a red triplane, followed closely by another Camel. The first Britisher seemed to me to ground his wheels, and hesitate as if about to land and then continued on across the valley to safety. Opposite the brickworks the German rose sharply to 200 feet or so, began a right hand turn and nose dived into the ground.

I was one of the first 20 or 30 to reach the scene of the crash, and can still clearly see the tall, closely cropped fair-haired Baron lying on his back amongst the ruins of his plane.

Once again we have the distant slant view by Shankland, and from his position it is probable that his feeling that May had attempted to land his machine was due to the fact that the Camel did not climb to escape but flew parallel to the ground as the Gunner viewed it, and assumed it was trying to land. An optical illusion?

In one of May's later accounts of the action he confirmed that at times during the chase down the valley he was so low he could have gone no lower. This supports the witnesses.

There is another account of a witness seeing May's wheels touch the ground. This came from E E Trinder, an observer with the 31st Battalion AIF, writing to Coltman from his home in Brisbane in January 1938. Trinder had been watching the whole action through a pair of Zeiss binoculars, for his job was to report all daily happenings and movements on the Battalion sector and noting map references etc. This morning his FOP was situated on the spur of Corbie [Morlancourt] Ridge overlooking (ie: from where he could see through his binoculars) both the villages of Vaire-sous-Corbie, which was held by his battalion, and Le Hamel, occupied by the Germans.

> ... I watched their progress over the British side of the lines, both planes [sic] firing at intervals, when I was astonished to notice both planes change direction towards our OP. As they came close the British marked plane was only one length and a half ahead of the German plane which was shepherding the British plane towards the ground. As they came within 40 yards of the OP the British pilot endeavoured to land, his wheels on the plane touched the ground on two occasions, but he had too much speed to land, as he certainly would have capsized. He went over the side of the hill for a few hundred feet. The German was on his tail during this landing movement; the British plane then skimmed the grass and rising went directly towards a wood, which was 150 yards from the OP. Immediately on

Aerial view taken in July 1996 with Vaux-sur-Somme bottom left, Welcome Wood middle distance far right and the brickworks middle distance centre.

reaching the wood - the planes were no higher than 50 feet - a burst of bullets from a Lewis gun situated in the wood was fired and the German plane momentarily wobbled and then crashed to the ground. The British plane flew straight on and passed over the town of Corbie. I can honestly say they were the only two planes that were seen over the Ridge that morning, and who fired the burst from that Lewis gun I cannot say. If I had known who the pilot of the red plane was at that particular moment he crashed, I would have certainly broke a record to be in for a souvenir.

This seems yet another case of the short appearance of Brown's Camel below in the valley being hidden by the lip of the Ridge from a viewer higher up. When combined with the mist over the valley, the sun to the south, we can see quite clearly how people standing in different locations and concentrating on the two main antagonists can report seeing contradictory things if interpreted as applying to the chase as a whole.

Another Australian correspondent with John Coltman in late 1937 was Jack O'Rourke, also from Brisbane. Being in another spot, apparently about a mile further to the east than Trinder, he was most emphatic that the *second* Camel did the damage:

> ...anyone suggesting that there was not a third plane in Richthofen's fatal dive is very definitely wrong. The third plane was on Richthofen's tail quite long enough to have caused this great airman to go to his death.

LEFT: The church at Vaux-sur-Somme taken in July 1996; May nearly led von Richthofen into the tower after the chase along the canal and coming out of the mist above the water.

BELOW: The wooded slope of the Morlancourt Ridge (facing north) taken in 1918, as the river turns from north-west to south; to the right is the marshy flooded area and Corbie is in the foreground. (The canal is just out of view to the right.)

I was standing not more than 50 yards from where the pursued Camel flattened out from its life or death dive and could plainly see the pilot looking round to see if Richthofen was following. On looking up for Richthofen I found that his guns were not firing and that he seemed to have changed the angle of his dive and that he had another plane on his tail. His machine seemed to wobble and considerably slacken its speed as the other British plane left him and returned to the dog-fight. This would naturally convey to one that the second British pilot was satisfied he had got his man.

Major H C Rourke MC was another of Coltman's correspondents, whilst serving at the Royal Military College, Duntroon, Australia in 1937. He was atop the Morlancourt Ridge, east of the brickworks, on the 21st, with the 27th Field Battery AIF:

I was standing in the mess dug-out on which was mounted an AA Lewis gun. After the battle had been going on for some minutes I saw a Camel dive towards the ground. It was followed at once by the red triplane. As they got near the ground they were both obscured by trees and a ridge to the south-east of the battery. Shortly afterwards three planes (two Camels and the red triplane) came into view from the south-east and commenced chasing one another round the trees. The triplane was engaged by a large number of ground AA Lewis guns including my gun, whenever it was safe to fire. One Camel disappeared early and Richthofen appeared to be getting the better of the other. Finally the last Camel appeared to break off the fighting and fly off in the direction of the aerodrome.

Richthofen manoeuvred his plane round the trees for a short time, as if looking for his opponent, and then flew due west straight up the Corbie ridge, generally above the Corbie-Bray road. He was flying about 200 feet above the ground and was being engaged by a large number of Lewis guns. As he passed over the ridge the nose of the machine was almost pointing straight up in the air. He then dived suddenly and appeared to crash nose first.

Up in the sky from a distant slant view, LeBoutillier saw Brown make his attack exactly as described on the plaque in the military club in Toronto where the Triplane's seat, etc, is on view. LeBoutillier stated that he saw Brown's tracer strike the Triplane but he did not say where, presumably because the slant view would not have allowed him certainty. Apparently he said in later life that he saw the bullets strike the cockpit area, but one has to wonder if by that time he was adjusting his view to fit the known facts? At the very least the tracer passed by close enough for von Richthofen to see the trails of smoke.

Lieutenant Wood heard shouts from the field kitchen in the trees on the slope below him. Bullets from the air had struck the mobile stove; one of them had holed the stew-pot and part of his platoon's mid-day meal was streaming out through it onto the ground. The hungry men must have noticed that the third aeroplane was facing in their direction at that time for they cursed its pilot roundly and in no uncertain terms! This is further confirmation that Brown attacked the Triplane from the south-east; that is on its left side.

As no bullet holes were later found in the tail or the rear of the fuselage, on the basis of probability it may be presumed that some of Brown's bullets hit the Triplane's wings and that von Richthofen saw the smoke of the tracer from the others pass by. After the forced landing, one soldier who looked at the Triplane stated that the interplane struts on one side had suffered damage. Unfortunately he did not clarify which side or how he thought the damage had occurred. Whether the Baron heard the Rak-ak-ak sound, saw tracer smoke, heard/saw bullet holes or was hit towards the end of Brown's long burst, his subsequent behaviour establishes that he believed he was being attacked from the left. Even if he saw no indication of the whereabouts of his attacker, the position of the sun to his left and the Ridge face to his right heavily favoured the left.

Von Richthofen's immediate and ingrained reaction would have been to turn and face his attacker who would logically be somewhere up there in the sun on the left and who was most likely correcting his aim at that very moment. To hesitate meant to be shot down. People who have claimed to have fought against him in combat all confirm how quick his reactions were. The first shot fired in his direction and he was gone.

However, on this occasion, being too low down to roll over and dive away, plus the risk of a collision if he turned left to face the attack, he 'broke' sharply to the right. There were two good reasons for this 'breaking' direction. The first was that it would put more distance between himself and the bullets coming his way. The second one was also the reason why Brown stopped firing and began turning left – to avoid the mid-air collision. Other than stories which depend entirely and absolutely upon bullet holes which never existed, no information has been found to gainsay LeBoutillier who claims to have seen the 'break'. Whilst von Richthofen was occupied, May had been handed an excellent chance to escape. Unfortunately he did not see the chance and continued to zig-zag.

The topography, prudence and combat technique dictated that Brown make a gradual turn to the south-west (his left) immediately after firing. In this way he would not present himself as a target to the Triplane pilot and could lose his excess speed on his way up and round the south of Corbie before continuing into a right-hand turn to the north and home. If May was then still in danger from the Triplane, he would yet be in a good position to spot the two aircraft and engage the German again as they dropped down the northern side of the Ridge. It should be noted however that it is not easy to relocate an aircraft once it has been lost from sight. May was in a camouflaged machine but even a distant red aeroplane would not be that easy to find, always provided Brown was looking in exactly the right direction and distance. Like forced-landing drill – never take your eyes off the field selected or you'll never find it again.

Oliver LeBoutillier later confirmed that Brown did as described above and pointed out that during his long, gradual climbing turn to the left, Brown's wings would have obscured the view of the Triplane and he would not have seen what followed. That Brown believed that he had wounded the German pilot, is indicated by his reports and actions later that day. Unfortunately, having lost sight of the Triplane, it would not be so easy for Brown to find it again as might be imagined.

Both of Brown's combat reports (he made out two due to reasons which will be explained later) state: 'He went down vertical.' But unfortunately neither one of them says when or beginning from where. One thing is certain, it was not immediately after; the Triplane was not high enough for it to do so. His flying log book entry is equally silent on this point. According to LeBoutillier the descent followed some time afterwards. The other witnesses to Brown's attack agree with that.

If von Richthofen had been killed by Brown's long burst, the red Triplane would have crashed beside the river between Vaux-sur-Somme and Corbie, or certainly on the southern slope of the Ridge. Its engine would probably have still been running at normal power. A wounded von Richthofen could recover control and fly for some time; how long and how well was another matter. Those who query whether he was hit at this stage, either by Brown (who in any event was the wrong side of the Triplane to inflict the mortal wound) or from ground fire from the Ridge, must explain why the Baron did not immediately turn south to south-east, towards the German lines, rather than face the climb over the Ridge.

Wounded or untouched, as may be, whilst von Richthofen was completing his evasive action, he would already have been looking for his attacker. He would have noted that the aircraft which had caught him by surprise had overshot at high speed and would not be back for a while. Assuming that the Baron had mistaken his ground position, he would have believed that the heavily defended zone between Vaux and Corbie was yet a couple of miles away. The only Allied airfield around was the one north of Vaux, formerly used by 3 AFC as a landing ground, but which had been evacuated three weeks earlier. Apart from the now departed Camel which had attacked him, there was no sign and not much likelihood of any unfriendly activity. The Camel that he had been about to despatch was still zig-zagging away. It was further ahead than before but not too far to catch. There was time for one more try. The continued zig-zagging agrees with Lieutenant May's later statement that he did not see Brown's attempt to rescue him.

On the basis of airmanship, a pilot of Brown's calibre would not have made unnecessary manoeuvres in an aeroplane close to self-disintegrating speed. If he was doing anything at that moment other than sweating, it was most probably trying to check May's present situation. This is supported by Lieutenant J Quinlan on the Morlancourt Ridge who reported having seen an aeroplane travelling west about half a mile beyond the far side of the river. The probability is that after Brown's Camel had slowed down enough to restore normal control pressures, he looked back to his right. In the time taken to do this, he would have travelled about one mile. May would have travelled less than that, but to find May's olive-brown Camel and the red German Triplane against a dark background, Brown needed first to know approximately where they were. Looking into three-dimensional space is one thing, finding something is another.

Whilst Brown was distracting von Richthofen from May, Lieutenant Mellersh had succeeded in escaping from the two Triplanes which had forced him down to hedge-hopping height. All that is known of Mellersh's movements from then onwards is that, as he passed near Corbie on his way home, he saw a red Triplane crash nearby. He did not say to his right or to his left. He then looked upwards and saw Brown's streamered Camel above him. However, based on LeBoutillier's statement that Mellersh was flying ahead of him and off to his right, one has to assume from this that Mellersh had to be south of the river and if he was indeed flying north-west in the direction of Bertangles, then the Triplane must have been off to his right and within his view.

The total elapsed time between Brown ceasing fire on the Triplane and Mellersh seeing him overhead would have been about 30 seconds, depending on exactly where Mellersh was.

There would be nothing unusual for an aeroplane with a severely wounded pilot to fly, under control, for some time before crashing. There were many cases during the war of a pilot dying of wounds within minutes of making a successful landing. It would have been nothing really extraordinary for Brown to catch sight of the red Triplane in a steep descent about 30 seconds after he had fired on it and about half a mile from the place where he had done so.

Although neither of Brown's combat reports nor log book mentions the subject, he later affirmed that he had seen the red Triplane crash at Sainte Colette. To quote: 'May saw it, Mellersh saw it and I saw it.' If 'it' included the steep angle of the Triplane's initial descent and not just the cloud of dust which followed, the source of the phrase: 'He went down vertical,' is explained. Brown never publicly clarified exactly what he saw and there is no record that he was ever asked to do so.

As Jasta 11 pilot, Leutnant Richard Wenzl, flew past Corbie and Hamelet on his way back to Cappy, he noticed a small aeroplane on the ground. When combined with von Richthofen's failure to return and Leutnant Wolff's sighting of him low down in the same general area, he recalled that the small aeroplane might have been red in colour. The suspicion arose that something unfortunate must have befallen their leader.

Upon hearing this unwelcome news, Hauptmann Willi Reinhard immediately ordered three aircraft to be refuelled and dispatched to check what Wenzl had observed. Wenzl, who knew the exact spot, Walther Karjus and Wolfram von Richthofen were the pilots. From this excursion much confusion was to arise later for they were attacked by Sopwith Camels and heavy machine-gun fire from the ground between Vaux and Corbie. For a few minutes any combination of Triplanes and Camels chasing one another could be seen, and more than one was reported.

Richard Wenzl managed to confirm that there was a red-coloured aeroplane on the ground but he could not get close enough for positive identification. He was surprised to see a second aeroplane on the ground not far from the first one and was certain that it was not lying there when he passed by earlier. Nobody else mentioned it on either side and not much credence was given to his observation until 1993 when Private Frank Wormald revealed that he had watched it come down. There are no obvious British casualties to fit this second aeroplane, so perhaps if indeed there was one it was merely someone force landing, with only slight damage or engine failure. It had nothing to do with the matter in hand, except that the sudden possible appearance of a pilot may have led to further confusion amongst the soldiery on the Ridge and may be behind a tale which eventually developed into the fable, which achieved official status, that Lieutenant Mellersh landed in a nearby field.

In mid-April 1918, for some reason, 209 Squadron had run out of Army Form W 3348, Combats in the Air [reports] and the Recording Officer (RO), Lieutenant Albert Shelley RNVR/RAF, a 28-year-old peacetime accountant and auditor from Sydenham, south-east London, had perforce to use a locally made substitute. This was to influence later events. Upon returning to Bertangles, Captain Brown, together with colleagues, made their reports to the RO, who typed them up for posterity; one original and the usual number of carbon copies, on this unofficial form. Brown, in his report, cited Lieutenant Mellersh as witness to the crash of a red Triplane. The text of Brown's report reads like a run-of-the-mill description of a High Offensive Patrol (HOP) in which contact with the enemy had occurred, and is phrased in the 'least said, fewer questions asked' style. (Not unusual in any of the dozens of other squadrons in France.) The only location mentioned is map reference 62D.Q.2 which delineates an area to the immediate west of the village of Cerisy. The only altitude given for the events described in the report is 5,000 feet. No additional information is given as to where or at what height: 'I got a long burst into him..' took place. There would have been nothing out of the ordinary in catching sight again, 30 seconds later, of an earlier target now going down out of control, therefore, 'He went down vertical and was seen to crash by Lieut. Mellersh' was a clear and concise statement of fact. With each day's paperwork to be closed out at 1559 hours and much of it sent to 22 Wing soon afterwards, the RO would long ago have mentioned the merits of brevity to everyone. That no particular care was taken with the phrasing is illustrated by an obvious un-corrected error. The '2-seater Albatros' which was shot down by Lieutenant M S Taylor if referred to as '2 Albatrosses'. In the upper right quadrant of the substitute combat report, Major Butler added in ink – 'Decisive'.

Apparently, at some time after these forms and carbons had been removed from the typewriter and separated, Captain Brown learned that Lieutenant May had also witnessed the crash of the red Triplane, so the RO, in order to maintain alignment on all sheets, one by one subscripted onto the original and each copy, the additional words: 'and Lieut.May.' On the second and later carbon copies the additional words are in fact in far neater letters than the blurred text in the main body which gives the impression that somebody added them later on a different typewriter. This logically brings into question when the addition was made. An examination of a photocopy of the original shows no difference in the type face and provides the clue as to what probably happened. It is most unlikely that Lieutenant Shelley would have made such an addition after Major Butler had appended his signature and comment. However, the report is definitely an altered document and as such, incurred someone's displeasure later that day, or perhaps on the morrow, when its contents acquired unexpected importance.

The two pages of 209 Squadron's Record Book which cover from 1601 hours on Saturday 20 April to 1559 hours on Sunday the 21st, state that on 21.4.18 Captain Brown had a 'Decisive combat with red Triplane at 62D.Q.2 (See Combat Report)'.

Major Butler's comment in ink was altered at Wing or Brigade level to 'Indecisive' by the pencilled addition of a suffix 'In'. The probability is that soon after lunch, Lieutenant-Colonel W J Cairnes, who had already taken over some of the duties of Lieutenant-Colonel F V Holt, the 22 Wing CO, whom he would replace later that week, was made aware that two RE8 crews of 3 Squadron AFC had also been in action with a red Triplane at about the same time and place and, while they had made no claim initially, were now wondering whether they had indeed shot it down. A further complication arose when word arrived that a red Triplane had been shot down by anti-aircraft fire from the 53rd Australian Battery and the 24th Machine Gun Company, also at about the same time. It must soon have become obvious to Cairnes that all four claims referred to the same aeroplane.

In a letter written by the then Major-General L E Beavis in the 1960s he confirmed, that in the late afternoon of the 21st, a senior RAF officer, who may be assumed to be Lieutenant-Colonel Cairnes, accompanied by a pilot who may well have been Brown, visited his dug-out at his Field Artillery site near Bonnay. They came to investigate the downed Triplane (and it has been suggested that Brown saw von Richthofen's body laid out on a casualty-clearing stretcher, which Beavis himself had earlier sent up to Sainte Colette. Also that Brown then had an attack of nausea). Beavis, however, did not have any recollection of Brown going into his dug-out. The 53rd Battery's Daily Record Book (or War Diary) does not mention the visit of an RAF Lieutenant-Colonel, and a locally important one at that. No witness has reported seeing Cairnes or Brown risk his life to long-range snipers or an artillery shell by going out into the open at Sainte Colette to inspect the Triplane. Indeed, its position in the field was deemed to be so dangerous that 3 AFC Squadron salvage crew crawled out to it to decide how best to retrieve it. The only visiting officer definitely known to have gone to Sainte Colette for a short while at that time was Lieutenant W J Warneford, who was in charge of the salvage crew. He and his men surprised everyone by calmly advising that they had arrived to collect the German aeroplane which had been shot down by an RE8 of their Squadron. Officers did not wear name tags on their uniforms in those days. Unless a visiting officer were brought into direct contact with an NCO or private soldier, they would be unlikely to learn his identity, except through rumours.

COMBATS IN THE AIR.
– * – * – * – * – * – * – * – * – * – * – * – * – * – * – * – * – * –

Roy Brown's first combat report.

NO. 209 SQUADRON.

DATE.... April 21st 1918.

Type & No. of Aeroplane. Sopwith B.R. B 7270.

Time. 10. 45 a.m.

Armament. Two Vickers Syn. Guns.

Locality. 62D Q 2.

Pilot. Capt. A. R. Brown, D.S.C.

Duty. H.O.P.

Height. 5.000 feet.

Result: Destroyed.
Driven down
out of control.
Driven down.

Remarks on Hostile Aircraft: Type, etc,

Fokker Triplane, pure red wings with small black crosses.

NARRATIVE.

(1)   At 10. 25 a.m. I observed 2 Albatross burst into flames and crash.

(2)   Dived on large formation of 15 - 20 Albatross Scouts D 5 and Fokker Triplanes, two of which got on my tail and I came out.

Went back again and dived on pure red triplane which was firing on Lieut. May.   I got a long burst into him and he went down vertical and was observed to crash by Lieut. Mellersh. and
Lieut. May.
I fired on two more but did not get them.

A R Brown
Captain.

Major.
Commanding 209 Squadron.R.A.F.

Some idea of the confusion of names on that day may be gained by information given officially to author Floyd Gibbons stating that it was Lieutenant Mellersh of 209 Squadron who conducted the salvage operation! Major Beavis vividly recalled receiving many visitors *the following day*.

In the light of his own observations, Major Beavis did not take much notice of Captain Brown's assertions that he had shot the Baron down, especially as Warneford was already saying 3 AFC had got von Richthofen and he was well aware of the claims of his own gunners, Buie and Evans. Following on from this, a heated discussion between Brown and Lieutenant Ellis, of the 53rd, got to such a state that Ellis ended up by calling the Canadian pilot a bloody liar, a remark for which Beavis told Ellis to apologise. This remark was to turn up again, totally inverted in *Liberty* magazine and in the serialised newspaper article – *My Fight with Richthofen* – in which Brown is made to say Beavis was the liar, although he is also said to have made the remark behind the Major's back.

Because of Major-General Beavis's revelations, the pages of the 53rd Battery Daily Record Book, and the confusion of officers' names as described above, the recollections of 22 RAF Wing personnel at Poulainville aerodrome, that the first time Brown saw von Richthofen's body and suffered his well-publicised attack of nausea was when the Crossley tender driven by Mick Worsley arrived back there with it on board, sound as though they might be correct.

When Captain Brown's letter to his father, dated 27 April, is considered, confirmation appears. Brown wrote in reference to preparations at Poulainville for the first medical examination that it was' the first time he had seen von Richthofen's corpse.

It should be noted that, from statements later made by Brown, he believed that he had put several bullets into the Baron's back in the area of the left shoulder, that they had passed downwards and forwards through the heart and had exited through the abdomen on the right side.

The Combats Annex to 5th Brigade's Summary of Work of the 21st, issued that evening, describes events from 1601 hours on the 20th until 1559 hours on the 21st. For 209 Squadron only the 'decisive' combats of Lieutenant Taylor and Lieutenant Mellersh are listed. 3 Squadron AFC and 209 appeared to be making a duplicate claim for a certain red Fokker Dr.I, therefore, Captain Brown's claim, and that of Lieutenant Barrow, had been omitted from the Annex for the day in question. 22 Wing, to which both squadrons belonged, had not resolved the matter due to some unexpected complication with the Australian 5th Division.

Brigade had decided to make some enquiries before taking a decision. Prudence dictated placing the matter before the common superior, the HQ of the British Fourth Army.

Authors' Note

In the 1960s an attempt was made to discredit Gunner George Ridgway's testimony by alleging that the chimney which he had climbed was not at Sainte Colette but at the town of Heilly.

The chateau, where the Sector HQ was located, was near the town of Heilly, and not surprisingly that part of the Front was known as the Heilly Sector. When the present authors drove past the chateau in 1996, it was empty, abandoned, the wrought iron gates were chained shut and its once beautiful garden was overgrown with weeds. In statements concerning the Triplane's forced landing site, many witnesses had referred to the brickworks chimney as the Heilly Sector Chimney. Unfortunately, Ridgway, whilst describing his location had, on one occasion, omitted the word 'sector'.

The town of Heilly is deep down in the valley of the River Ancre on the north side of the Morlancourt Ridge. There is indeed a tall chimney in the industrial section at the south-west edge of the town, but the top of the chimney is more than 100 feet below the top of the Ridge. A person who climbed that far up it would have a grand view of the fields surrounding the town and of the River Ancre, but not much else. That has been cited as proof that Ridgway was fibbing.

However, no signals officer who valued his job would run his wires AWAY from their destination or down the back streets of a town. That eliminates the Heilly town chimney immediately from both the technical and logical points of view of communication with the various Battalion HQs in the Sector.

When researching his book, Carisella looked into the chimney issue. Ridgway's son was running a tourist hotel in Amiens at the time – the Australian Hotel – and fortunately, his father, on a visit to France had shown him exactly from where he had watched Brown diving to the attack. The son personally took Carisella to the place – Sainte Colette brickworks. (See photos on pages 43 and 60.)

CHAPTER FIVE
Ground Fire – The Third Claim

The ground action against Manfred von Richthofen's Fokker Triplane began with Lieutenant-Colonel Whitham's soldiers firing at it with their rifles as it passed over Vaux-sur-Somme. Captain Brown then made his rescue attempt. Further west, at a pontoon bridge over the Somme canal, where it passes behind a large farm house, Sergeant Gavin Darbyshire's repair party also subjected the Fokker to rifle fire. Due to the bends in the river and the pre-occupation with work, the machine-gun crews hidden in the vegetation along the slope of the Morlancourt Ridge did not realise in time to respond that an enemy aeroplane was following the Camel which was approaching low down beside the river. It was not a common occurrence for German aircraft seldom chased Allied aircraft beyond the front lines.

The height at which May's Camel and von Richthofen's Fokker were flying may be judged from a statement by Lance Corporal Victor Ewart who was with the 56th Australian Battalion. Victor Ewart wrote in October 1937, from his home in Lakemba, NSW:

> At the time I was attached to No.12 Section, No.11 Platoon, C. company, in reserves. Our position - or possies - were along a narrow road skirting a hill or plateau overlooking a valley running parallel with the road. Across this valley, known to us as Death Valley, was Villers Bretonneux. I wish to emphasise the fact that we were on the side of a hill overlooking a valley. The rest of our Battalion was scattered over the crest of the hill above and behind us. When the Baron chased the British 'plane past our position he would be below the crest of the hill and therefore would be open to rifle fire which was concentrated on him from above and behind us. There were many men who had a shot at him and it is my contention that the Baron was brought down by an infantryman of the 56th Battalion AIF, whose identity will never be known. There were only two aeroplanes in the immediate vicinity, the chaser and chased. The Baron would only be about 70 feet from me and about 75 feet from the bottom of the valley when I shot at him with my rifle at an angle of about ten

> degrees. The men who were firing from above and at the rear of my position would be firing down on him; this would coincide with the medical evidence that he was fired on from above or from the air.

As described in detail in Chapter Two, the two aeroplanes were then confronted by the sharp left turn of the Ridge face where the Somme changed direction from west to south just before Corbie. Continuing straight ahead they made a steep climb followed by a half right turn to the north-west. Private Ray McDiarmid of the 8th Brigade, who later claimed to have been near the top of the Ridge, stated that he had seen the situation in time to open fire at the Triplane. He later ruefully said: 'Unfortunately I did not lead far enough [aim in front of it] and my shots went behind.'

Authors' note. Private McDiarmid tells a convincing story including that his helper with the Lewis gun obtained a souvenir from the red Triplane later that day; so it is certain that the correct event is being described. Unfortunately McDiarmid did not specify exactly where he was when he fired, and it has been assumed that he was on the wooded north slope at the time.

However, two aspects do not fit correctly. First; his unit, the 30th Battalion, 8th Brigade, 5th Division, was stationed south of the River Somme. Second; if he had been seconded to help out north of the river, his statement that after he had ceased firing, a machine gun to his left opened up raises some questions. McDiarmid's firing position would have faced south, therefore the Triplane would have crossed his front from left (east) to right (west) on its way towards the 53rd Battery position.

All in all, it looks as though he was south of the canal but close to it. His helper would have had to cross the pontoon bridge behind the farmhouse and then ascend the slope. The time required to do that fits with the souvenir obtained; a piece of sheet metal from the Triplane's petrol tank. Hardly one of the first items to be garnered.

Sergeant Gavin Darbyshire, 9th Engineers, down at the pontoon bridge, saw the first two aeroplanes climb the Ridge and heard several successive bursts of machine-gun fire. From his home in

Chinkapook, Australia, he wrote in October 1937:

> Early that morning I was in charge of a
> party repairing pontoon bridges on the
> Somme, directly behind a farmhouse. Just
> after daylight a German 'plane flew low
> along the canal and stirred us up a bit.
> Later, as we were busy at our work... we
> heard a machine gun burst and saw a plane
> coming our way. As I always considered a
> live engineer was much more useful than a
> dead hero I ordered all under cover. On
> looking out I saw the plane was one of
> ours flying very low, then behind it, and
> just above the trees, I saw a three-winged
> German plane firing madly at the one in
> front. We all hopped out and some of the
> chaps took pot shots with rifles at the
> Fokker, so close that we clearly saw the
> pilot. At this stage I am certain that
> the German was so interested on his job
> that he did not know where he was.
>
> Now I consider this the acid test. The
> leading plane turned slightly towards a
> rather high ridge used by artillery OP,
> some of which I built; the German
> followed. At this stage we heard the roar
> of another plane going flat out at least
> half a mile further back from us. I then
> turned to look at the two leading planes
> just going over the ridge, heard a burst
> of gunfire and the Fokker stopped in its
> stride and did the first half of the loop
> then straightened out and fluttered down
> out of our sight as if doing a pancake
> landing. By this time the third plane was
> just approaching the ridge.
>
> All this was vividly stamped on my
> mind and I was amazed later to hear
> that he was brought down by a plane as
> the chaser was not firing at the time
> the German stopped.

These bursts of machine-gun fire Darbyshire heard would have been Private McDiarmid and those about to be described. The third aeroplane was no longer in sight; it must have slipped past overhead or behind him a little earlier with its engine throttled back whilst his men were firing their rifles at the Triplane and hoping that the Camel in front of it would clear the trees as it climbed. Several witnesses later commented on the motion of the Triplane in flight at this time. The interesting aspect is that they all used the word 'unsteady' which suggests that they may have read something about it during the interim.

Sergeant Cedric Popkin of the 24th Machine Gun Company, assisted by Private Rupert Weston and Private Marshall, had also opened fire with a Vickers gun before the Triplane passed over the crest of the Ridge. Several different map references, two of them being prefixed 'approximately', have been given for the location of this gun. Three of them when plotted on an April 1918 map are down beside a road at the bottom of the Morlancourt Ridge and appear to be incorrect as Sergeant Popkin could not have fired downwards on the Triplane from any of them. The explanation for this mix-up is to be found in Chapter 17. The fourth reference, given by Popkin himself, is: '.. in 62D.J.19.d, about 600 yards from the crash site of the Triplane.' This location would have permitted all the actions described by the Sergeant as having taken place that morning. (See maps on page 105.)

Sergeant Popkin's Vickers gun was either mounted on a post or on one of the special, tall tripods which had been developed for anti-aircraft work. He later claimed that the 'unsteadiness' of the Triplane was the result of his shots having struck the aircraft. He added, with all honesty, that the Triplane 'recovered' shortly afterwards. This would be typical aircraft behaviour when flying in and out of a zone of severe turbulence such as would occur at that point of the Ridge on a windy day.

The noise of the aircraft engines and the ground fire alerted the troops for some distance around. Bombardier Secull picked up his rifle. This was the best he could do for, although he was in charge of the 53rd Battery's two anti-aircraft Lewis guns, Gunners Buie and Evans were rostered for duty that morning as already stated. All three men had already been alerted by Sergeant Hart's orderly to prepare for action. Buie was positioned at 62D.I.24.b.65.36 and Evans at 62D.I.24.b.73.43. The 53rd and 55th gun crews, who were hidden beneath camouflage netting, stopped work and watched. (See map on page 54.)

Some witnesses said that the German pilot was firing heavily at the Camel. Buie later said: 'He was blazing away.' Others said that the Fokker pilot several times leaned forwards in the cockpit and then fired a very short burst. Lieutenant-Colonel Fitzgerald said that each burst contained only two or three shots. One soldier, Private Smith, stated that whilst the German was passing over his head, he fired not a single shot. When the Triplane's machine guns and ammunition belts were examined later, their condition indicated that only the last three observations were correct, and in that order. The suggestion has been made, and there is good reason to accept it, that it was at this point that von Richthofen's right-hand gun stopped

VAUX-SUR-SOMME
CHURCH

DARBYSHIRE'S
PONTOON BRIDGE

BEND IN
THE CANAL

LEFT: Aerial view of Vaux-sur-Somme and showing the pontoon bridge over which Brown flew after firing at the Triplane.

ABOVE: Close-up of the pontoon bridge and the farm buildings.

completely and that he decided to head for home.

Richthofen, who, one has to say, may not yet have noticed that ground fire was being directed at himself (although this seems unlikely, it is perfectly possible if everyone aimed like Private McDiarmid), had started a turn from north-west to north-east whilst May continued straight ahead to the north-west. When they first came into accurate range of the two Lewis guns manned by Buie and Evans, May's Camel had been interposed between them and the chasing Triplane. Gunner Buie later acknowledged that the first to get a clear shot was Evans. As the low flying Triplane proceeded in its turn Buie also got a clear view and opened fire. Buie was very specific that the Triplane was flying towards him

The pontoon bridge, facing north.

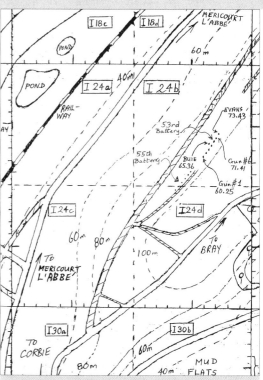

Enlarged area showing the position of the 53rd and 55th Batteries and the locations of Gunners Buie and Evans.

a little to his right. Evans's evaluation of his own situation is not on record.

Although the Triplane was an easy target, it was by no means so easy to hit. Being low down and close to Buie and Evans, the Triplane was changing position rapidly relative to them and they had to swing their Lewis guns quickly both horizontally and vertically in order to follow it. An added complication, which might not have occurred to them (they were not trained, expert anti-aircraft gunners) was that the Triplane was not moving in the direction it was headed. The Triplane was headed approximately north at 110 mph (165 feet per second, approx) and the air by which it was supported was moving west at 25 to 30 mph (38 to 45 feet per second). The gunner, who merely allowed for the speed of the Triplane, would, by the time he had pulled the trigger, find that the pilot's body had moved about seven to nine feet to the west and his shots would therefore strike somewhere (like the same seven to nine feet) out on the right wings.

Using short bursts, Buie fired a whole pannier (drum) of 47 rounds at the Triplane. Assuming that he and Evans did allow for the strong east wind (blowing the Triplane to the west) the first shots of either gunner would have struck the pilot almost frontally in an upwards direction unless he had been twisted around in the cockpit at the time, checking his rear. Buie's final burst would have been about 45° upwards relative to the ground but, due to the Triplane's angle of bank, would have struck the pilot somewhere between horizontally and slightly upwards relative to his seated position in the cockpit. It is important to bear in mind that a Lewis gun has a much tighter pattern than a Vickers gun, and at close range it is normal to find three or four bullets in any target that has been struck squarely, ie: not hit near the edge.

That the two gunners did not allow for the sideways motion of the Triplane is suggested by Gunner Buie and others nearby claiming to have seen 'splinters' flying from the Triplane's tail. This is another case of the deceptiveness of a slant view. Unlike most British aircraft, the Triplane's fuselage and tail were made from welded steel tubes covered with fabric. There was some plywood used for the fairing around and behind the cockpit but, during the later examination, no bullet holes were found in it. Indeed, looking at photographs of the tail when the machine was at Poulainville, there are no signs of any bullet holes at all.

The Triplane's wings were made from wood and fabric. The wide interplane struts were also made

ABOVE: **Lewis machine gunner, with gun on tripod, supported by his spotter with telescope. Note camouflaged 18-pounder gun.**

ABOVE RIGHT: **Lewis gun.**

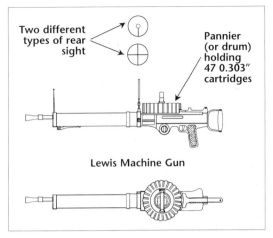

from wood. Splinters torn from any of these would have slowed down enough to become visible as they flew by the tail. Von Richthofen made an immediate turn to the right. With a pilot of his skill and combat experience this would have been a flat turn. A little known trick outside the flying fraternity was to skid sideways by applying rudder and opposite aileron. In the Baron's situation, his best move was to apply right rudder and left aileron; this would double his rate of sideways travel relative to the direction in which the nose of his Triplane was pointed. To climb would have been fatal in that the Triplane would then be following a predictable flight path. His tactic was obviously fruitful for a while but a few hundred yards away, a trained and highly successful anti-aircraft machine gunner who knew that trick, and could make rapid mental judgement of by how much to lead the target and how much to allow for the wind, was watching and biding his time. His name was Vincent Emery, his helper was Jack Jeffrey.

A few seconds after the right turn of the Triplane, Gunner Buie saw it begin to act strangely. In later years, Buie told his nephew, Morris, that he did not replace the drum and fire again because there was no point in it; the Triplane was obviously finished. Private Frank Wormald, who was standing beside Buie, later claimed to have seen Buie's tracer: '... *going like a red streak towards the cockpit and striking the pilot's chest.*' He added that the pilot made a motion rather like shrugging his shoulders and then sat up erect in his seat. Without doubt Wormald saw Buie's tracer heading towards the Triplane but to affirm where it hit would have been a conclusion based upon later information

that there was a large hole in the Baron's chest. There is simply no way a man on the ground would be able to see much more than the top of the pilot's head (flying helmet) in a Triplane coming straight at him, sitting behind a large engine, twin machine guns and a windshield and cockpit fairing!

In their short machine-gun trench at Sainte Colette beside the Corbie to Bray road, Privates Emery and Jeffrey saw the two aircraft separate as the Triplane turned away from the Camel and headed in their direction (from north to north-east). These two soldiers were part of four Lewis-gun crews on assignment from the 40th Battalion, to defend the supply routes to the front from surprise German air attacks. Emery was an expert anti-aircraft gunner with four German aircraft already shot down to his name, and like the professional he was, he swivelled the Lewis gun, aligned it on the target and accustomed his eyes to the light and the distance. Private Jeffrey placed a spare pannier ready for use.

With the Triplane now flying almost directly towards them, heading east along the Ancre (north-western) side of the Ridge, at low altitude, it appeared that Private Emery was about to become an 'ace'. Ironically, von Richthofen may have just spotted the Australian 18-pounder guns on that reverse slope. Gunner R L C Hunt, who was part of the crew of No.6 gun, the one furthest north, claims that the red Triplane passed overhead, between guns No.5 and No.6. This would place Buie and Evans obliquely below it, Evans being on its left and Buie on its right. Buie was behind gun number four and Evans beyond gun number six out on the far left (north-east) side. The camouflage netting over the guns would not be very effective against observation from as low down as that. To enable the exact location of the two batteries to be determined had been one of the main reasons JGI group had been called into the area, to help, by clearing the sky, German two-seaters to spot them. If he had seen them, it may have gone through his mind in those last moments that this information was something urgently needed.

The two gunners waited for the triplane to come closer. It was shortly to do so in a most unexpected manner. They heard Vickers gunfire, Lewis gunfire and a lot of rifle shots from the fields to their west. The noise would have been a little delayed in reaching them due to the distance and the strong east wind. It would appear to have been at this time that von Richthofen realised exactly where he was, especially if he had seen those 18-pounders a moment earlier. He was approaching a very tall chimney made to look like a tin whistle by shell holes blown in it, and joined to a building

which stood almost alone in a field. Until now it had been below the skyline and had blended in with the dark background. It could only be Sainte Colette brickworks. There was no other tall chimney isolated like that for miles around.

The machine-gun firing had ceased, and apart from the odd rifle shots, which Lieutenant Wood later claimed came from his platoon, things had become quiet. The Triplane began another right turn and started to climb. If it continued along that path, it would shortly be right side on to Sergeant Popkin's Vickers gun. The Sergeant prepared to open fire for the second time.

Private Scott, a signaller who watched the action, stated that: 'Hundreds of soldiers were firing rifles at the Triplane.' Private Ernest Boore, Private Henzell and Trooper Howell, later claimed success (see Appendix K).

Privates Emery and Jeffrey, and Lieutenant George M Travers, later described how the climb had suddenly steepened sharply and the Triplane almost turned over to the right. They heard the engine roar. Many others, who also saw the event, interpreted it as a steeply banked climbing attempt to escape. The wind and the distance made von Richthofen's initial increase to full climbing power seem to belong to the violent pull-up and twist. Not being fighter pilots, the viewers did not realise what they had just seen. It was the instant when von Richthofen's body reacted to a spasm following a sharp stab of pain, caused by a severe wound on a right-handed person. The uncontrollable muscular contraction caused his grip to tighten on the stick and his arm to jerk it back and to the right.

BELOW: The site of the 53rd Battery taken in July 1996, facing north. The Morlancourt Ridge is off to the right while the road runs from Corbie to Méricourt-l'Abbé.

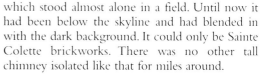

ABOVE: Aerial view of the 53rd Battery position, showing the Corbie to Méricourt-l'Abbé road, and the town of Bonnay centre left (facing north).

This reaction was well-known to the ace fighter pilots on both sides. The Baron's brother, Lothar, and A G Lee (in his book *No Parachute*) both describe how they attacked an enemy aeroplane and whilst firing at it saw it nose up steeply. This, they both wrote, was a sure sign that the pilot had been hit.

Authors' Note: Dr.-Ing Niedermeyer pointed out the muscular contraction phenomenon, and it was confirmed by Doctor José Segura MD when his opinion was requested. The reader has only to imagine a sharp dig in the ribs to understand the reaction.

Private Emery stated that he saw the pilot stiffen and then appear to collapse in his seat. Gunner Ridgway said that the pilot's head fell over to the left. As Emery did not hear any machine guns firing at this time, he assumed that one of the rifle shots had struck the pilot. He then heard the distant noise of a Vickers gun. However, it must be borne in mind that, due to the wind and the distance, sound was not synchronised to sight; it was, in fact considerably delayed in Emery's direction.

Major Blair Wark VC, the second-in-command of the 32nd Battalion, who watched the sudden climb, made a statement in 1933 which agreed basically with Private Emery, in that he said:

> The fatal shot came from another machine gun than those with the 53rd Battery and the 24th MG Company [Popkin], but definitely from one firing from the ground. A number were firing at the plane.

Gavin Darbyshire, watching from below by the canal, seeing the events from one side, saw the loss of forward motion resulting from the pull-up and twist of the Triplane. He described the pull-up as that performed at the beginning of a loop; the Triplane then nosed down and disappeared below his line of vision. Darbyshire added:

> [The Baron] was either hit from the ground or his machine was put out of control from the ground, as when the burst came his forward flight stopped as if he had run up against a brick wall.

Written in 1937, Darbyshire's words are completely original and could not have been swayed by anything he might have read, as later 'witnesses' may have been. Many of the latter have mentioned the word 'stagger' or the 'plane staggered'; the repetition of this word staggered suggests a common source. Staggered does not make aeronautical sense either.

The Triplane was seen to cease its apparent attempt to escape and to 'wallow around' in the sky. The Triplane turned half left, which would have been into the wind, and as a result of the delayed sound, an apparent reversal of a logical sequence was noted by witnesses in that the propeller was seen to slow down and the engine note was heard to change; in that order. In retrospect it can be seen that von Richthofen began preparations for a forced landing in the nearest open space; the field at Sainte Colette where Captain Turner and Lieutenant Wood had their respective FOPs.

Based upon the testimony of witnesses who observed the beginning of the descent of the Triplane and of others who examined it afterwards, it appears that the following then happened.

Upon recovering control of his machine and realising that the wound which he had just suffered was serious, von Richthofen immediately initiated standard, emergency procedure. He needed to get down quickly before he passed out, and to get medical help, even from the British. He turned into wind, looked for and found a suitable field nearby and decided to land there. He automatically took steps against fire following a possible mishap in a rough field by closing the fuel valve, (the equivalent of the throttle on an Oberursel or Le Rhône rotary engine) opening the vent valve of the pressurised petrol tank, and switching off the magneto. To use the cool air as an aid to maintain his fading faculties he pulled off his flying goggles. They fell overboard and were picked up by Private E E Hardaker of the 11th Brigade, who kept them for many years; they were later acquired by Pat Carisella. The watchers from the 53rd Battery saw the Fokker, which was obviously on its way to earth, disappear behind the trees to their east. Behind those trees lay the field with the FOP across the road from the brickworks with the tall chimney. Thereafter began the rush of soldiers to the field at Sainte Colette.

Both the 53rd Battery gunners Buie and Evans, and the 24th MG Company's Sergeant Popkin, entered claims for downing the red Triplane. It is worth noting that Gunner Buie truly believed he had put several bullets frontally into von Richthofen. In civilian life he lived by fishing and by hunting wild fowl. He was known locally as a 'crack shot'. In December 1959, the magazine *Cavalier* published an article entitled: *I Killed Richthofen* which contains the following assertions by Robert Buie:

> Richthofen was struck in the left breast, abdomen and right knee. The wounds were all frontal. Two separate medical... reports agreed that the fatal chest wound was definitely frontal.

Gunner Evans also believed that he had put some bullets into von Richthofen. In a letter to his mother, Evans asked her to tell his Uncle Bill that he could still shoot straight. It has to be assumed too, that soldiers returning from the crash site, having seen the blood down the front of Richthofen's body and on his knees, tended to confirm frontal hits. With both Buie and Evans adamant that they had hit the pilot frontally, they had nowhere else to go with their stories.

In Sergeant Popkin's report, dated 24 April 1918, he stated after seeing the body he believed that at least three machine-gun bullets had struck the body, one in the ribs at the side and a couple through his chest. Later, according to a telegram sent by him dated 16 October 1935, to C E W Bean, the Australian historian, he explained that the first time he opened fire on the Triplane it was travelling directly towards him [coming from the direction of Vaux] and at a lower level than his gun position; the second time it was passing by a little way off and higher up [atop of the Ridge] with the right-hand side of the machine towards him. In the first case he would have been aiming downwards and in the second case, upwards.

Unfortunately for Popkin, the paperwork for his claim was not made out immediately. With a type of black humour it can be said that this was fortunate for General Sir Henry Rawlinson otherwise his dilemma that evening would have been four official claims, not three.

CHAPTER SIX
The Rittmeister's Forced Landing

At least nine soldiers witnessed the forced landing of the Triplane from nearby, and many others from afar. Depending upon how familiar the distant witness was with the aircraft and with slant views, is how he interpreted what he saw. Some later stated that with a dead pilot in the cockpit, the Triplane made a perfect landing and rolled to a stop undamaged. The latter fiction seems to be preferred by film directors.

It is worthy of recognition that every one of the descriptions provided by the nine soldiers appears to depict a totally different event from the one described by Squadron Leader, (later Air Vice-Marshal) Francis Mellersh at an RAF Staff College lecture in 1931. To quote him:

> Suddenly the Triplane did two extremely rapid 'flick' rolls and crashed straight into the ground with full engine on... I flew right over it after it had crashed, however, and saw that it was a complete wreck.

The nine with the close view were:

Lieutenant Turner and Gunner Ernest Twycross, Artillery Officer and Signaller respectively, who were in the Royal Garrison Artillery FOP at Sainte Colette.

Two army signallers, Privates Len Dalton and Harvey, who were mending a telephone cable near what the local farmers call a sugar beet pie. That is a pile of sugar beets partially buried in a pit. The earth removed is then placed on top like a pie-crust. In that environment, the sugar beets both soften and sweeten at the same time. The pie was actually in the field where the machine came down. Both men later stated that the Triplane: '... landed in front of us.' They did not say *crashed*.

Two army signallers, Privates Vernon Elix and Jock Newell, who had just finished burying a telephone cable across the Corbie to Bray road.

Gunner George Ridgway, and Privates Emery and Jeffrey who had also seen most of the air and ground actions.

Again making a montage of what these various witnesses say they saw, it is most probable that the following occurred.

With von Richthofen having switched the engine's single magneto OFF, the forward motion of the Triplane was now driving the propeller

against the compression of the engine. This absorbed a lot of energy and acted as a dive brake thus providing a steep descent without an increase in speed. An unintentional tribute to von Richthofen's airmanship was given by a soldier who was of the opinion that the Triplane was obviously out of control since it came down sideways. Again, the witness, not being an aeroplane pilot, did not realise the import of what he saw; viz von Richthofen was alive. He had put his Triplane into a side slip so as not to overshoot the field. This steepened the angle even more. From a distant front or rear view in which no forward motion would be seen, the Triplane would appear to be descending almost vertically which matches Brown's description.

The trees on the west side of the field now hid the Triplane from all the machine gunners except Private Emery who, without having fired a single shot, watched his almost-5th-victory arrive at his feet as if by special request. Except for Lieutenant Wood's platoon, the soldiers who were in that general area were carrying drums of wire, pliers, screwdrivers and field telephones at the time. Privates Elix and Newell thought that the Triplane was planning to strafe them so they downed tools and dived for cover. It is doubtful, therefore, whether anyone fired at the Triplane in the last part of its descent even though the late Ed Ferko suggested it as a possibility.

Doctor José Segura MD, pointed out to the authors that regardless of which geographical position the Triplane had been in, the pilot's reaction to the wound would not have differed. At landing speed the muscular contraction would have caused a spectacular nose-up stall followed – in most cases – by a horrendous crash and fire.

Private Ridgway, from his 20-foot high perch on the chimney side, saw the end of the show as well. At about tree-top height, von Richthofen ceased side-slipping and placed the Triplane in landing attitude. One of two things happened next. Either due to weakness he lost the strength to hold the 'joy stick' back (on an aeroplane without a trim wheel the force required can be considerable) or, with or without fast fading faculties he misjudged his height. The landing wheels hit hard. The impetus pushed the tail down

ABOVE: The Sainte Colette brickworks, facing north. The Triplane came down in this field.

RIGHT: Gunner Ernest Twycross – the first soldier to reach the crashed Triplane. He saw von Richthofen die.

and the Triplane, which still had just enough speed to fly, took off again in a nose-high attitude. It climbed to about 12 feet above the ground losing speed as it went. Von Richthofen took no corrective action and a classic novice pilot landing stall, followed by a dropped wing took place. At the time of the stall, the driving force of the air pressure on the propeller became less than the resistive force of the engine compression; the engine and propeller ceased to rotate. The Triplane was not high enough off the ground for the nose to drop very far. The undercarriage and the lower left wing took the worst shock. The wheels splayed outwards as the rubber shock-absorbers parted inside the fairing, which looked like a small fourth wing between the wheels, and the legs were pushed backwards. One leg is said to have separated from the fuselage. The soldered seams of the petrol tank and the oil tank parted and the liquids began to escape. If the petrol tank had still been pressurised at this time, the fuel would have sprayed out and most likely caught fire, hence opening the tank vent valve at the right time was an important part of emergency landing drill. With unbalanced resistance to forward motion as it slid along the ground, the Triplane made a ground loop to the left of about one and half turns.

The Fokker finally became stationary with its nose pointing towards the town of Bonnay (west), and resting, with its tail canted upwards, two or three feet away from the 'sugar beet pie'. We know this because Private Emery later recalled being able to walk between the 'pie' and the front of the machine, so the Triplane had not actually ended up with its nose into it.

During the short glide the engine had cooled somewhat which was fortunate as petrol was still leaking from the tank. One blade of the propeller was broken off. The machine was quite easily repairable; airframe mechanics at flying training schools dealt with worse mishaps every week.

The names of those who claim to have been amongst the first to reach the downed Triplane form an impressive list! A point of interest is that of the myriad of claimants, none could recall who was actually the first. A half-clue came from one who said that it was some chap he did not recognise and that he must have been from some other unit stationed in the area.

In 1996, quite by chance, the mystery man was revealed to the authors, as having been Gunner Ernest Twycross of the Royal Garrison Artillery (RGA). His testimony strongly supports that of Privates Dalton and Harvey; namely that the Triplane did not slam into the ground and smash itself to pieces but made a reasonable landing. It also, once and for all time, definitely settles the dispute as exactly when Manfred von Richthofen died.

The RGA had two mobile 18-pounder guns on the Corbie to Bray road which were firing on targets of opportunity. Lieutenant Turner, who was in command of them, was 'spotting', from his Sainte Colette observation trench about 150 yards from the sugar beet pie. His assistant was Gunner Twycross, a signals specialist. No sooner had the Triplane stopped than Turner instructed Twycross to climb out and take the German pilot prisoner before he could set his aeroplane on fire.

As the gunner reached the cockpit, the pilot, who was covered with blood, gurgled or gasped three words and then died. The first two sounded like: 'War es.' . The third one was definitely 'Kaput'. It can be safely assumed that he said: 'Alles Kaput' meaning 'It's all over for me, I'm finished.' Gunner Twycross, smelling the petrol, hearing the ticking sounds made by hot metal as it cools down, and seeing several soldiers running towards the aeroplane, prudently returned to his post.

Ernest Twycross's son had taken his father on a nostalgic visit to the old battlefields of France in June 1970 (he was suffering with cancer and was to die in 1973), and upon reaching the Corbie-Bray road the old soldier asked his son to stop and he looked out across the field in front of the brickworks:

I did not know why he wanted to visit this area, and, after stopping the car he said they had had a forward OP near here (pointing to the fields next to the road) and: 'we used to tether our mules along this road with chains' he said. He then told me that he and his officer witnessed a fight between three aircraft, two RAF and one German Triplane. My father said the Triplane appeared to be in trouble and he and his officer watched it force land under control by the side of the road. As the aircraft appeared to have landed intact my father was sent to capture the pilot and aircraft before the pilot destroyed it. My father had no idea who the pilot was. He arrived at the aircraft which in my father's own words, had come to rest against a pile of 'mangel wurzles'. The pilot was still alive and my father's intent was to capture him and to get him out of the cockpit because of the smell of petrol and the engine was ticking as it cooled down. The pilot gurgled or gasped: '... kaput,' and died. He said the words sounded like 'War es kaput,' but with the noise around he couldn't be sure, but 'kaput' came into it. A few moments later Australian troops and an officer arrived and my father left the site. It was only afterwards that he learnt that the pilot was von Richthofen, a famous German aviator.

As to how steep the Triplane's descent really was, once again slant views can be deceptive. The observer for the German 18th Feld Artillerie Regiment, Leutnant Schönemann, (in the church tower in Le Hamel) reported that it was so steep that the pilot could not possibly have survived the crash. On the other hand, Leutnant Fabian, 16th Artillerie, viewing from a different angle, reported a good landing but added that the pilot had remained in the cockpit. Infantry Leutnant Koster, from yet another viewing angle, reported that a red Triplane had glided down to a landing. Other German artillery men, looking through range-finders, saw Allied soldiers running towards the downed Triplane. Unfortunately some German soldiers and airmen remembered a newspaper propaganda story from the previous year which stated that the British had offered riches, his own personal, private aeroplane and a medal to the airman who could kill the German national hero who, so it was written, was terrifying their airmen. The reported glide to a good landing and the running soldiers provided a useful basis for an anti-British propaganda story that von Richthofen stepped down from the cockpit with his hands up and was murdered for bounty by the first men to reach the Triplane. The story, which has several versions, has been re-cycled every two or three decades as 'new evidence'. It is just about due to be 'discovered' again!

Sergeant E C Tibbetts, of the 53rd Battery, who had been walking along the Corbie-Mericourt road while watching the final stages of the chase, thought the Triplane had made a remarkable landing and wondered whether the pilot had just lived long enough to bring it down in the field in front of the brickworks.

Possibly the second soldier to reach the Triplane was Signals Sergeant Norman Symes, an Australian. In December 1982 he told the *Sydney Sunday Press*:

I looked straight into the dead pilot's face. A fine looking fellow he was, despite the wound on his forehead. Beside the dead man in the cockpit lay a loosely bundled parachute. I gathered it up and ran it to HQ. I am claiming no credit; I didn't shoot at him. I didn't even have my pistol with me.

Sergeant Symes neither saw nor heard of the parachute again and wondered what had happened to it. Many denied, and some still deny, that it ever existed which makes the Heinecke parachute harness that von Richthofen was wearing somewhat inexplicable! From other sources it is understood that some of the girls in Corbie and Amiens might have been able to help Sergeant Symes with his enquiries.

While the parachute was used by balloon observers of both sides, Allied airmen were not allowed such luxury. However, German airmen had just started to use them and a number would save their lives in the coming months – provided they worked, which wasn't always guaranteed; however, there is no record of any airman returning his parachute with a complaint.

The pilot of the Triplane was identified as the German top-scoring ace, Rittmeister Manfred Freiherr von Richthofen. Souveniring of the Fokker began immediately the word spread around who the pilot was. Some lucky soldiers with pocket knives acquired sections of wing fabric with the German insignia; Private Wormald was one of them having run over from the Buie/Evans machine-gun location. It was a little risky to go near the Triplane as an occasional short shot from German artillery to the south was arriving nearby. One soldier hearing a 'crump' and

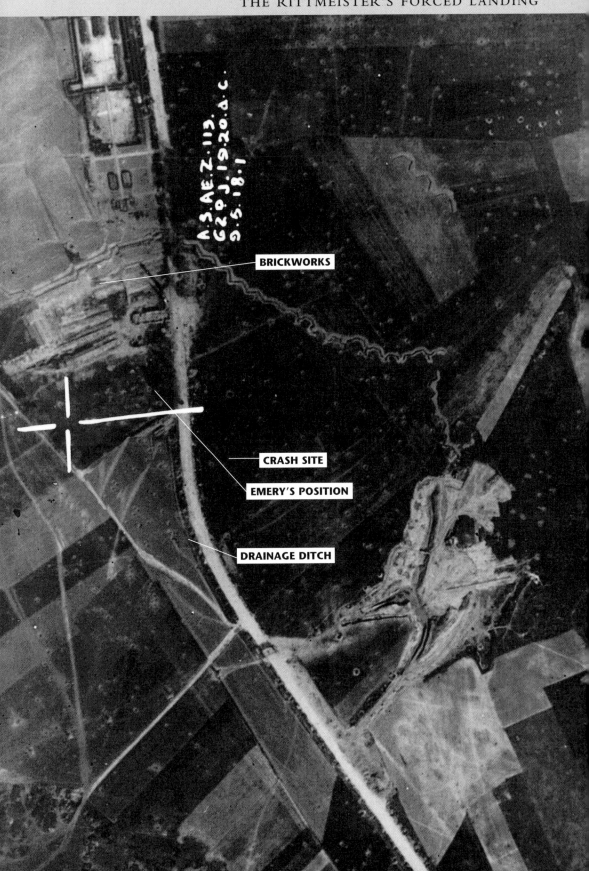

BRICKWORKS

CRASH SITE

EMERY'S POSITION

DRAINAGE DITCH

feeling something strike him thought that he had been wounded. His colleagues did not feel that being hit by a flying piece of sugar beet merited much compassion or sympathy. An officer, Captain E C Adams of the 44th Battalion AIF, came along and shooed the crowd away; mainly for the soldiers' own safety. Guard was mounted over the Triplane to prevent further looting but unfortunately its members were chosen from volunteers for the task!

In this area, 3 Squadron AFC, to which all Allied or German crashed or force-landed aircraft 'belonged' by official writ, was asked to come and collect its property. Enemy aircraft brought down inside Allied lines were never retained by the army however they were acquired. They were handed over to the RAF and most would be given an RAF 'G' number.

At 1400 hours, approximately, the 3 Squadron aircraft recovery team, commanded by Lieutenant W J Warneford and supervised by Air Mechanic 1st Class (later Warrant Officer) Alfred Alexander Boxall-Chapman appeared. The Lieutenant, who appears to have been detained at Battalion HQ during the progress of the work, was, in some inexplicable manner, assumed by some

unidentified officer to have been Lieutenant Mellersh of 209 Squadron. Amongst the troops, rumour seems to have identified him as the pilot of the Camel who had come to thank Gunners Buie and Evans for having saved his life. The next day, the visitor's name to some, was Lieutenant May; to others he was Captain Brown. These errors found their way into official reports, and personal letters, and much confusion this created. (see Appendices C and D.)

A photograph of the Triplane taken the next day has sometimes been used to depict the 'wreck'. It was taken after the aeroplane had been 'ratted' by souvenir hunters and then partially re-assembled specially for the pictures.

The Headquarters of the British Fourth Army were duly informed that the 'Red Devil' himself had been shot down and killed.

Indirectly, the broken firing pin in the right-hand gun was to have unfortunate consequences upon the beliefs of those who looked at von Richthofen's body that afternoon and evening. Because of the firing pin defect, von Richthofen had loosened his safety harness so as to be able to reach forward to re-cock the machine gun each

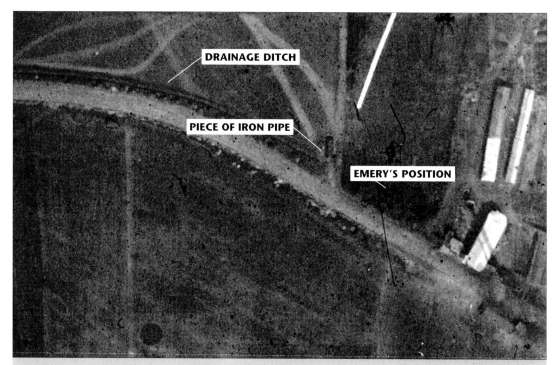

Section of the field where von Richthofen came down taken on 6 April 1918. The brickwork buildings to the right are where Emery and Jeffrey had their gun position in between the piece of iron and the brick storage yard. The drainage ditch north of the road can be seen, while positioned in the field in the foreground is the sugar beet pie by which the Triplane came to rest, facing WNW.

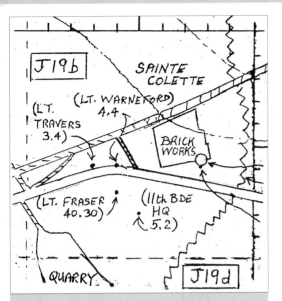
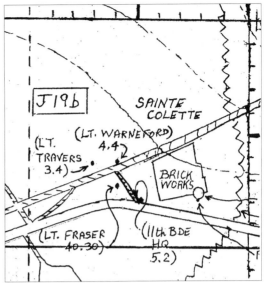

These two sketches illustrate the problem created by plotting April 1918 map references on a August 1917 map. The result is that the Triplane is shown to have come to rest north of the road instead of in the field to the south of the road.

time it stopped. Upon the final impact with the ground, his unrestrained body was thrown forwards allowing his face to impact the gun-butts which projected back into the cockpit. There was a lot of blood around, which appeared to have flowed from the mouth. Private Emery said that von Richthofen looked like a stuck bullock; the blood reached down to his fur overboots and had actually soaked into the top of one.

Injuries were observed to his mouth, to his neck, behind his right eye (some say left), to his legs, to his abdomen, to the front of his chest near his left shoulder and inside his right armpit. Depending upon the haste and/or the expertise of the spectators, all of those injuries or merely the last two, were taken to be gunshot wounds. When one takes into consideration the hundreds of shots which were fired at the Baron during the last two minutes of his life, that was not unreasonable.

The actual location on the ground where the Triplane came to rest has been the subject of much unnecessary dispute. The co-ordinates were estimated by all concerned based on their April 1918 issue Field Map 62D. The nearby roads do not run due north-south or due east-west which influences even the most careful judgement. Under the circumstances, they did quite well. Absolute accuracy was not required for their purpose; surveying instruments would have been needed to do better.

The dispute arose due to the point reference grid on the 1916 and 1917 maps of Military Zone 62D having been over-printed slightly out of position. The error was corrected on the 1918 edition by shifting the horizontal lines about 100 yards to the south. If the location given by Lieutenant Travers – 62D.J.19.b. – is plotted on a 1916 or 1917 map, the pinpoint will be found to be NORTH of the Corbie to Bray road. Fortunately, aerial photographs show some type of sheds on the north side which proves those who gave the reference used the April 1918 edition. The allegation that the place where the Triplane came to rest is uncertain, is another case of a controversy having been created out of thin air. The spot was definitely SOUTH of the road and the exact position is known to within 50 yards.

According to the Baron's mother, Kunigunde Freifrau von Richthofen, the Kaiser had taken a firm decision to order the Rittmeister to fly no more after achieving his 80th victory. Previous efforts by 'higher authority', to use the Rittmeister's own words, had been circumvented or simply 'forgotten'. This time it was final. In her book, *My War Diary*, the Baroness describes how on the morning of Sunday 21 April 1918 the news reached the Kaiser that Manfred had scored his 79th and 80th victories the previous day, thus doubling the score of his former mentor and staffelführer, Oswald Boelcke. Before he could issue the edict on Monday the 22nd, news arrived that the Rittmeister was missing. The door of fate turns on very small hinges.

CHAPTER SEVEN
Salvaging the Triplane

In order for British aircraft designers fully to understand the capabilities of and technical innovations in German aircraft, an evaluation unit had been established. Under this scheme, all downed German aircraft fell under the jurisdiction of the Royal Flying Corps, and after 1 April 1918, the Royal Air Force. Each Wing had a salvage crew which would proceed to the site, dismantle the aeroplane (providing it wasn't just a heap of burnt wood and metal) and take it to a designated aerodrome where it would be examined, and if required, and still in flying condition, shipped to England for performance evaluation. The same organisation also retrieved all force-landed British aircraft and inspected those seriously damaged in battle or for any other reason.(1)

Between 1100 and 1200 hours on 21 April, as the Camels of 209 Squadron landed back at Bertangles, they were carefully examined for combat damage. 1st Air Mechanic Boxall-Chapman, the 3 AFC Squadron airman who would soon be ordered to go to the crash-site of Richthofen's Triplane, was examining May's Camel D3326 which had sustained an unusually large number of bullet holes. If any main structural member had been damaged, it would need to be returned to the Central Workshops at the Aircraft Repair Depot (ARD) near Amiens. However, the Camel had evidently only suffered fabric damage, which would be quick and easy to repair as it was used by him the following day for the morning patrol.

Towards the end of his examination, Boxall-Chapman received a summons to return to Poulainville aerodrome, which was close-by, to join Warneford's salvage party, which was preparing to depart to retrieve the downed Fokker.

Before he arrived there, Lieutenant Donald L Fraser, the intelligence officer of the 11th Infantry

Brigade, assisted by Corporal Norman Ramsden, Corporal J Homewood and Private Frank Wormald, had removed von Richthofen's body from the cockpit and placed it on the ground nearby. It lay there until removed by the salvage crew. Private Emery obtained a neat pair of Zeiss binoculars which had been about his neck, while Private Jeffrey acquired a short-barrelled 9 mm German officer pilot's Luger pistol.

Major Beavis, having sent the battery's folding stretcher to Sainte Colette, later recalled receiving the body back at his dug-out. He reported the crash, and that he was holding the body, at his HQ – the 14th Artillery Brigade. When Lieutenant Warneford of 3 AFC arrived with the salvage party, he told Beavis that Richthofen had been shot down by an RE8 of their Squadron, which Beavis thought was '... ridiculous.'

The following description is taken word for word from a letter written by Boxall-Chapman on 28 May 1936, which the authors consider more accurate than accounts written by him 25 years later and which, prior to publication, may have been edited. In the letter he mentions the encounter between May, von Richthofen and Brown, but this can only be hearsay. The salvage crew consisted of Warneford, Sergeant Richard Foales, and airmen J K Kitts, Joseph Waldron, Colin Collins and Boxall-Chapman. Boxall-Chapman, who lived in Lincoln in 1936, recorded in a letter to John Coltman:

> .... six of us set off to the scene of the crash in broad daylight, as it was thought that the pilot may still be alive (we usually salvaged plane's at night as 'Jerry' had a habit of strafing the crash).
> We arrived at the battery, climbed the hill and went forward about ¼ mile when the plane came into view, and low and behold it was a red Triplane, the Red Devil. We now knew the reason for the daylight job. 'Jerry' was not shelling it.
> Now picture the scene; on our right the Battery, on our left a destroyed sugar factory [1], in front a red plane stuck into the end of a

(1) The British authorities did not realise some of the true potential of German aircraft until after the war. For instance the synthetic petrol used by the Germans had a far higher octane value than the petrol issued for British aircraft, which gave them a better rate of climb. All tests in England, of course, were conducted using standard British aircraft petrol.

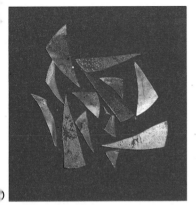

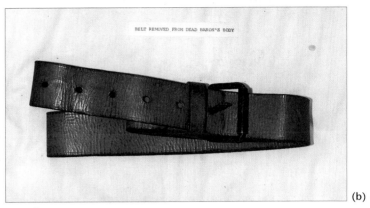

BELT REMOVED FROM DEAD BARON'S BODY

(b)

GUN LOCK FROM MACHINE GUN

(d)

(a) yellow glass from one lens, broken some years later.

(b) von Richthofen's leather belt.

(c) von Richthofen's handkerchief - note initials – and scarf.

(d) breech block from von Richthofen's right-hand gun, No.1795.

(e) von Richthofen's flying goggles.

'potato pie' [2] (potatoes piled up and covered with earth), an occasional shell flying well over our heads, and now and then one searching for the Battery, with a shell on bursting smelling of pineapples (gas).

About ½ a mile further in front was our trenches [3] with 'Jerry' immediately in front again, and we could plainly see the smoke of discharge of the German artillery, so you can see the plane was an easy mark if he cared to shell it, but never a shot was fired at it.

We halted about ¼ mile from the plane and myself and another [Private Collins] went forward. We walked about 200 yards and then started to crawl the remainder. When we arrived at the plane we first examined the pilot's identification disc, it was the Red Devil.

We noticed he had a dark ring round his neck [4] (broken neck) and a cut on his forehead. The force of the crash threw him on to his guns which cut his forehead and broke his neck. There was blood on his right side and so we traced the bullet hole, there was one in the right side of the cockpit (standing at tail and looking forward) but none on the other side, so I traced the track of the bullet; it entered half way down his right side, passed upwards and outwards, coming out behind his left shoulder. (No bullet fired from the air could have travelled in this direction.)

We then tried to remove the body, but found it too heavy for us so we decided to get a rope. My companion returned to the party for a rope, and whilst he was away I made an examination of the plane. I noticed that the ignition switch [5] was in the off position; this fact puzzled me until I read his book, wherein he states that he always switches off his engine when in trouble (a very wise precaution to prevent fire if the plane should crash). There was ample petrol in his tank. I next examined his guns, these were twin Spandaus [6], mounted together, there was ample ammunition; but opening the breech of the first gun, I found what I took to be a discharged shell [7], stuck in the chamber; the second gun

was exactly the same (when our armourers stripped the guns after the machine had been salved it was found that both cartridges had been struck and failed to explode); this is the most difficult if not impossible stoppage to clear in the air [8]; from examination of the cartridges later it was evident that he had attempted to clear his guns by cocking and firing, but without success, and very fortunate for May.

The propeller was smashed [9], so was the three right-hand planes and undercarriage but the three left-hand planes were intact [10].

When my companion returned with the rope it was fastened under his armpits [11] and with the assistance of the whole party, the body was drawn back. It was then placed upon a stretcher and carried back to the Battery and laid under the protection of the cliff face. We then returned to the plane, and by placing a false undercarriage under it we were able to draw it back to the trailer, on which we loaded it and returned to camp [12]. I never saw the body again out of its coffin.

It was getting dark when we arrived back in camp, and further examination of the plane was impossible; a guard was placed on it, but when I returned to complete my examination in the morning there was nothing left except the bare spars, even the guns had been removed by souvenir hunters [13], but I was fortunate to get both cartridges out of the guns, one of which I gave to the CO, the other I still have.

This is a faithful picture as I saw it, could I have found my diary I would have been able to give the names of the party that was with me.

Notes: [1] The factory actually made bricks, not sugar.

[2] The 'pie' was composed of sugar beets, not potatoes. As the Triplane was now touching the 'pie', it seems that an attempt had already been made to move it, or at least turn it around.

[3] The trenches were some short French ones made a year or more earlier. They did not form a line. On that part of the front, the River Somme and the cover provided by the Morlancourt Ridge obviated the need for continuous static defences.

[4] The dark ring most likely came from the grease

soaked into the collar of von Richthofen's flying suit and would appear to have been washed off during the preparations for the official medical examination. To avoid frostbite, airmen put a thick layer of grease over the exposed skin. With constant head turning, it would spread around. Von Richthofen's neck was not broken.

[5] The 110-hp LeRhône rotary engine, from which the 110-hp Oberursel was copied, had only one magneto. Many publications have 'corrected' Boxall-Chapman's word 'magneto' to 'magnetos' which raises the question of the value of editing a witness's words.

[6] Spandau is the name of the city where the German machine-gun factories were located. The type of gun used on the Fokker Dr.I was a belt-fed Maxim adapted for air-cooling and known as the LMG 08/15. LMG (Luftgekühlte Maschinen Gewehr, type 8, designed in 1915.)

[7] The word 'shell' refers to a cartridge. Boxall-Chapman's reference to the ample supply of ammunition remaining tallies with witnesses who said the Triplane pilot was firing very short bursts or none at all, as opposed to those who stated the German pilot was 'blazing away with both guns.'

[8] To clear this fault the defective cartridge needed to be removed from the breech without the belt slipping. The vibration of the engine virtually guaranteed slippage. Ground-based Vickers gun crews considered the correction to be a two-man operation.

[9] The propeller was actually broken, not smashed. One blade had snapped off. Captain LeBoutillier's mechanics unbolted the propeller remains from the engine and carved a walking stick for Boots.

[10] The left and right in the letter are based upon the viewer looking at the Triplane from the front, which is how Boxall-Chapman would have seen it as he approached Sainte Colette from the 53rd Battery. In later letters, he was more precise. As seen from the pilot's seat, the port (left) wings were the damaged ones.

[11] Some people have stated that the rope was attached to von Richthofen's parachute harness. Boxall-Chapman, being the man who tied the rope, should have the best recollection.

[12] Some people have stated that the Triplane was dragged back across the field by a rope. This would be virtually impossible to do as protruding broken pieces would dig into the ground, which in itself wasn't smooth. The late Cole Palen, who more than once had to remove a similarly damaged replica Dr.I from Old Rhinebeck airfield in a hurry, told the authors that the Dr.I was not

heavy; it was awkward. Ten men could pick it and carry it easily. With a dolly beneath it (a false undercarriage) and a rope attached to the dolly, only one man would be required to steady the starboard (right) wings whilst the others, from a sheltered position tugged the rope.

[13] The two machine guns were recovered and are to be seen in photographs taken on the morning of the 22nd. They both disappeared again shortly afterwards.

John Coltman replied to Boxall-Chapman and asked a few additional questions to which the latter replied in June 1936:

> From my examination of the machine and enquiries made, I would say that the machine made a good landing considering there was a dead pilot on board. The idea of the plane being pulled back gently by a rope is 'rubbish'. The body was pulled back by a rope as I stated in my previous letter.

On 29 January 1918, Leutnant Eberhard Stapenhörst of Jasta 11 had force-landed his Fokker Dr.I (144/17: RAF 'G' No.125) inside British lines and had been unable to destroy it. The machine, which was only slightly damaged, was repaired and extensively test-flown. There was no need for another one, therefore Richthofen's 425/17 held no particular interest. For this reason no serious action was taken to prevent extensive souveniring whilst the Triplane was at Sainte Colette waiting to be loaded onto a trailer, nor later at Poulainville.

The missing fabric and instruments (it looked as though rats had been at it) had to be explained somehow to HQ, so the time of the 'Evening Hate' was advanced to suit and the 'damage', while at Sainte Colette, attributed to that. A 'box barrage of fire by the Germans to allow the pilot to escape' was invented by others which was illogical as, given the inaccuracy of the badly worn barrels of most German guns, they were more likely to kill him than save him. The special outer clothing worn by airmen precluded long distance running and two miles was a bit far for von Richthofen to travel through enemy-held territory dressed solely in his pyjamas, which were the only clothing he was wearing beneath his flying gear.

Private Emery, the AA machine gunner nearby, confirmed that the Germans did not aim a barrage at the downed fighter, although several stray shots intended for other targets landed nearby.

At Poulainville, the remains of the Triplane

RIGHT: Control column from Richthofen's Triplane. Top left are the two recangular gun triggers marked L & R. On top is the coupé button for the magneto; on the right is the finger grip and on the left is the auxiliary throttle control. The holes at the base are for the cables from the throttle and triggers.

were filmed on the morning of the 22nd by The Army Film Unit and used in a newsreel. The written narrative was translated into French and Portuguese (and perhaps other languages). Half a dozen 'still' photographs were also taken. The photography clearly shows that there are no bullet holes in the elevators or the top of the fuselage behind the cockpit. The fabric from the rudder (both sides) had been 'liberated' by this time but the owner of one side (originally in the possession of Captain Brown) assured the present authors that there are no bullet holes through it. Diving on the Triplane at 190 mph, which itself was travelling at about 110 mph, Brown was closing at around 80 mph (ie. about 40 yards per second). During his long burst of fire – recorded as five to seven seconds – he would have reduced the distance between the two aircraft by approximately 240 yards. Which means he must have opened fire at about 300 yards, and ceased at 50.

To test the theory of Brown having seen his bullets striking the Triplane (see Appendix E), the authors set up a red-painted piece of plywood, with holes drilled in it to represent .303 bullet strikes. As opposed to the actual event, the experiment was under ideal conditions; there was no aircraft 'shake or vibration' causing problems at either end, ie: the piece of plywood was stationary. The sun was positioned behind the viewer and shining on the plywood.

By using accurate measured distances with a 100 foot tape measure, it was found that beyond 60 yards the bullet holes could not be seen! This clearly establishes that the story given that Brown, who commenced firing at long distance, saw his bullets striking the Triplane's tailplane and then corrected his aim, is pure fabrication.

Similarly, von Richthofen's head turning to see who was attacking him, is equally disproved, for at a distance of over 100 yards, a dark helmeted head half buried in a cockpit with face covered by goggles and muffled against frost bite, cannot be seen to turn.

The many journalistic renderings in post-war pulp magazines and the like where various lines of bullet holes were 'stitched' across the tail, up the fuselage decking and into the pilot's back, are

thus proven to be pure fabrication and drama. It is well known that the bullet pattern from an airborne machine gun tends to resemble that of a shot gun effect, and does not produce a straight line of bullet holes (except in the movies).

There were so few bullet holes in the Triplane that in later years one soldier described Private A D Craven, one of the soldiers at the scene of the crash, as having been lucky enough to obtain a piece of fabric with a bullet hole through it.

Sergeant John Alexander, the 3 AFC Squadron photographer, took 'still' photographs of von Richthofen's body. He later commented that it was awfully cut about and added that the German had been shot through the chin, the heart and the legs. To cover the scale loss produced by photography, he made an exact size sketch of the chest wound which he apparently believed to have been the principal one. He also 'dusted' the facial injuries with baking soda and pulled the dislocated front teeth back in place before taking the photos.

The cartridge which Boxall-Chapman took from the Triplane's breech and kept was sent to John Coltman (on loan) in the summer of 1936. Coltman was so intrigued that he sent a detailed description of it to the German Reichsarchiv in Potsdam. They replied on 29 July, stating that the numbers on the bottom related to:
S67 – marks of the type of case;
P – the mark of the Polte factory at Magdeburg;
11 – month of manufacture (November);
17 – year of manufacture (1917).

TOP LEFT: Detail of the muzzle of an LMG gun showing the air cooling jacket, recoil booster and the flash suppressor. (Inset: sketch of the base of the cartridge from the Triplane's gun.)

TOP RIGHT: Detail of the LMG gun showing the cocking handle.

ABOVE LEFT: Twin LMG 08/15 (Made in Spandau). The cable of the synchronising mechanism can be seen between them.

ABOVE RIGHT: Von Richthofen with the flying goggles he normally wore but they were not the ones he used on the fateful day.

RIGHT: The Triplane's engine showing no damage to the cylinder-heads indicating that the engine had stopped prior to the crash-landing. Viewed from the rear. Those heads that are not visible in this picture can be viewed in the colour picture earlier (page 9).

Two well known photos of the 'well-souvenired' Triplane at Poulainville aerodrome, surrounded by men of 3 Squadron AFC. Of interest is the complete lack of bullet holes in the elevators and the fuselage decking behind the cockpit, despite the damage sustained by the souvenir hunters.

In the lower picture the officers are: (left to right) Lts C W Gray, F J Mart, N Mulroney, A V Brown, T L Baillieu, R W Kirkwood, A L D Taylor, A E Grigson, M Sheehan, – guard –.

CHAPTER EIGHT
The Commander-in-Chief's Dilemma

The information which the Commander-in-Chief of the British Fourth Army, General Sir Henry Rawlinson, had received until now was a little confusing. General Sir John Monash, who commanded the 5th Australian Division, had been told that the Red Devil (as he was often called by the front line troops) had been shot down by an RE8 reconnaissance aeroplane. General Sir William Birdwood, who commanded the Australian Corps within the Fourth Army, had heard quite a different story. His Aide, Captain McGrigor, made the following entry in his diary for the 22nd:

> Great excitement yesterday afternoon as Baron von Reichtofen [sic], the great Bosche [sic] flyer who is said to have accounted for 80 of our machines, met his fate yesterday near here, being brought down by machine guns of one of our batteries at about 500 feet up while swooping on the tail of one of our reconnaissance machines. He was killed dead having about five bullets in him, and there is no doubt but that he is the famous pilot all Bosche communiqués have been making so much of the last few months. There is a lot of dispute as to who actually shot him down, but the machine gunners of the battery have finally established their claim. Went over to see his plane in the afternoon, it was a red triplane, but owing to the crash and the multitudinous souvenir hunters who got at it before the flying people, there was really very little of it left. Crowds of French troops still on the roads behind us, all moving north. Rode over and dined with Jack Cunningham [1] at No.65 Squadron; the talk was all about Reichtofen's death, and they all swear that he was brought down by a plane and not from the ground. Had a most cheery evening finishing up with a good game of poker, did not get back until 1.15.

[1] Major J A Cunningham, CO of 65 Squadron and soon to command 65 Wing; a former RFA officer he had been a pilot since 1912 and ended the war as a Lt-Colonel DSO DFC, Croix de Guerre, Chévalier of the Order of Léopold.

The time came around for the official British 4th Army Daily Report on Activity and Availability of Munitions, dated 21 April 1918 to be issued. Under Item 11 – General, it stated:

> Baron von Richthoffen [sic], the well-known German aviator, was brought down and killed by a Lewis Gun mounted over 53rd Battery A.F.A. His machine, a red triplane, crashed on the road 1,000 yards north of Vaux sur Somme. Baron von Richthoffen on the previous day accounted for his 80th Allied machine. An account of the circumstances under which he fell is attached as an appendix.

It would appear that the three claims which had been making their way up through the chain of command arrived at the HQ of the Fourth Army shortly after the Daily Report was issued. They were brought to the attention of Sir Henry and may be briefly described as follows:

The claim from 3 Squadron AFC, Lieutenant Barrow, was based upon a burst of Lewis gun fire aimed frontally at the Triplane as it dived on the RE8. This would encompass about one third of a drum of bullets fired at about ten rounds per second. A standard drum held 47 rounds.

The claim from 209 Squadron, Captain Roy Brown DSC, was based upon a long burst of fire from twin Vickers guns aimed from above and from one side in a dive towards the left rear of the Triplane. This would encompass about 50 to 70 rounds from each gun, ie: 100-140 in total.

The claim from the 53rd Field Artillery Battery AIF, Gunners Buie and Evans, was based upon several short bursts of fire from two Lewis guns aimed semi-frontally, that is upwards and a little from the right of the Triplane's direction of flight. Gunner Buie had fired 47 rounds but gunner Evans's contribution is unknown.

At least there was agreement on one point between all stories, official and unofficial. The Baron, no matter how his name was spelled, had been struck by a fair number of bullets. This introduced a factor which might possibly be decisive; the types of the bullets in the body. The 53rd Battery claimants were using 'rifle' bullets and 'tracer' only. However, in the case of 3 AFC and 209 Squadrons, about 80% of the bullets fired would be 'rifle' bullets, about 10% would be 'tracer' while the final 10% would be 'explosive' or 'armour piercing' rounds. The exact mix depended upon the preference of the airmen concerned; this would help.

With such a vast difference between the angles of fire and the possible presence of a type of bullet not employed by the 53rd Battery gunners and/or of the two squadrons, an expert medical examination of the body should be able to determine which of the three claimants was truly responsible for bringing down the Fokker. Even if the bullets were not found, each type made a wound of a highly distinctive nature.

The medical services of the British Fourth Army were headed by Major-General O'Keefe. Colonel John A Nixon, (one incorrect reference cites a Colonel Dixon) whose title was Consulting Physician, and Colonel Thomas Sinclair, whose title was Consulting Surgeon, reported to him. These officers were highly qualified professionals and, in addition to administrative duties, they dealt with the more difficult cases at the Fourth Army Hospital in Amiens officially known as the 42nd Stationary Hospital. The basic arrangement was that Field Dressing Stations at the front would send casualties on to the nearest Field Hospital. The latter moved with the front line position and were considered to be mobile hospitals. These, in turn, would send serious cases to a Stationary Hospital. This, in the case of the Fourth Army, was the 42nd in Amiens. Those whose recovery would be delayed would, after initial treatment, be sent back to 'Blighty', as Britain was nicknamed. This resulted in the term 'a Blighty wound', which some regarded as a blessing in disguise.

Sir Henry Rawlinson requested Colonels Sinclair and Nixon to examine the Baron's body. On the basis of probability, it may be assumed that at that late hour the Colonels yet had things to do that evening. A message had to be sent to Poulainville to have the body prepared for an examination on the morrow and an Aide would need a little time to arrange the necessary transport to the airfield. Ordinarily Colonels do not 'hurry', and the body would still be there in the morning.

Sir Henry was to be disappointed. When the two medical men returned the next day, they brought disquieting news. The first item was that 22 Wing RAF had jumped the gun by sending over the new Medical Officer (MO), Captain N C Graham, RAMC, from its Field Hospital, accompanied by his predecessor, Lieutenant G E Downs, RAMC, who was preparing to depart for England. They conducted an examination of their own on the evening of the 21st. Although 22 Wing Routine Orders do not cite Downs as surrendering his functions until the 25th, Graham had in fact taken over as Wing Medical Officer upon arrival on the 20th. He signed the medical report on von Richthofen as: 'MD i/c 22 Wing.' As one of the interested parties, and with the knowledge that the matter had been referred 'upstairs', this was improper procedure.

The second item is best told in the words of Colonel Thomas Sinclair as written on 17 October 1934: 'Our verdict disposed of all these claims.' The reason for this surprising statement was that the injuries to von Richthofen's body did not, in the slightest degree, have any relation to the quantity, direction and angle of fire described by a single one of the three claimants. Even Air Mechanic Boxall-Chapman's opinion was at variance with the facts.

The controversy had begun, and, in the opinion of Major Beavis, given in 1934, many of the arguments concerned items which were so self-evident or had been witnessed from close up by so many soldiers at the time, that nobody had bothered to write them down.

CHAPTER NINE
The Wandering Wounds

Over the years, due to lack of concrete information, a good deal of emphasis has been placed on finding out the type of wound inflicted on the Baron by means of an attempt, based on the assumed time of his death, to reverse-calculate the exact time he was hit.

This was complicated by argument concerning the exact nature of the wound. The evidence collected by John Coltman, supplemented by Gunner Twycross, has clarified the entire situation and definite times can now be given for both the wounding and the death.

So much attention, which can now be shown to be inaccurate, was previously placed on the wound, that it tended to cloud what actually happened. Therefore, in order to clarify this to the reader and historian, later chapters, which are based on more complete up-to-date knowledge both of ballistics and pathology, go into this quite deeply.

With rare exception, those who looked at the body in the cockpit, on the ground beside the Triplane or at any other time prior to the medical examinations, seem to have held to the first impressions which they initially adopted. It is said that those impressions last the longest, and this seems to be the case with the injuries to Manfred von Richthofen. This is clearly illustrated in the statements made by the major participants ten years (Brown), thirty years (May) and forty years (Buie) after the event. 209 Squadron pilots, Lieutenants Robert Foster and Francis Mellersh, who, although not major participants were closely associated with the events, have followed the same pattern in their official pronouncements.

The wide variations in opinion displayed by the participants as to the number, position and direction of the wound(s) have been used, in several instances, to give the impression that doubt still exists as to its (their) nature. This is not too difficult to achieve if the 'information' is gathered from books and articles published around 1930, and/or from later works which have used them for reference and therefore were unintentionally flawed from the outset. Who for example would have questioned Gibbons' original book, or information still to be found at the Public Record Office at Kew, or even supplied by Air Ministry!

In September 1937, John Coltman received a letter from a former officer with the 150th Brigade Royal Field Artillery, G N Farquhar, stationed on the northern slope of the Morlancourt Ridge just to the south-east of Heilly. While it is not possible to fathom how much of the action he saw on 21 April, he does make a very interesting statement:

> .... although at the time I had no doubt whatever that I had seen Richthofen killed (from a distance of only about 150 yards) I have read so many and such conflicting reports of his death in the past nineteen years that I begin to wonder whether I really saw it happen.

Gunner Robert Buie, one of those who claimed to have shot down the Baron, was quoted in December 1959 by the magazine *Cavalier* as having written as follows:

> Over the past forty-two years I have read some strange accounts of what was supposed to have taken place in the action, and each has been more fantastic than the preceding one. Some of those who looked at von Richthofen's body before it was removed from the cockpit, saw no further than the large quantity of blood which appeared to have flowed from the mouth.

It appeared to them that *von Richthofen had been shot frontally through the mouth*. At some point the comment was added that *the bullet had exited behind the left eye* some said *behind the right eye*.

While the body was lying on the ground outside Major Beavis's dug-out at 53rd Battery, several men looked at it. One was Gunner E A Bellingham of the 53rd, who wrote in November 1937 from his home in Victoria, Australia:

> Just about sundown or a little later, they [the salvage party] came back with the plane and the body. He was laid down on the grass in front of the major's dug-out. He seemed to have a good many bullets in him. There was a crowd of people there claiming to have brought him down.

When Major Beavis received the body in his dug-out he at first accepted the head wound story but, after a more leisurely look, he later reported that same day:

> The wounds in the pilot's body were mainly
> in the chest and stomach. Apparently the
> first bursts of fire were effective. Both
> guns inflicted wounds on the pilot, in my
> opinion. If the enemy plane had not been
> turned off by our fire, it would have
> been able to drive down the British plane.

This did not explain the injuries to the abdomen which some claimed to have seen, so as the story in the report was passed on, it changed to: *Von Richthofen had been killed by bullets which entered through his left shoulder, passed downwards through his chest from left to right and exited through his abdomen.*

An airman, R Schofield, on clerical duties at 22 Wing HQ in 1918, wrote to a London newspaper in the 1930s as follows:

> I saw both 'combat reports' of the officer
> concerned, and only a medical examination
> of the body finally proved that the fatal
> shot was fired from above – through the
> shoulder and heart.

That is the basic theme of the beliefs expressed in later years by Captain Brown, Lieutenants Wilfred May, Francis Mellersh and Robert Foster.

Some people seeing or hearing of the large wound in the left breast, which matched a close burst of Lewis gun fire, assumed an exit wound in von Richthofen's back. The story then became: *von Richthofen was killed by a bullet which passed through his heart from front to back.* This version is the basic theme of the beliefs expressed in later years by Gunner Buie, Sergeant Popkin and Lieutenant Ellis.

A close-range shot from that direction would have pierced the body and made a hole in the back of the pilot's seat. Such a hole was duly invented.

To some people the large lesion on the left breast looked suspiciously like the exit wound of a single bullet rather than one of multiple entry. On the understanding that the bullet had passed through von Richthofen's heart, an entry point was required in the middle of his back which in turn required a bullet hole through the back of the seat. Such a hole had already been invented and so the tail now began to wag the dog:

> There is a bullet hole in the seat back
> which proves that von Richthofen was
> killed by a bullet through the heart
> fired from behind.

First Air Mechanic Boxall-Chapman, and Captain Roderick Ross (who was Boxall-Chapman's CO in overall charge of Salvage Operations and who later inspected the Triplane at Poulainville) had earlier formed the opinion that a single bullet had entered the body, low down on its right side, had passed upwards and forwards through the chest and had exited behind the left shoulder. This story then seemed to disappear into oblivion. The simplest explanation of this, and therefore the most probable one, is that Boxall-Chapman was obviously wrong as no-one had claimed to have fired at the Fokker from that direction.

The following description of the wound(s) were publicly made by the major participants:

Gunner Robert Buie, *Cavalier* magazine, December 1959:

> In the crash Richthofen's face had been
> thrown against the gun butts and suffered
> minor injuries. Blood had come from his
> mouth which indicated at first glance
> that a fatal bullet had pierced a lung.
> According to the popular versions, death
> came from a single bullet which had
> entered his back and passed forward
> through the chest.
>
> This is not true. Richthofen was struck
> in the LEFT BREAST, ABDOMEN and RIGHT
> KNEE! I examined these wounds as his body
> lay on a stretcher. His fur-lined boots
> were missing, as were his helmet and
> goggles and other personal effects, these
> having been taken by souvenir hunters
> before his body arrived at the battery.
> He was wearing red silk pyjamas under his
> flying clothes.
>
> The wounds were all frontal. Their
> entrances were small and clean and the
> exit points were slightly larger and
> irregular in the back. Later, Colonel
> Barber of the Australian Corps and
> Colonel Sinclair of the Fourth Army, both
> medical officers, made separate examinations
> of the body and their reports agreed that
> the fatal chest wound was frontal.

Authors' note: It should be pointed out that Buie's identification of the medical examiners is only partially correct, and that his information concerning their verdicts is totally wrong.

Sergeant Cedric B Popkin. Official Report dated 24 April 1918:

> I saw at least three machine-gun bullet
> holes through his body; one in his ribs at
> the side and a couple through his chest.

Lieutenant A B Ellis (53rd Battery). Story from the Australian 5th Division, dated 1927:

> Men hurried to the spot and found the body of their renowned and gallant enemy lying dead among the ruins of his Triplane. It bore frontal wounds on the knees, abdomen and chest.

Captain A R Brown DSC, *Ottawa Citizen*, 2 December 1925:

> Captain Brown said that the story published in German newspapers that Richthofen had landed safely behind the Canadian lines and had afterwards been shot by two men of the 149th Battalion was 'absolute nonsense'.
>
> There was an enquiry and it was found that the bullets had been fired from above. It was definitely established that Richthofen had been shot from the air. One bullet entered the left shoulder, passed through the heart and came out through the abdomen.(1)

(1) Medically the *abdomen* means more than the front of the belly. It covers the sides and the rear.

Authors' note: This fully agrees with Captain Brown's 1920 description of his attack on von Richthofen. It should be noted that the path of the bullet, as described, requires the entry point to be considerably higher than the exit.

Ottawa Citizen, 5 February 1931:

> In the Mount Royal Hotel last night Roy Brown was questioned about who had brought down the crack enemy airman. He answered: 'I have no bones to pick with those who think they brought him down, they were quite right in believing they did. Their guns were on the ground and trained up at an angle. They saw him coming, they fired, and he fell.
>
> But the autopsy revealed the bullets had hit from above and behind. The Royal Air Force recognised me as the man who brought him down. I was right on his tail at the time I shot. Therefore, either Richthofen was flying upside down and backwards, or else I brought him down.

Authors' note: In this second interview Captain Brown confirms the direction of his attack as given on the plaque at the Canadian Military Institute, by implication, and that his earlier statement that the entry wound was in the left shoulder meant the rear of it. The expression 'flying upside down and backwards" should be noted.

Lieutenant W R May. *The Edmonton Journal*, 11 January 1919:

> The preface to an interview with Lieutenant May contains the following statement probably excerpted or paraphrased from his remarks on the encounter with Manfred von Richthofen. 'A post mortem later revealed the fact that the Baron had met his fate by a bullet through the heart fired from above.'

The Edmonton Bulletin, 9 July 1919:

> In about an hour we heard for sure that it was the Red Baron. He had been shot through the heart and instantly killed. The bullet had entered his shoulder and went down through his heart thus establishing beyond a doubt that it came from above and was fired by Captain Brown.

The Canadian, which is published in Carleton Place, Ontario, where Captain Brown was born and lived, told its readers on 15 October 1936:

> You no doubt know the remainder of this story – how the Australians and other people claimed he was shot down from the ground. However, Baron Richthofen's body was examined, and it was found that the bullet passed through his shoulder and down through his heart. The bullet was fired from above, and could not have been fired from the ground. Captain Brown was officially given credit by the Royal Air Force.

Canadian Aviation, April 1944:

> A short time ago we heard that the red tri-plane [pilot] was none other than Baron von Richthofen. His body was examined and it was found that one bullet had passed through his heart from his shoulder down, which proved conclusively that Roy shot him.
>
> Richthofen would have to have been in a partial loop for the ground gunners to accomplish this feat.

Authors' note: the expression *in a partial loop means upside down*. Captain Brown had also used that analogy as referred to above.

Lieutenant R M Foster. Memoirs, date unknown but around 1930 when he was a Squadron Leader RAF:

> The doctor's [sic] report showed that the bullet which had killed Richthofen had come from above and behind and so tallied with Brown's account of his attack on the red Triplane. To support the Australian

claim, von Richthofen's aircraft would have had to have been in an inverted position close to the ground, whereas it struck the earth at quite a slight angle and was by no means smashed to pieces. To us it was conclusive that the pilot had been killed in the air and that the aircraft had carried on in a shallow dive till it hit the ground. At any rate, Brown was definitely awarded the kill.

Authors' note: The expression *inverted position*, meaning upside down has now appeared for the third time. The use of: 'To us.....' in the phrase '*To us it was conclusive*', etc. is of interest. Foster appears to be referring to some kind of a discussion with his colleagues at some time after the event.

Lieutenant F W J Mellersh, RAF Staff College, 1931, when he was a Squadron Leader RAF.

Doctors reported that Richthofen had been hit by two bullets, which had been fired from above and behind. They further said that in their opinion the shot could not have been fired from the ground.

Official Press Release, Australian HQ, France, 23 April 1918:

It was a dramatic end to a great fight. The German champion crashed smashing his machine to smithereens. Only one bullet was found in his body, and that had gone straight through the heart, entering on the left side.

Baroness Kunigunde Freifrau von Richthofen, *Toronto Star*, 6 July 1936:

On 5 July the baroness was interviewed in Toronto by R C Reade. During the conversation he mentioned, 'a portion' of the seat from her son's triplane was nearby. The incorrect downgrading of the exhibit to a mere 'portion' destroyed any interest the Freifrau might have had. She merely commented: 'The pieces which have been kept would make two aeroplanes. I should like to know [what happened] but I am afraid I shall never know.'

But, [Reade remarked] the evidence seems to be clear that the bullets entered the aeroplane from above. 'But I have been told,' said she, 'that at the moment he was making what they call an Immelmann roll. He was upside down. So he could have been shot from the ground and appear still shot from above.'

The present authors refer the reader back to the statement of G N Farquhar and R Buie on the first page of this chapter. If the Triplane was indeed 'upside down' when the ground gunners fired at it, not one of them, nor any witness, has ever mentioned it in any comment or statement.

As late as 1964, a major article in *The Canadian*, told its readers:

In the Royal Canadian Military Institute in Toronto, is the seat from Richthofen's DR-1 [sic]; a bullet hole is in the back of the seat, slightly upward and to the right.

The Canadian, whose writer had obviously never seen the exhibit upon which he was expounding, elaborated a little on the theme as follows:

A controversy as to who brought down Von Richthofen began. The Australians claimed they did, with small arms fire from the trenches, but evidence decreed the fatal bullet was fired from an aircraft, since the shell [sic] struck the Baron from an upward angle to the rear and to the right - from where Captain Brown pressed the firing button.

With information, such as the above examples (to cite but a few) being given to the public over the years, in which Captain Brown's own words *above* and *left* have been changed to *below* and *right*, it is no small wonder that there is indeed a controversy.

Further evidence of error is that Lieutenant May's several writings show that he and von Richthofen were just skimming the surface of the water at that time, which would hardly leave height for Captain Brown to be below him.

The basic common factor in what the major aerial participants appear to believe is that the shot(s) came from above, behind and from the left, whilst the ground participants believe that they came from the front and the right. The exceptions are 1AM A A Boxall-Chapman, Lieutenant Warneford and Captain Ross of 3 Squadron AFC, who all saw the bullet hole in the starboard side at the front part of the fuselage. The curiosity is the repetition of the *upside down* analogy by 209 Squadron pilots.

The hint, by Lieutenant Foster, that some kind of discussion took place after the actual event and that a conclusion may have been reached, could be connected with the repeated use of the analogy upside down and the mention of a 'board' on the plaque made for the 1920 exhibition at the Canadian Military Institute.

Von Richthofen preparing for flight with the fur overboots he was wearing the day he was killed.

The fur overboots worn by von Richthofen on 21 April are now on display in the Australian War Memorial in Canberra. One of them contains a small area at the top edge where the fur is matted with dried blood. This would be at the wearer's upper thigh height. The fur overboots appear to have had at least one previous owner, a British pilot, who claimed after the war to have been wearing them on the occasion von Richthofen shot him down.

Over the years it has been assumed that the fur boots were all that the Baron was wearing on his feet and legs but these were in fact over-boots which would be worn over his shoes. The actual shoes worn by him that day were taken by Corporal J A Porter, of 3 AFC Squadron, who even wore them in France, but after the war forwarded them to the Baroness.

An official of the Australian War Memorial who had noted the bloodstain made the unfortunately phrased statement that: 'one boot bore evidence of the fight.' His words were instantly interpreted as indicating the presence of a bullet hole and thus 'new evidence' was created. In 1972, Mr A J Sweeting, Acting Director of the AWM confirmed no such hole existed.

It is to the medical examinations and the type of bullet that hit von Richthofen that we must now turn our attention. So much has been written about the examinations in the past based upon partial information that a modern up-to-date analysis based on present day knowledge of ballistics and pathology is needed to present the information in a logical and understandable manner.

CHAPTER TEN
Background to the Medical Aspects

Prior to the publication in 1969 and 1970 of the books by Pasquale Carisella/ J W Ryan, and Dale Titler, the number of medical examinations performed on Manfred von Richthofen's body was rarely cited correctly. The number and the combinations of the doctors who made them is like a lottery, and the three separate and completely independent medical reports were often combined

which time the bullet has stabilized, there is a little loss of velocity over the next 300 yards.

When a 0.303" Mark VII cartridge is fired from a Lee-Enfield rifle, the bullet, which weighs 174 grains, leaves the muzzle at 2,440 feet per second (1,664 mph) spinning at 2,930 RP Sec (175,800 rpm). The trajectory of the bullet is approximately as depicted below (not to scale):

into one apparently composed to stress a particular aspect. The 'midnight' medical examination by the new 22 Wing MO, Captain N C Graham and his predecessor, Lieutenant G E Downs, is emphasised, whilst the 'official' examination by the most highly qualified specialists from the British Fourth Army hospital in Amiens (known as No.42 Stationary Hospital), is disparaged. The third examination, literally the 'accidental' examination, again made by a highly qualified specialist (in fact the Deputy Director of Medical Services for the Australian Imperial Force – ie: the top man in France who, for reasons that need not be stated here, happened to be at Poulainville), is ignored. The true sequence of events seems to be unknown by the general public. This is not surprising given the many television programmes, plus magazine and newspaper articles which over the years have re-cycled the flawed material of the 1930s.

Characteristics of 0.303 inch Rifle Bullet Wounds

The British Army 0.303" Mark VII rifle bullet is a variant on the Spitzer type. This is an aerodynamically shaped fully metal jacketed lead bullet with a pointed nose. The shape causes minimal aerodynamic drag with the result that after the initial 100 yards flight, by

Note. The rpm of the spin decreases 5 to 10% per second of flight time. The progressively slowing bullet will take three to four seconds to cover one mile depending upon the air density of the occasion.

The portion of the trajectory where good accuracy is normal (400 yards) is covered at a nominal 2,300 feet per second (1,568 mph). According to an official RAF publication for fighter pilots, after a bullet has covered the initial 400 yards a progressive loss of velocity begins. At 800 yards travel over half of the initial velocity has been lost, with a corresponding decrease in 'hitting power'.

This supersonic speed is the cause of the Rak-ak-ak sound when bullets from a Vickers, Lewis or German machine gun pass nearby. The design of the bullet's shape places the centre of gravity towards the rear to obtain maximum effect. Were it not for the spin imposed upon the bullet around its long axis by the rifling of the gun barrel, the rearward centre of gravity would cause serious directional instability. A little instability does remain, however and, in technical terminology, the bullet is said to *yaw in flight*. In the vernacular, the pointed nose wiggles a little but the direction of travel is accurately maintained. The rearward centre of gravity is the reason why spent Spitzer-type bullets fall from the sky base first.

The following information applies to all persons wounded by a German or British Spitzer-type 1914–18 bullet. Once a Spitzer bullet encounters the resistance (drag) of human (or animal) tissue, the rapidly slowing spin is no longer able to maintain it in a nose-forwards position for more than about four to six inches of penetration. The four inches of penetration is representative of bullets fired from 600 to 800 yards, and the six inches for bullets fired from 100 to 500 yards. However, it should be borne in mind that other variables might consist of worn barrels on whatever gun is firing the round whether it be a Lewis gun, Vickers gun or a short Lee-Enfield rifle. Also, each of those types of gun produces a different rate of spin. A Spitzer-type bullet which enters and exits tissue of an arm or a leg would be nose first all the way. A front-to-back (or back-to-front) penetration of the chest or abdomen, being about eight to ten inches of flesh, would initiate a departure from the nose-forward attitude well before the exit of the bullet through the outer skin on the far side. At ranges of 1,000 yards or more, the spin rpm and the velocity will be so low that the change of attitude will begin very early. The increased 'drag' as the nose progressively tilts away from the direction of travel, results in a greater loss of kinetic energy per inch travelled. This is converted into increased damage to the tissue surrounding its path as it goes through the body.

This change of attitude is known as 'tumbling'. Tumbling does not mean turning over and over, but merely one half turn around the short axis in which the bullet changes attitude from nose-first to tail-first. The centre of gravity is now at the front, and will remain there. Assuming a 175,000 rpm strike at 2,300 feet per second, for a bullet to reach a fully tumbled condition (base-forwards) requires a passage of about 18 inches through human tissue.

Assuming that prior to striking a human body the Spitzer-type bullet has not been damaged, the entrance wound will be small and round. If the strike was perpendicular to the skin (ie: it has struck squarely) the abrasions around the periphery of the entrance wound will tend to be equal. However, if the bullet has struck the skin at an angle other than perpendicular, the entrance wound will frequently be oval and the abrasions around the edge will be unequal; any heavier abrading present at the edge of the wound will tend to indicate the angle whence the bullet came.

A fully tumbled or partially tumbled bullet will present a blunt surface to the inside of the skin at the exit point. The skin being elastic in nature will absorb a lot of energy before permitting the bullet to pass through. The resulting exit wound will be 'torn' rather than 'perforated'. It will be very much larger than the entry wound.

A Spitzer bullet, which during the process of tumbling touches a fairly resistant bone, can suffer a major change of direction. The direction in which it is deflected will depend upon whether the nose or the tail of the bullet touched the bone, and at which radial angle it was tumbling at the time. In all cases a major loss of kinetic energy will simultaneously occur, ie: the bullet will slow down considerably and the tendency to tumble will increase.

Between the ranges of 400 and 800 yards, Spitzer-inflicted wound paths will be identical in appearance although penetration will vary. During flight the spin rpm and the velocity have decreased, but not by enough to be obvious in their effect upon stability. Range cannot be determined with any certainty from the wound between those distances as premature tumbling may have many causes.

If a Spitzer bullet is fired from more than 800 yards at the trunk or abdomen of a man who happens to be wearing heavy clothing, the spent bullet is quite likely to be found resting in between his skin and the said clothing just below the exit wound. Bullets are frequently found at a soldier's waistline, trapped where his trouser belt holds his shirt against his body. Sometimes the bullets fall out when the victim is moved. During the time that the bullet travelled side-first, ripping through tissue and organs, the friction had already converted so much of its kinetic energy into tissue damage that, after overcoming the elasticity of the skin, the remaining energy was absorbed by the elasticity of the garments.

If the range exceeds 1,000 yards, it is quite likely that a tumbled Spitzer bullet will not exit the trunk or abdomen. At ranges below 150yds, a 0.303″ British Army Mark VII rifle bullet (Spitzer) is travelling at more than twice the speed of sound and will literally self-destruct shortly after impact. This creates an effect similar to an explosive bullet and results in a distinctive type of wound.

Unlike a bullet fired from a 45 (0.45″) automatic pistol, which merely increases a little in diameter (due to compression) as it passes through human tissue, and may be said to bore a hole, a Spitzer type carves a channel once it slows enough to tumble. In addition to the channel itself, the kinetic energy absorbed by surrounding tissue during the carving action results in extensive internal damage. More information on this aspect is given in Chapter 12.

Many people have been shot frontally in or through the heart with a pistol and have survived. A shot fired from the side by a British Army 0.303″ weapon would have a far different result.

CHAPTER ELEVEN
The First Medical Examination
(The Midnight Preview)

On the evening of 21 April, Major Blake, the CO of 3 Squadron AFC, received word from 22 Wing HQ that Lieutenant-Colonel Cairnes (1) was sending the new Wing MO, Captain Norman Clotworthy Graham RAMC, to his aerodrome to examine von Richthofen's body. One must assume that Cairnes was in hopes that at least the dispute between the two squadrons under his command could be resolved before the 'top brass' (the Fourth Army Consulting Surgeon and Consulting Physician) arrived on the morrow. Judging from the after duty hours activity which then took place, the 3 AFC medical orderlies received instructions to clean the body up a bit and to lay it out neatly.

During this activity, the senior orderly, Corporal Edward McCarty, discovered a spent bullet inside the clothing at the front of the body. Actually it fell out unexpectedly, so he could not say precisely where it had been lying. Others saw him pick it up and heard him comment on it; this eliminates the discovery being a later 'tall story' on McCarty's part. The body had been moved around quite a bit since the Baron died, so exactly where the bullet came to rest is unknown. The knowledge as to between which layers of clothing it was resting was also lost when it fell out of its own accord. McCarty's belief was that upon exiting the body, further travel of the bullet had been arrested by the bulk of a leather wallet which he found in the breast pocket of an inner garment. The details are somewhat garbled and in the light of the knowledge that von Richthofen pulled his flying suit on over his pyjamas, it is more probable that the wallet was in an inside pocket of the suit. This would also explain the fact that those who had earlier searched the body for valuables and had found a large sum of French money, had missed the wallet. The bullet was not pristine; it bore a sharp indentation indicative that it had struck something hard at some stage.

During the 1960s the late Pasquale Carisella succeeded in finding the 'owner' of the wallet and obtained four excellent photographs of it; one of each of the shiny leather surfaces: two exterior and two interior views. Author Bennett has seen these photos and can affirm that none of the four faces bears any mark or dent whatsoever. It therefore would appear that the final energy of the bullet was consumed in breaking through the skin and possibly the pyjamas, and that it came to rest against the inside of the heavy fur-lined flying suit.

There were two other mentions of a bullet on the body, curiously enough both by members of Sergeant Popkin's gun team, Privates Weston and Marshall. Weston said that it was on the left side partially embedded in a book. It may have been hearsay for, in extensive correspondence with historian Frank McGuire, he never mentioned it. Sergeant Popkin told C E W Bean, the Australian Official Historian for the 1914-18 war, that Marshall had taken a bullet from the body. Marshall was killed later on in the war; however, it is strange that no one else has mentioned such an interesting 'find' on his part. The most probable explanation is that either Marshall or Weston saw the bullet and decided to leave it well alone. Corporal McCarty found it later on that evening.

At about 2330 hours, Major Blake and his Recording Officer, Captain E G Knox, arrived at the tent-hangar where the body had been laid out. They were accompanied by Captain Graham and his predecessor, Lieutenant Downs, who was to leave France four days later to take up a posting in England. The captain had arrived just the previous day, Saturday the 20th, and had immediately assumed his new function.

The two MOs, without doubt, had heard from Lieutenant-Colonel Cairnes about his visit with Roy Brown to the 53rd Battery, and it is logical to assume that Major Blake had already spoken to them about the red Triplane which Lieutenants Barrow and Banks had forced out of the fight over Le Hamel. The task before the two doctors might be a fairly simple one; namely a dispute between three bursts of machine-gun fire; all from 50 to 350 yards range, but from completely different angles towards the Fokker.

(1) Lt-Col Cairnes arrived at 22 Wing from Home Establishment on 17 April and would take full command from Lt-Col F V Holt on the 25th.

82

Whilst they made their examination, about 20 officers from 3 AFC watched from a respectful distance. One of them was Lieutenant Banks, the RE8 observer who had a stake in the game.

The first unexpected discovery was that far from having been the victim of a burst of machine-gun fire, only one bullet had struck the body. What had been taken to be a multiple bullet entry wound was actually the exit wound of a single bullet. The other 'bullet wounds' all turned out to be impact injuries, sustained in the cockpit during the crash landing.

According to witness testimony received by Dale Titler, Lieutenant Downs noticed something about the body which suggested to him that the bullet had not followed a straight path from the entry point to the exit point. The nature of this 'something' has, unfortunately, never been disclosed.

In an attempt to discover what that 'something' might have been, the present authors consulted three gunshot wound specialists; one in Canada, one in England and one in Australia. They all indicated that when dealing with a Spitzer-type bullet, the entrance wound will often give an indication of the angle at which the bullet struck the victim. If it strikes the skin perpendicularly, its sharp point, followed by an aerodynamically-shaped increasing diameter, will make a neat round hole and the abrasions around the inner edge of the hole will be equally distributed. As the angle of impact moves away from the perpendicular, so will the hole become progressively unequal. The exception will be if the bullet has struck something else first and has either become deformed or has begun to tumble.

Dale Titler's witness also revealed that Lieutenant Downs had tactfully suggested to Captain Graham that perhaps the bullet had dog-legged on its way through the body (possibly via touching the spine). Whether he drew Graham's attention to the entry wound is unknown. The witness continued that Graham, after looking at the size of the exit wound which was much larger than the entrance one, was of the opinion that it was still not large enough to have been caused by a bullet which had deflected off the spine. This was not exactly true, for the size of an exit wound in the trunk or the abdomen made by a Spitzer-type rifle bullet depends mainly on a combination of its spinning rpm at the time of impact and how far it has travelled through the body tissue.

Two of the three claimants said that they had fired from 50 to 100 yards range. The third one had opened fire at 350 yards range (noted as long range by his standards) and had ceased fire at about 50 yards range. The wound characteristics, being identical between 400 and 800 yards, would not reveal the range at which the shot was fired. The distance travelled through body tissue rapidly reduces the rpm of the spin [from the rifling] which permits the bullet to begin to tumble (change from point-first to base-first travel). The conversion to a partially tumbled or fully tumbled attitude will be helped by an interference such as glancing off the spine. *However, given the distance travelled by that particular bullet, it would have tumbled regardless of which of the two paths it had followed.* In the straight-through instance, the rate at which tumbling progressed to the base-first attitude was principally a function of the rpm of its spin. In the dog-leg instance (off the spine) the straight-through situation was modified by how much encouragement the glancing had given to the progression of the tumbling. Captain Graham, being totally unaware that the bullet had been found and that it bore, according to the man who found it, a sharp indentation, and because of the rudimentary knowledge of ballistics in those days, had considerably over-simplified the situation.

In the light of today's knowledge, Captain Graham's error is easily explained. If one looks at a bullet travelling a 'short' distance through, say, a limb, and being provoked into early tumbling by deflection or glancing off a bone, the point of exit may well coincide with the maximum extension of the temporary cavity which is then unable to close and thus remains open in the form of a horrendous wound. It would appear it was this sort of injury to which Captain Graham was referring.

With a bullet travelling a longer distance through a body, as in von Richthofen's case, the temporary cavity had time to close down again by the pressure of the surrounding tissue. The exit wound therefore is considerably smaller. Ballistic pathologist, Doctor David King, pointed out to the authors that the exit wound, as described on von Richthofen's body, conformed exactly to what he would have expected to see resulting from a Spitzer bullet having taken a long path laterally through his trunk.

The sketch on page 84 shows this and a fuller explanation will be found in Chapter 12.

The cause of death had definitely been established; a single bullet through the chest which had caused massive damage to vital organs in its path. Whether, as it tumbled, it had passed in a straight line from entrance to exit points or had dog-legged, the final result would have been the same although the organs damaged and the symptoms would have been different. Downs gave

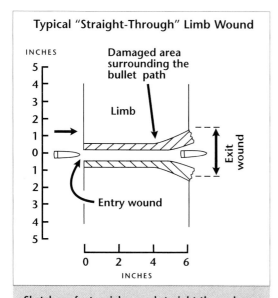

Typical "Straight-Through" Limb Wound

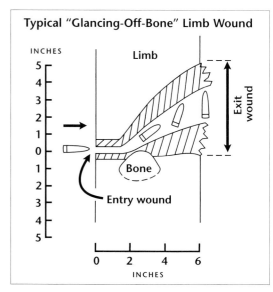

Typical "Glancing-Off-Bone" Limb Wound

Sketches of a typcial wound straight through a limb, and one deflected by an arm or leg bone.

no argument and co-signed the report which, although obliquely mentioning his suspicion, presented no opinion against it.

The next morning, Monday 22nd, they wrote the following combined report to 22 Wing RAF HQ:

> We examined the body of Captain Baron von Richtoven [sic] on the evening of the 21st instant (April 1918). We found that he had one entrance and one exit wound caused by the same bullet.
>
> The entrance wound was situated on the right side of the chest in the posterior fold of the armpit and the exit wound was situated at a slightly higher level nearer the front of the chest, the point of exit being about half an inch below the left nipple and about three quarters of an inch external to it. From the nature of the exit wound, we think that the bullet passed straight through the chest from right to left, and also slightly forward. Had the bullet been deflected from the spine, the exit wound would have been much larger.
>
> The gun firing this bullet must have been situated in roughly the same plane as the long axis of the German machine and fired from right and slightly behind the right of Captain Richtoven. (1)
>
> We are agreed that the situation of the entrance and exit wounds are such that they could not have been caused by fire from the ground.

The wing span of an aeroplane in those days was greater than the length of its fuselage. The *long axis* referred to would be close to that of an imaginary line drawn along the middle wing of a Triplane from tip to tip. When the 'joystick' was pushed forward or pulled back, the Triplane would pivot around that line, hence the name *axis*. Depending upon the attitude of the Triplane at that time, the *long axis* could have been inclined in any direction. The two MOs, who are using engineers' terminology, are stating briefly that the right-hand side of the Triplane was almost squarely facing the gun that fired the fatal shot wherever that gun may have been. They are relating the gun to the attitude of the aeroplane – not vice-versa.

Some, who have not realised the import of the long axis statement in the third paragraph, have claimed (mistakenly in the authors' opinion) that the final sentence contains the unwarranted assumption that a fighter aeroplane always flies straight and level, and Captain Graham and Lieutenant Downs have been accused of both outright bias and of gross stupidity because of it. However, a moment's reflection suggests that the MO of an entire Wing, which included several squadrons of fighter aircraft, would be well aware how they were flown and would be most unlikely to imply such nonsense, especially in writing to a superior officer. There surely had to be more to it than that.

If one takes the same starting point as being

(1) It is amazing how many people at this time did not know how to spell Richthofen's name. We have had Reichtofen, Richthoffen and now Richtoven.

We examined the body of Captain Baron VON RICHTOVEN on the evening of the 21st instant. We found that he had one entrance and one exit wound caused by the same bullet.

The entrance wound was situated on the right side of the chest in the posterior fold of the armpit: the exit wound was situated at a slightly higher level nearer the front of the chest, the point of exit being about half an inch below the left nipple and about three quarters of an inch external to it. From the nature of the exit wound, we think that the bullet passed straight through the chest from right to left, and also slightly forward. Had the bullet been deflected from the spine the exit wound would have been much larger.

The gun firing this bullet must have been situated in roughly the same plane as the long axis of the German machine, and fired from the right and slightly behind the right of Captain RICHTOVEN.

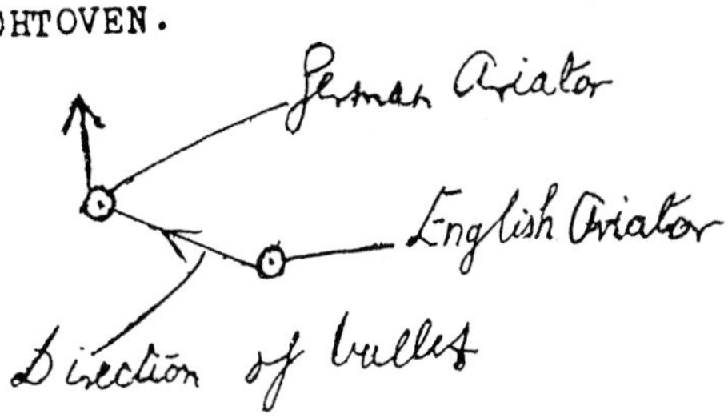

German Aviator

English Aviator

Direction of bullet

We are agreed that the situation of the entrance and exit wounds are such that they could not have been caused by fire from the ground.

Capt. R.A.M.C.
M.O.i/o 22nd Wing, R.A.F

Lieut. R.A.M.O.

In the Field.

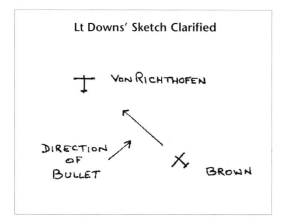

Lt Downs' Sketch Clarified

Von RICHTHOFEN

DIRECTION OF BULLET

BROWN

the situation before the MO's, it becomes obvious that they would not have any reason to make a general statement, as they had only one ground fire claim to deal with. To them, the fatal shot, not being a frontal or semi-frontal wound through the chest with exit through the back, eliminated the claim of the 53rd Battery. There was also the matter of the tight pattern fired by a Lewis gun at close range versus the single bullet which struck the Baron, and a ground-based Lewis gun was much steadier than one mounted on a vibrating aeroplane.

The final statement was as far as they were prepared to go; anything deeper was dangerous territory. RAMC Lieutenants and Captains do not pre-empt Army Medical Services Colonels, unless they wish a posting to some far away place with a strange sounding name and lots of flies! The statement represents the conclusion of their examination; it is not just a comment. Once it is read as referring to the claim by the 53rd Battery, their report becomes clearly impartial.

The sketch which they appended to illustrate the third paragraph (The gun firing this bullet ....), required knowledge of the bullet hole in the right-hand side of the fuselage at the front end. Such knowledge could only have come from a briefing on that point, probably from Major Blake who would have learned about it from Captain Ross, his Armament Officer. The snag was that the lines on it did not exactly match the angles from which Captain Brown or Lieutenants Barrow and Banks claimed to have fired at the Triplane. However, who could be sure of the exact attitude of the Triplane in the air at that time? There was the added complication of the harness which the pilot had loosened to work on his defective machine guns. Was he sitting erect or leaning forwards when he was struck? There is no indication that his right

arm may have been raised as he worked the cocking handle of his guns, for at the moment he was struck he would already have given up on that and have been in the act of pulling up and away. The 'hot potato' of 209 Squadron versus 3 AFC remained on the griddle.

Unnecessary *confusion* has been created by the paraphrasing of the conclusion to the point that it is common belief that the words are: '.... the shot could only have been fired from the air.' This completely alters the point that the MOs were trying to make (rightly or wrongly) that the 53rd Battery's claim was inconsistent with the facts.

A copying error occurred in the transcript sent to C E W Bean, the Australian Official Historian, so that it read: '.... below the *right* nipple ...' instead of: '.... below the *left* nipple ...'. Either that or the writer was mentally viewing von Richthofen from the front where the left nipple would be to the writer's right. Bean caught and corrected the slip but some of the others, who received copies of the flawed transcript, used it *verbatim*. The origin of statements such as: 'Von Richthofen was shot in the back of his right shoulder and the bullet exited through his right breast ...', becomes obvious.

By the morning of the 22nd, 3 AFC had withdrawn its claim; the time of the encounter of their RE8s with the Triplanes was too early. By default, this left Captain Brown as the remaining contender – from the air.

At some time that morning, the Recording Officer of 209 Squadron (Lt Shelley), obtained an Army Form W3348, Combats in the Air [reports] and re-typed Captain Brown's earlier one in a more presentable manner. The subscripted words: '.. and Lieut. May.' became part of the line itself. No words were changed; that would have been illegal, but some additions were typed into the top left hand corner, viz:

```
Engagement with red triplane
Time: about 11-00 a.m.
Locality, Vaux sur Somme
```

Captain Brown signed it. Major Butler approved it and this time annotated it: One Decisive.

The better-looking report was also dated 21 April 1918 and was submitted to 22 Wing on the 22nd together with post-1601 hours documents referring to the 21st. In the Air Ministry file it is numbered later than the 209 Squadron reports received by the 5th Brigade on the 21st.

Also on 22 April, 3 AFC Squadron submitted its War Diary entry for the 21st. The relevant portion is transcribed below:

> Two machines of this Squadron encountered the Circus about the same time as the Baron was shot down although they were not concerned in the actual shooting down of the celebrated enemy. Lieuts. Garrett and Barrow, and Lieuts. Simpson and Banks were proceeding to the line for the purpose of photographing the Corps front when they saw the enemy triplanes approaching. Lieut. Simpson and Banks were the first to be attacked by four of the triplanes. The observer fired 100 rounds at point blank range at the E.A., one of which was seen to separate and go down. The others withdrew and attacked Lieuts. Garrett and Barrow. The observer in this case got in 120 rounds Lewis, in bursts and another of the E.A. was seen to go down out of control. Both pilots then proceeded over the line and carried out their task of photographing the whole Corps front....
>
> In the meantime reports had come from the Infantry that one of the triplanes shot down in the general combat which had ensued between our scouts and the enemy circus after they had been driven off by the the RE8s of this Squadron, was that of Baron von Richthofen. The Lewis gunners of the 5th Divisional Artillery, A.I.F. claimed the honour of firing the shot which brought him down, but after the matter had been carefully investigated, the award was made to Captain Brown, of No. 209 Squadron, RAF.

The entry was written by the RO, Captain E G Knox (a former Sydney journalist) and signed by the CO, Major Blake. The phrasing indicates that 3 AFC was no longer pursuing Lieutenant Barrow's claim. Another interesting fact at this early stage is that Knox apparently knows, or at least indicates, that the Baron was killed by a single bullet! It also makes the first known official reference to an 'investigation'. Major Blake will return to the story in the final chapter.

Any investigation which took place in the evening of the 21st or the morning of the 22nd would hardly have all the facts at its disposal. Such a hurried affair clashes somewhat with the impression given on Brown's plaque in Toronto where he refers to a Board, and with the statements made by Foster, May and Mellersh on the same subject. The clash has complicated earlier attempts to study what some have referred to as the Official Board of Enquiry for the descriptions appear to refer to two different meetings.

The solution to the puzzle is actually quite simple; there were two different meetings. The first one was on the evening of the 21st and the second one on 2 May, the day after Captain Brown entered No.24 General Hospital at Étaples. The details appear later in Chapter 15.

The Graham/Downs medical examination report was not a model of precision. The wording – 'a slightly higher level' and 'in roughly the same plane' could without any difficulty have been made clearer. The second example given is particularly deficient in that 'above' or 'below' is not specified. The report also contains two 'abouts' and one 'we think'. Even worse, they had missed an injury caused by the very bullet whose path they had studied.

Historian Frank McGuire told the authors of an amusing story about an attempt (not his) to locate Captain N C Graham after the war in order to obtain his first-hand comments on the examination. A RAMC Captain Graham was found without too much difficulty and he said that he remembered the incident quite well. Unfortunately the story which he told matched an inaccurate one published some time before. Further investigation revealed that his initials were not N C, nor had he been in France in April 1918!

CHAPTER TWELVE
The Fatal Bullet's Path
(Permanent and Temporary Bullet Path Cavities)

The term **Permanent Cavity** refers to the tissue that lay in the immediate path of the bullet. Basically, it is the bullet hole all the way from start to finish as found after the event. Once the skin has been penetrated, the diameter and shape of this

cavity depend far more upon the shape and the metallic composition of the bullet which made it than upon its diameter; 0.45" or 0.303" for example.

After an initial penetration which can be anywhere between two and six inches, depending upon several factors, a Spitzer Mark VII 0.303" British army type rifle bullet begins to tumble. As the bullet transitions from the point-forwards attitude to side-forwards attitude, the 'tunnel' inside the body being bored by it will be progressively enlarged up to at least 1¼" diameter

BELOW LEFT AND RIGHT: Male torso indicating entrance and exit points, and showing the axillary lines on the left.

BOTTOM: Permanent and Temporary Bullet Path Cavity.

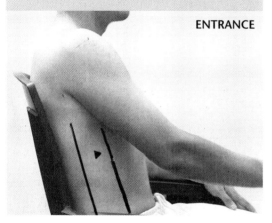

ENTRANCE

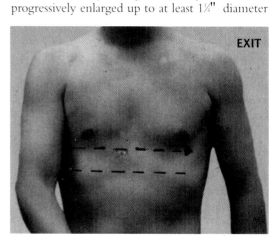

EXIT

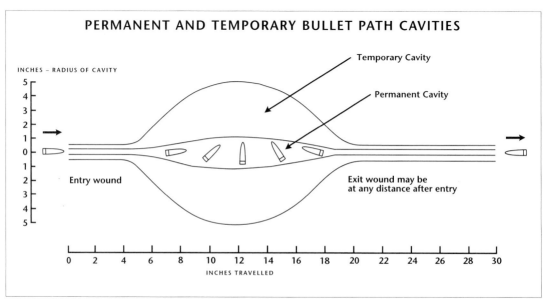

PERMANENT AND TEMPORARY BULLET PATH CAVITIES

Temporary Cavity

Permanent Cavity

INCHES – RADIUS OF CAVITY

Entry wound

Exit wound may be at any distance after entry

INCHES TRAVELLED

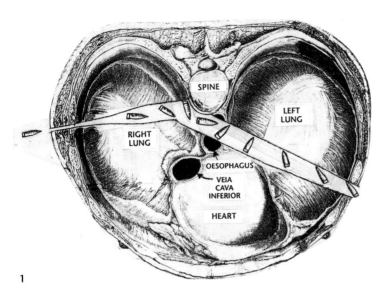

1

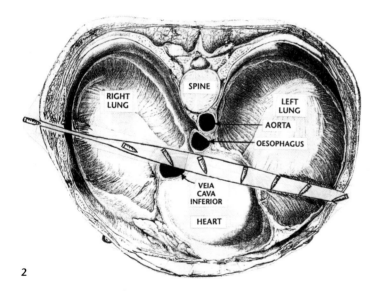

2

latter expands as the bullet passes along and thereby compresses the surrounding tissue. If said tissue is elastic in nature, it eventually returns, undamaged, to its original shape.

However, if the tissue surrounding the permanent cavity is hard in nature (such as the liver) and cannot absorb the compression, severe damage, generally of a permanent nature, occurs.

The Two Possible Paths Of The Fatal Bullet

To avoid congesting the bullet path illustrations with lines, the temporary cavity is not shown. It is not difficult to imagine it as being there, and thus to comprehend the severe nature of the wound, straight or deflected, incurred by von Richthofen.

1. The permanent cavity as might be caused by deflection from the front of the spine as suggested by Lieutenant Downs and confirmed by Colonel Sinclair and Colonel Nixon (See Chapter 13), *then later re-confirmed by Colonel Barber.* (See Chapter 14)

The bullet is depicted tumbling clockwise horizontally. It could just as easily have tumbled vertically or anti-clockwise in any combination. The effect would be roughly the same.

2. The permanent cavity as might be caused by a straight through path as per Captain Graham's opinion.

The bullet is depicted tumbling anti-clockwise horizontally. Clockwise and/or vertical are equally likely, and with similar effect.

(the bullet measures 1 ⁵⁄₁₆th" from top to base). Any tissue in its way is literally turned into pulp, which is why probing a wound on a corpse beyond four inches is not recommended. As the bullet continues changing attitude from side-forwards to base-forwards, the diameter of the permanent cavity (the correct name for what we have termed the 'tunnel') progressively decreases back to about 0.303" although the bullet may exit the body before this state is reached.

The term **Temporary Cavity** refers to the tissue surrounding the permanent cavity. The wall of the

CHAPTER THIRTEEN
The Second Medical Examination
(The Official One)

On the morning of Monday 22 April, Colonel Thomas Sinclair, Consulting Surgeon, and Colonel John A Nixon (not Dixon, as sometimes recorded), Consulting Physician, both of the Army Medical Services and accredited to the British Fourth Army, arrived at Poulainville aerodrome.

From a letter (quoted later in this chapter) it is clear that, similar to Lieutenant Downs and Captain Graham, they had been briefed on the circumstances of the three claims; that is type of weapon, number of rounds fired, angle of fire, and the presence of just one bullet hole in the fuselage of the Triplane and the fact that it was in the right-hand side at the front end by the cockpit. Like their predecessors, they were both unaware that the fatal bullet had been found, and more important, where it had been found.

Before proceeding with the description of the Official Medical Examination, two explanations of the terminology used therein are required.

1. Rifle Bullet

0.303" Mark VII with Spitzer-shape nose and cylindrical body. Standard British Army issue in WW1 and WW2. Used in Lee-Enfield rifles, Vickers machine guns and Lewis machine guns.

Six other types of Spitzer-shape bullets were used in WW1; three examples are tracer, incendiary and armour piercing. The other three types were for use against balloons and airships. Each one of the seven inflicted its own distinctive variety of wound upon the human body.

Ground-based machine guns fired a mixture of rifle bullets and tracer bullets in ratios varying between 4:1 and 10:1 as per the gunner's preference. Aircraft machine guns were loaded with rifle bullets interspersed with tracer and other types, depending upon the intended purpose. The ratio used reflected the individual pilot's preference.

The characteristics of a wound, when matched against the types of bullets loaded into different weapons firing simultaneously at a target, can sometimes indicate which one was responsible for it.

2. Axillary Lines

The word *axilla* means armpit. Basically, when a person is standing in the military *attention* position,

the front of the arm will agree with the *anterior axillary line* down the trunk and the rear of the arm with the *posterior axillary line*. In medical terminology these are definite linear positions on a human body. For example: the intersection of the eighth rib and the anterior axillary line is an exact (or pinpoint) location, not an approximate one.

The two Colonels also noticed something about one or both of the wounds which hinted that the bullet had followed a 'dog-leg' path from entrance to exit. Again, no indication remains of what they saw but, unlike their predecessors, they took their impression seriously and decided to investigate it.

There is a difference of recollection among the orderlies who were present as to whether Colonel Sinclair (the surgeon) used a medical instrument or a piece of fencing wire, which he found nearby, to probe the wounds in order to establish the path of the bullet. It certainly was not a piece of barbed wire as has sometimes been written (see Chapter 14) that would be absolutely useless for the purpose. Probing will not establish a precise direction and therefore its result is not accepted, for instance, in a judicial court. However, it will often give a general direction which may well serve the purpose of the occasion.

The present authors have been advised that where a Spitzer-type rifle bullet is involved, provided that it still has its pointed nose undamaged and facing forward when it strikes flesh, and has not started to tumble, the first inches of penetration will be quite likely to provide an acceptable indication of the angle at which it struck the body. After tumbling has begun, probing becomes meaningless. To evaluate damage, or lack of it, to internal organs, the body must be surgically opened. In this case it appears that a general direction, which agreed with their original suspicions, was established to the satisfaction of the examiners. They proceeded no further.

Colonel Sinclair and Colonel Nixon's report, dated 22 April 1918, was as follows:

> We have made a surface examination of the body of Captain Baron von Richthofen and find that there are only the entrance and

THE SECOND MEDICAL EXAMINATION

exit wounds of one rifle bullet on the
trunk. The entrance wound is on the right
side about the level of the ninth rib,
which is fractured, just in front of the
posterior axillary line. The bullet appears
to have passed obliquely backwards through
the chest striking the spinal column, from
which it glanced in a forward direction
and issued on the left side of the chest
at a level about two inches higher than
its entrance on the right and about in
the anterior axillary line.

    There was also a compound fracture of
the lower jaw on the left side, apparently
not caused by a missile - also some minor
bruises on the head and face. The body
was not opened - these facts were
ascertained by probing the surface wounds.

Authors' Note.

Careful, leisurely measurements made on a male
body of equivalent build to Manfred von
Richthofen have revealed that the difference in
height between the two wounds, which the
colonels estimated at 'about two inches', would
actually have been on the high side of two, not the
low side.

The colonels learned from the examination that
only one bullet had struck the deceased, that it was
of the rifle-type, (so it could have been fired by any
one of the three claimants) and that whilst inside the
body, it seemed to have been deflected by about 30
degrees. Knowing that only one bullet hole had
been found in the side of the fuselage of the Triplane
and that its location agreed with the position and
direction of the entrance wound, they decided that
not just one, but all three of the claimants were
disqualified. This left the verdict wide open and gives
the lie to allegations that their report was slanted
against Brown. A long stretch of imagination is
required to declare an 'open verdict' as biased.

The Colonels' report in effect disqualified all
three candidates as each claimed that he had
inflicted many hits from his machine gun(s) fired
from 50 to 350 yards range and from a specific
direction, but none of them had claimed to have
fired from anywhere near the right hand side
'roughly in the plane of the long axis' (to borrow a
phrase from Graham and Downs).

The twin Vickers machine guns mounted above
the vibrating engine of Brown's Sopwith Camel
would, at all times, give a cone-shaped pattern of
fire, hence the need to get close in order to hit a
target. At 300 yards range, and further, the spread
would be rather wide and a hit with a single bullet
was actually more likely than with half a dozen. This

was a strong point in his favour. Unfortunately there
was the matter of the bullet hole in the front end of
the right-hand side of the fuselage. Its alignment
with the entrance wound indicated that von
Richthofen's trunk had not been twisted round to
his right when the bullet struck him; he had been
sitting straight, or close to it, in the cockpit. The
bullet which struck him could not have been fired
from 'above, behind and from the [Triplane's] left
rear' as per Brown's claim.

The bullet had approached the Triplane from
slightly below and from slightly in front on its
right-hand side. Its point of origin could only be
determined exactly if, at the time it struck, the
precise attitude and direction of the Triplane in the
air were known. At this stage, that aspect had
received little, if any, attention. The field was now
open to claims from anybody who had fired a rifle-
type bullet from anywhere between 400 and 800
yards range towards the right-hand side of the
Triplane. In truth, the finding of the bullet inside
the Baron's clothing indicated that the shot had
most likely come from a distance of 600 to 1,000
yards, but because Corporal McCarty had kept the
finding of the bullet to himself, it did not come into
the equation. So today we can state it was NOT a
short range shot.

The two colonels' report differed markedly in
style from the first one in that the position of the
entry wound and of the exit wound were given in
anatomical terms and therefore, both medically and
forensically, defined exact locations. However, their
examination did not mention bullet wounds in the
knees and legs which some still believed to be
present. This has been held against the completeness
of their report despite the most probable cause of
the apparent omission being that the injuries in
question had not been caused by bullets – or caused
at all! Most of the stories of the supposed chest and
leg injuries seem to have stemmed from initial
viewing by troops at the scene of the large amount
of blood discharged from Richthofen's mouth. This
had naturally gushed onto the front of his flying
suit, the top of his legs, his knees and soaked into
the upper part of one of his fur overboots. They did,
however, settle the matter of the injuries to the
mouth and face, which had also, in the early stages
been said to have been caused by gunfire.

In October 1934, Doctor J A Nixon, by then a
well-known physician in the Bristol area of
England, received a query on von Richthofen's
death from a Mr Linder. The question(s) which Mr
Linder asked are unknown but the following two
paragraphs excerpted from Doctor Nixon's reply
are self-explanatory.

Death of Baron von Richthofen

```
Colonel Sinclair (consulting surgeon to
Fourth Army) and I were sent for to go to
an aerodrome at Bertangles in order to
decide if possible to which of several
claimants the credit of bringing down
Richthofen belonged. An Australian
squadron claimed that they had engaged
his whole Circus (well known by their
coloured planes) and singling out their
leader had riddled him with bullets till
he crashed. Another squadron (British)
said that they had been previously
engaged with the 'circus', and that they
had disabled Richthofen's plane before
the Australians came on the scene.
Finally a machine gun battery on the
ground maintained that he was escaping by
flying low until he came within their
range and had poured an incredible number
of hits into him.
  Our verdict disposed of all these
claims. The plane had only been hit by
one single bullet which had passed through
the fusillage [sic] and entered the chest
in the middle of the right axilla.
Travelling horizontally it had struck the
front of the vertebrae and glanced off,
probably into the heart, but we did not
open the body to make our examination.
Enough had been established to dispose of
all' the claims we had heard. No one had
claimed to have come alongside of
Richthofen and fired horizontally at him.
All this account is my own first hand
observation.
```

The word 'all' in the last sentence quoted above is sometimes challenged on the ground that by the time Colonel Nixon arrived at Poulainville the section of fuselage fabric with the bullet hole in it had most probably already been removed from the Triplane which might well be true. The most likely explanation is that he received information from an officer who had personally seen it, probably Captain Roderick Ross, the Armaments Officer with 3 AFC, who had no connection with the 53rd Battery. Like Lieutenant Warneford and 1AM Boxall-Chapman, he belonged to the Australian Flying Corps, so they had no axe to grind. They had all seen the bullet hole in the fuselage long before it assumed importance, and certainly had not invented it.

It appears that Colonel Nixon was never really satisfied as to what had happened to the Red Devil. At the end of his letter to Mr Linder he mentions that he had heard a rumour which properly fitted the trajectory of the bullet, and he emphasises that it was merely a rumour, that whilst the Baron was flying along, a British two-seater aeroplane drew up alongside without him noticing, and the observer killed him. For this to be true, one would need to imagine von Richthofen, over enemy territory, flying along admiring the scenery or reading the morning paper at the time. Obviously this is the tail wagging the dog again. The story has been created in reverse; the starting point being the true trajectory of the bullet relative to the Triplane.

Surprisingly – or by now perhaps not surprisingly – Doctor Nixon's 'rumour' without the earlier paragraph of his letter quoted above, has been published more than once as a 'new discovery' or 'new evidence', and Lieutenant Banks of 3 Squadron AFC has even been named as the observer in question despite the only time he encountered the Baron being half an hour before the latter was killed.

An interesting corollary to the above is to be found in the Obituary of Colonel Thomas Sinclair given below:

Carleton Place Herald
Vol. 91, No. 23, November 27, 1940
Credited Roy Brown With Downing Richthofen

Belfast, Nov. 25 – Col. Thomas Sinclair, 81, Conservative Member of Parliament for Queen's University here for 17 years, died today. He retired from the House of Commons two months ago. It was Col. Sinclair who as consulting surgeon of the British 4th Army in the First Great War gave credit to Capt. Roy Brown, former Carleton Place boy and Canadian aviator, for the shooting down of Baron Manfred von Richthofen, German flying ace.

Richthofen's plane crashed in a dog fight. He was chasing a young British pilot when Brown got on his tail. The three planes dived within range of the ground fire of Australian troops. The latter claimed the Baron as their victim. Colonel Sinclair officially examined von Richthofen's body and, from study of the flier's wounds, concluded that he had been brought down by Brown.

The Carleton Place *Herald* cannot be faulted for this flawed Obituary, which was written in Northern Ireland. Whoever wrote it appears to have a vague recollection of the tale as told in *The Red Knight of Germany* (see Appendix D). The young 'British pilot' of course, is Canadian Lieutenant May, whom Gibbons had earlier described as an Australian from Melbourne, but surely a Canadian newspaper should have known enough at least to correct or highlight this error about one of its sons?

The sad aspect is that with the best of intentions, when anniversaries occur, the flawed information is re-cycled even in newspapers of high standing, and thus gains new life.

CHAPTER FOURTEEN
The Third Medical Examination
(The Extra One)

During the German's March Offensive, and the Allied effort which stopped the Germans from taking Amiens, there had been a scandalous shortage of bandages, dressings and medication in the Field Advanced Dressing Stations and the Main Dressing Stations. This was due, in great part, to the confusion of the retreat and the *ad hoc* measures taken to stem the German onslaught.

A renewal of the German attack was expected towards the end of April (it actually began on the 24th) and Colonel George W Barber, the Deputy Director of Medical Services, (the AIF's top Medical Services man outside Australia), who was based at Villers Bocage just north of Amiens, was determined that, this time, the AIF men at least would lack for nothing in the way of immediate treatment.

Accordingly, in early April, he began a series of personal inspections of the advanced and the support medical facilities. On 21 April, accompanied by Major C L Chapman AAMC, he inspected the 12th Australian Field Ambulance unit. On the morning of the 22nd he went to Bertangles where he (quote): 'Conferred with the Officer Commanding [the] 3rd Australian Flying Squadron re his medical requirements.' The officer would have most probably been Major Blake whose aeroplanes were at nearby Poulainville aerodrome.

Upon arrival he learned that Baron von Richthofen's body was at the aerodrome lying in a 3 Squadron tent hangar at Poulainville. His programme for later that morning, to inspect 3 AFC's Dressing Station, thereupon suffered a short postponement. It was too good an opportunity to allow to pass by.

Colonel Barber and Major Chapman arrived at the tent hangar just as the medical orderlies were cleaning up after the examination by Colonels Sinclair and Nixon. The story of what happened next is best described in Barber's own words in a letter to C E W Bean 17½ years later:

October 23rd, 1935

My Dear Bean,
With reference to your letter of Oct. 14th, I was Inspecting this Air Force unit and found the medical orderly washing Richthofen's body, so I made an examination. There were only two bullet wounds, one of entry and one of exit of a bullet which had evidently passed through the chest and the heart. There was NO WOUND of the head but there was considerable bruising over the right jaw which may have been fractured. The orderly told me that the Consulting Surgeon of the army [the Fourth Army] had made a post mortem that morning. I asked him how he did it as there was no evidence. The orderly told me that the Consulting Surgeon had used a bit of fencing wire which he pushed along the track of the wound over the heart. I used the same bit of wire for the same purpose. So you see the medical examination was not a thorough one and not a post mortem in the ordinary sense of the term. A bullet hole in the side of the plane coincided with the wound through the chest and I am sure he was shot from below while banking. I sent a full report to General Birdwood at Australian Corps and I have often wondered what became of it.
                    With kind regards,
                    Yours sincerely,
                    George W Barber

P.S. Of course a proper PM might have been made after I saw the body but I never heard of it and do not think so.

In a letter to a British Military Publication circa 1930, Major General Barber supplied information identical to that given above but with one addition:

The report that it [the body] was riddled with bullets is absolutely incorrect. There was one bullet wound only and this was through the man's chest. I formed the opinion that it had been fired from the ground and struck the airman as he was banking his machine, because the exit of the bullet was three inches higher than the point of entry.

Whatever written contribution Major Chapman made for posterity is also now lost except for a quotation: 'The bullet came out about three inches higher than it went in and might well have been shot from the ground.'

Because Colonel Barber's written report appears lost, and without secure knowledge of what was in it, beyond the affirmation that only one bullet had struck the body and that the other so-called wounds were all impact injuries, there are no known actions of his which can be taken as first hand discoveries. His major contribution was ordering Corporal Ted McCarty, the medical orderly, to undress the body completely and thereby setting beyond doubt that there were no other bullet wounds anywhere on it.

It is obvious from the content of Barber's letter that he had received information from others on the circumstances of the Red Devil's demise, not the least of which was the bullet hole in the fuselage, which he may or may not have been shown but was obviously told about. Corporal McCarty certainly had watched what Colonel Sinclair had been doing because he knew of the piece of wire and because in later years he mentioned that the bullet had dog-legged inside von Richthofen's body. It must have been common knowledge amongst all the orderlies that the Fourth Army Consulting Surgeon had said so, and he would carry much more weight with them than the new 22 Wing MO. McCarty still remained quiet about the bullet which he had found in the clothing. One has to wonder about this all the time. If he had been an ordinary 'erk' one might excuse it, but being a medical orderly he must have known of its possible importance. He was apparently not looking for any trouble that might arise, and the longer he remained quiet the more he would be unable to admit to his find. Initially he had told others there were at least three bullet holes in the body, so perhaps finding just one bullet didn't seem overly important at the beginning. Or perhaps it was purely a case of having a great souvenir and he was going to keep it!

It could be said that Colonel Barber's letter agrees with Graham and Downs in that the shot came from roughly in the plane of the long axis, although he goes a little further than they did by indirectly pointing out that said axis might well have been inclined at the time. On another point he appears to agree with Sinclair and Nixon for, although there is no record that Colonel Barber's probing confirmed Sinclair's conclusions, there are no reports or rumours that he disagreed with them. Not even amongst the post-war recollections of the orderlies.

That afternoon, von Richthofen's body was interred with full military honours. The pall-bearers were pilots from 3 AFC Squadron, one of them being Lieutenant Banks. The next day, RAF aeroplanes dropped photographs of the grave at useful locations over the German lines. One of the pilots selected was Lieutenant Robert Foster of 209 Squadron.

Back at Cappy, with the realisation that von Richthofen was not coming back, JGI's adjutant, Oberleutnant Karl Bodenschatz, opened a box kept in the office safe, in which he knew there was an envelope for just such an occasion as this. He opened it. There was a single pencil-written sentence, dated 10 March 1918 – just about six weeks earlier:

> Solte ich nicht zürück kommen, so
> Oblt. Reinhard (Jasta 6) die Führung
> des Luftgeschwaders über nehman.
> > Freiherr v
> > Richthofen
> > Rittmeister
>
> (Should I not return, Oberleutnant
> Reinhard (Jasta 6) is to assume
> command of the Geschwader.)

The Baron's obituary in *Flight* magazine was short and elegant: 'Manfred von Richthofen is dead. He was a brave man, a clean fighter and an aristocrat. May he rest in peace.'

Oberleutnant Wilhelm (Willi) Reinhard led JGI until 18 June 1918. On that date he handed over temporary command to Erich Löwenhardt in order to go to Adlershof, Berlin, to attend a flight test programme of the latest aeroplane designs. The aces were the test pilots and each one flew an aeroplane in mock combat with the others. On 3 July Oberleutnant Hermann Göring landed the Dornier DI, an all-metal framed biplane, and handed it over to Reinhard. During his flight in it, the top wing collapsed and Reinhard was killed in the crash. Thus was altered the course of history. Göring, the Staffelführer of Jasta 27, was promoted to lead Richthofen's JGI three days later, and after the war became Prime Minister of East Prussia, then finally Reichsmarschall, head of the German Luftwaffe, and in September 1939 Adolf Hitler's designated successor.

Von Richthofen's dog Moritz was adopted by Leutnant Alfred Gerstenberg, a former pilot in Jasta 11, who took him home to his farm. Many years later Moritz died there of old age. Gerstenberg became a Generalleutnant in the Luftwaffe in WW2 and died in 1959.

ABOVE: Ltn Alfred Gerstenberg, a former pilot with Jasta 11 until he was wounded in October 1917, who took care of Moritz after his master's death. Later a Luftwaffe General in WW2.

RIGHT: Von Richthofen with his dog Moritz.

The Basic Facts of Von Richthofen's Fatal Wound

1. It was inflicted by a Spitzer-type rifle bullet either fired by a machine gun or a rifle and travelled far enough through the Baron's body to begin tumbling. This created a large exit wound but not so large as others which Captain Graham had seen.

2. The general direction of the bullet path through von Richthofen's body was upwards. The exit wound (between the 5th and 6th ribs on the left side) was more than two inches higher than the entry wound (through the ninth rib on the right side).

3. The trajectory of the bullet in the vertical plane was slightly upwards relative to the side panels of the fuselage of the Triplane.

4. The trajectory of the bullet in the horizontal plane relative to the side panels of the fuselage was the subject of dispute.

Captain Graham, 22 Wing Medical Officer, who did not actually check the initial permanent cavity direction, gave an opinion that the bullet had come from slightly behind. Lieutenant Downs did not oppose Graham's opinion although earlier he had expressed doubts.

Colonel Nixon and Colonel Sinclair, after checking the initial permanent cavity direction, decided that the bullet had come from slightly in front.

5. Captain Graham gave the opinion that the bullet had passed in a straight line from entry to exit. Again Lieutenant Downs did not oppose Graham's opinion, although as before he had doubts.

6. Colonels Nixon and Sinclair, after checking the permanent cavity, stated that the bullet had dog-legged inside the body having been deflected off the front of the spine.

7. Colonel Barber's examination report has been lost – or at least not found. In a letter on the subject he affirmed that von Richthofen had been shot from the right. (See Chapter 14)

CHAPTER FIFTEEN
The RAF Board (So Called)

The First Medical Report was sent to 22 Wing RAF, while the Second Report went to the British 4th Army HQ. After being studied, each one received markedly different treatment.

The Board, referred to by Captain Roy Brown in the plaque made for the Toronto exhibit of the seat from the red Triplane, sometimes called 'The Board of Enquiry',' The Court of Enquiry' or either of those preceded by the word 'Official', represents the efforts of the Royal Air Force to evaluate the three claims. There is a marked similarity between the so-called official *Board or Court of Enquiry* and the weather in that everybody talks about it but nobody does anything about it. In the case of the Board of Enquiry (or the Court of Enquiry), historian Frank McGuire told the present authors: 'Everybody has heard of it, many refer to it, but nobody can produce it.'

Diligent research and advertising in aviation publications concerning the location of the records of it, or even knowledge of it, have obtained no reply. This does not mean that Captain Brown's reference to a Board is incorrect but simply that 'the tale improves with the telling'. The Board was simply 'promoted' first to a Board of Enquiry and then to a Court of Enquiry.

Listed below are six simple questions concerning the Board or Court of Enquiry. No answer can be found for any one of them.

1. WHERE WAS THE BOARD OR COURT OF ENQUIRY HELD?
2. ON WHAT DATE(S) WAS IT HELD?
3. WHO WERE ITS MEMBERS?
4. WHO TESTIFIED?
5. WHAT IS THE EXACT WORDING OF THE FINDING?
6. ON WHAT DATE WERE ITS FINDINGS PROMULGATED?

The many vague references to a gathering, or self-styled Board, of 209 Squadron pilots who put together all the information which they had on the death of von Richthofen, indicate that there was a serious discussion of the events of 21 April at some time after the event. At one time there was a document in the Public Records Office at Kew, in which a mention was made of such a discussion, but unfortunately it was a casualty in the massive theft of WW1 papers a few years ago.

However, Norman Franks made some notes from the document back in early 1968 from which we can see that the date of the meeting was 2 May 1918 (after Brown had left the Squadron). It seems that the 209 Squadron pilots who sat down to analyse the available evidence included May, Mellersh and Le Boutillier. These three at least, wrote down their reports, presumably for 'higher authority' again confirming that Brown had shot down the Baron. Another reference is still extant. On 15 October 1963, Edmond Clifford Banks, (the 3 Squadron AFC member) mentioned it, almost as an aside, in a letter to historian Frank McGuire which is quoted with his kind permission:

> The findings of the post mortem court held at our squadron with over twenty officers present was that von Richthofen could only have been shot down from the air.

Air Vice-Marshal Sir Robert Foster refers obliquely to such a gathering in his memoirs when he uses the word 'us' and not 'me', viz: 'To us it was conclusive that the pilot had been killed in the air.' Another indication of a group discussion is the commonality, in public statements or writings by Foster, May and Brown, of the pronouncement that for the fatal shot to have come from the ground, the Triplane would have needed to have been flying upside-down and backwards!

Descriptions of events can become twisted by retelling and/or passing from mouth to mouth, especially when being dramatised over a few rounds of drinks, but it is not difficult to fathom what is behind the following very strange story written down in 1992 by Wing Commander D L Hart who obtained it first hand in 1957 from one of the 209 Squadron officers who participated in the event described:

> Richthofen's body had come into the mortuary, as was the custom, for formal burial the next day, and that night there was a wild celebration at the end of the Red Baron, which they saw as bringing them a new lease of life. Who exactly

killed him was already very much debated, and when the senior officers had gone to bed the young officers argued the points since all who had participated in the fight were present. Eventually, it turned on the direction from which the fatal bullet had come, and after much indeterminate argument they fetched Richthofen's body from the mortuary, sat it in a chair in a normal flying position and inserted wires down the paths of the bullet wounds, then called upon their doctor to identify which wound had killed him. Once this had been done, they identified who had been in the position to fire it. The RAF claim was based on this evidence.

The final sentence seems to describe the claim too well to be mere co-incidence. In the main body of the tale, the errors of fact are numerous but do not destroy the premise that a discussion took place. One error, (4 below), indicates that the occasion was before the First Medical Examination was conducted by Captain Graham and Lieutenant Downs of 22 Wing.

1. Von Richthofen's body was not in 209 Squadron's mortuary but in a tent hangar at 3 AFC Squadron's aerodrome some distance away. However, we do not know whether the 209 Squadron pilots visited 3 AFC that evening for a general celebration or merely out of curiosity, and the hangar was merely referred to as the 'mortuary' for convenience of telling the tale.

2. The senior officers were very much out of bed between 2300 hours and midnight. The CO and the RO accompanied Graham and Downs during the examination which took place between these hours.

3. Before the examination some 209 Squadron pilots visited the tent hangar. It is far more likely that the discussion took place right then and there. Because of the wires being mentioned it seems much more likely that the tale is a mixture of this discussion and the doctors' subsequent examination, especially when mentioning the wounds being probed with wires.

4. Although the use of the word 'wounds' might indicate the belief that there were more than one, it can be assumed that all those concerned could see the entrance and exit wounds, provided the clothes on the upper torso were removed or at least opened. Even had they, at this stage, thought there were other, lower, wounds, the 209 Squadron pilots would have undoubtedly concentrated on the torso wounds as the cause of death, even if they thought wounds to the legs had been sustained.

The earlier Chapter, *The Wandering Wounds*, presented the curious fact that none of the 209 Squadron officers, who later made statements, appeared to know the correct direction of the wound, although the 3 AFC officers did. This suggests that the opinion of the 209 officers was formed before the first medical examination. Many 3 Squadron officers were present during that examination, so, logically they would know. That raises the point as to why the 209 Squadron junior officers did not learn the truth by the end of the week. A partial explanation is that the 22nd Wing Medical Examination report moved upwards, so they would not have seen it. Judging by the statements of the junior officers at the time, it appears that they were simply told that the report stated that only one bullet had struck the Baron and that it could only have been fired from the air.

Initially, it seemed to be clear that Captain Brown was the victor. There was a large multiple bullet entry hole in von Richthofen's left breast with the apparent choice of exit locations low down in the abdominal area on his right. Gunners Buie and Evans, as per their claim, had fired upwards, frontally and a little from the right; Lieutenant Barrow had fired frontally. Only Brown had fired downwards, from behind and from the left, and provided that von Richthofen had turned his trunk around and was looking behind to his left at the time, which was unlikely but not impossible, by default, he was the man.

That fits with Captain Brown being advised to present a neat report – the second one – and its being accepted higher up the chain of command. By the time the true direction became known to the RAF senior officers, the news had been released to the world that Brown was the hero, but it does not explain the persistent belief that Brown's bullet had struck von Richthofen in the left shoulder and had headed slanting downwards through his heart and out through his abdomen. There are only two hypotheses that fit. Either the 209 Squadron pilots did not believe the 22 Wing medical report or (as has already been mentioned above) they did not have exact knowledge of its findings.

One event points to the second hypothesis. In 1950, Captain May (his final wartime rank) expressed surprise upon hearing that the bullet had come from the right and had travelled upwards. The circumstances were as follows.

In 1949 a Rochester, New York, writer, Donald Naughton, was assembling information on von Richthofen's last flight. He had read what he believed to be Captain Brown's version of events in *Liberty* magazine, and wanted to supplement it with May's. The Royal Canadian Legion traced May for him and on 22 November, Naughton wrote to May asking him for his story. May's reply included an interesting statement:

> With reference to the medical report, the way you have it down does not add up. The one bullet is correct. It entered his back and went down through or near his heart. If it had gone in and then come out higher, it would have substantiated the Australian machine gunner's claim.

From Wilfred May's phrasing, it appears that he still did not understand what had actually occurred, 31 years later.

In 1918, all information given to the press had first to be released by the Official Censor, that is the origin of the expression 'a press release'. Major Neville Lytton, who performed that function, had just finished releasing a communiqué from RAF HQ on Captain Brown's victory over the Red Devil when in came the draught of a cable from Captain Charles E W Bean, the Official War Correspondent with the Australian 5th Division, in which the downing of von Richthofen was attributed to ground fire. Major Lytton sensed dangerous waters ahead so before releasing Bean's cable, he informed RAF HQ of its content. Major-General Sir John Salmond, the Commander-in-Chief of the RAF in France, was certainly aware that Brown had been proclaimed victor because the other two claimants had been eliminated. He was also aware that the ground upon which he stood in supporting the claim was not absolutely firm. The regulation obligatory Confirmation of Claim had not been provided by the artillery officer in charge of the sector where the red Triplane force-landed, in fact he had refused to do so. To make matters worse, the officer in question, Captain P Hutton, was English, not Australian.

The ground confirmation matter came up again in 1935 and Captain Hutton wrote: 'Later on the day [21st] the Air Force came to me for confirmation of their claim, which was then the rule, but I could not substantiate it.' ..... 'As anti-aircraft officer on the spot I claim to be in the best position to judge.'

By this time it was known in high circles that the Official Medical Examination report to the British 4th Army had given an open verdict, so there was neither help nor opposition there. The army was obviously not too sure of its position for there was no plain statement that Captain Brown did not fire the shot.

It is said that Sir John Salmond, who in his youth had heard of Prince Paris and the apple, decided that diplomacy and tact would be advisable. He suggested compromise; the Army and the RAF would share the credit. This has been denied but surviving evidence confirms that it was so.

A letter written by General Hobbs, some years after the war, states that he had passed the suggestion of a shared claim down the chain of command to Gunner Buie for his agreement or otherwise. Buie's answer was definitely otherwise, and Hobbs declined to repeat the exact words used. The General's answer to Sir John was a polite refusal.

RAF HQ decided to go ahead with full support for Brown's claim. It has been suggested that the certain increase in pilot morale would compensate for the possible fuss, which would soon die away. The horrendous loss of experienced fighter pilots to ground fire whilst ground strafing German troops and transport during the German's March Offensive was reflected in the high percentage of novices fighting in April. The two-seater squadrons too had suffered heavily.

Sir John was actually going out on the proverbial limb, but in view of the Consultant's open verdict, it did not look as though General Sir Henry Rawlinson's official enquiry would come up with much, if anything, which might 'saw it off'.

Unfortunately there was still the proverbial ticking bomb. Sergeant Popkin's claim remained temporarily dormant in a pile of papers on a desk at 24th Machine Gun HQ, and the sergeant was not very happy about it. In later years he was to write: 'I am afraid that my claim did not receive much consideration at the time.' On the 25th, his claim was to arrive at the top of the pile.

This claim had definitely been overshadowed by the three earlier ones for only a few soldiers had seen him firing and opinion, other than theirs, was that von Richthofen had already been hit by that time. Private Vincent Emery had not yet been questioned on the sequence of the bursts of machine-gun fire and the behaviour of the Triplane at that time.

RAF HQ are believed to have taken the following precaution. Officers of 209 Squadron are said to have been ordered not to talk about the matter, but beyond a hint from one or two officers, there is no proof that such an order was actually given. However, the definite fact remains that 209 Squadron did not say much in public that went beyond the accepted RAF version of what had happened although one definite slip occurred in 1931. It was the vast difference between Mellersh and Foster's eyewitness accounts of the Baron's forced landing. For Mellersh, see Chapter 6 and for Foster, see Chapter 9.

After the war, Roy Brown was discharged from the RAF on 1 August 1919. He acquired a farm at Stouffville, Ontario, and his neighbour, a Mr Brillinger, described him as a quiet and courteous man; far from the boor as he has been portrayed in films. They talked about many things concerning the war, but Roy never spoke of his encounter with von Richthofen. He died suddenly on 9 March 1944 when he was only 50 years old.

For ten years there was peace on the 'von Richthofen front'. In England and Canada it was generally believed that Captain Brown had ended the Baron's life. 209 Squadron even had its official badge approved by the College of Heraldry as a red eagle falling, symbolising the destruction of the Baron's red fighter.

In Australia it was generally believed that Gunners Buie and Evans had performed the deed. Then at the end of the 1920s four works of the pen appeared: *The Red Knight of Germany*; *My Fight with Richthofen*; the Australian *Official History of the War*, and the *British Official History of the War in the Air*. The lines became drawn and battle commenced.

CHAPTER SIXTEEN
Captain Bean Investigates

A careful reading of the reports from the first and second medical examinations shows them both as being serious attempts to be fair and impartial. Apart from the disqualification of the 53rd Battery in the first one, they were otherwise neutral and non-committal.

Concerning official military reports, three points must be borne in mind:

First: official reports move upwards through a chain of command. If another entity is involved, they will cross over at the top and work their way down until someone says: 'Stop'. Reports written by colonels are rarely seen by captains. In the lack of precise information, incorrect assumptions tend to be made at the lower levels of both ends of the chain of communication.

Second: constant paraphrasing alters the clearest of meanings; eg, 'Send me the brush which I left on the stairs,' in two repetitions during transmittal becomes, 'Send me the broom which I left on the steps,' and each person will swear that he changed nothing. The ultimate recipient will be looking outside the house for a large object.

Third: once an official attitude has been assumed, to reverse it is rather difficult even if it was flawed at some stage by incorrect assumptions or paraphrasing.

Upon the withdrawal of the claim by 3 Squadron AFC, the medical report written by Captain Graham and Lieutenant Downs left Captain Brown as the only horse in the race, but it did not state that he had won. The RAF, starting from Major Butler and proceeding upwards through 22nd Wing (Lieutenant Colonel F V Holt), 5th Brigade (Brigadier L E O Charlton) and RAF HQ (General Sir John Salmond) chose to interpret it as saying that he had. If the other claiments were not responsible, then obviously Brown was. Who could say when and how the bullet hole was made in the right-hand side of the Triplane, let alone who made it? The matter of how a shot fired obliquely downwards from the left could enter von Richthofen's abdomen on the right and then pass obliquely upwards through his trunk to exit on the left was not addressed. Captain Brown's neat-looking Combats in the Air report (the second one) was annotated 'Decisive' and started its journey into history. (An interesting point is that the signature on the second document seems to differ from the first one.)

General Sir Henry Rawlinson, upon receiving the open verdict report of his two senior medical officers, decided that further investigation was required. If none of the claimants had fired the shot, somebody else had, and judging by the talk going on, quite a few soldiers of the 5th Australian Division thought that one of their particular shots might have been successful. There was one sergeant in the 24th Machine Gun Company who was said to have filed a claim, but the General had not yet seen the papers.

If the finding of the fatal bullet by the medical orderly had been known to an officer, the field would have been narrowed considerably. With a new German attack known to be due any day, Sir Henry had nobody he could spare for such a seemingly non-essential investigation. He finally decided that the mantle lay on the shoulders of General J T Hobbs, the commander of the 5th Australian Division. His men had been involved, therefore, clearly any investigation fell within his bailiwick. General Hobbs in turn found the ideal man. A captain with no military duties, well educated and who was accustomed to inter- viewing people. Even better, it might get him out of his way for a few days. Not the chaplain, but the Official War Correspondent, Captain C E W Bean.

The investigation is best described in Captain Bean's own words. His diary entry for 27 April 1918, by which time Sergeant Popkin's claim had been received, reads:

> The British air service - some naval
> pilot who was half a mile away in the air
> - has claimed to bring down Baron
> Richthofen. It seemed to me so trivial a

Roy Brown's second combat report (with suspect signature [compare it with the earlier report]) and showing that Mellersh and May confirmed the Triplane crashing.

Combats in the Air.

Squadron : 209 R.A.F.

Type and No. of Aeroplane : Sopwith BR
B 7270

Armament : Two Vickers Syn. Guns.

Pilot : Captain A.R.Brown D.S.C.

Observer

~~Observer~~
Engagement with red triplane!
Time, about 11-00 a.m.
Locality, Vaux sur Somme

Date : April 21st 1918.

Time : 10-45 a.m.

Locality : 62 D Q 2

Duty : H.O.P.

Height : 5000 feet.

Result
Destroyed ....
Driven down out of control ....
Driven down ....

23

Remarks on Hostile Aircraft :—Type, armament, speed, etc.

Fokker triplane, pure red wings with small black crosses.

Narrative.

(1)   At 10.35 a.m. I observed two Albatross burst into
flames and crash.

(2)   Dived on large formation of 15 - 20 Albatross Scouts
D 5's and Fokker triplanes, two of which got on my tail
and I came out.

Went back again and dived on pure red triplane which
was firing on Lieut. May.   I got a long burst into
him and he went down vertical and was observed to crash
by Lieut. Mellersh and Lieut May.

I fired on two more but did not get them.

A.R.Brown.

Captain.

(one decisive)

Commanding ....Squadron.

matter who shot him that I had not
bothered to investigate the various
claims. However, Hobbs asked me to. He
says that there is a lot of feeling over
it - the German communiqué says that R
was shot from the ground. I said I must
see the actual men who claimed to do it.
So they were brought to 5th Division
Artillery Headquarters.

Gunner Buie and Gunner Evans say the
plane wobbled and swerved to the right,
and then speared towards the earth. He
crashed about 350-500 yards from the
guns. He was hit in chin, neck, chest and
left side and right leg. The wound in his
neck came out just below the chin. Lt
Doyle who was in the [gun] pit could see
bits flying off the plane.

Captain Bean's starting point was the verdict of
the Official Medical Examination which had
disqualified all three claimants. The 53rd Battery
had fired from the wrong angle and even if it had
been successful would have put more than one
shot into the Triplane's fuselage. Captain Brown
had fired from the wrong side, and Lieutenant
Barrow's claim had been withdrawn, due mainly
to timing.

After conversations with scores of witnesses,
the possibility developed in Bean's mind that the
two colonels had been too conservative and that
the 53rd Battery may indeed have been
responsible. Unfortunately he did not have the
benefit of a forensic interpretation of von
Richthofen's wound path from the point of view
of ballistics; in those days, that science was in its
infancy. He was not sure. Someone had done it,
but who? With so many soldiers firing at the
same time, and nobody with any real idea of
exactly which way the Triplane, in a gusty wind,
was angled at any given moment, there was no
simple answer.

He vacillated between the 53rd Battery and
the 24th Machine Gun Company, not to
mention scores of men firing rifles. Nobody can
fault him, for the Triplane's passage towards, over,
and beyond the 53rd Battery took but a
few seconds.

One uncertainty was nevertheless certain;
either the person firing the shot was an expert
who had correctly calculated a complicated
deflection angle, or it was a lucky shot from
someone who had made all the usual mistakes
and in his haste had fired so wide of the mark
that he had actually scored a hit.

Simple mathematics, as taught in anti-aircraft
gunnery school, supply the answer. A 0.303″

British bullet fired from a Lee-Enfield rifle, a
Vickers or Lewis machine gun, leaves the muzzle
at about 2,400 to 2,500 feet per second; in round
numbers that is 800 yards or about half a mile per
second. An aeroplane flying at 80 mph is covering
120 feet per second. So if a gunner is 400 yards
away from an aeroplane which is flying directly
across his line of fire (at right angles to him), he
must aim 60 feet ahead of the aeroplane in order
to hit it. But how to measure the 60 feet? That is
where knowledge and training come in.

An expert anti-aircraft gunner knows by
heart the wing span of the aeroplanes he is likely
to encounter. Back in those days, the fuselage
length was about 80% of the wing span, so a
Fokker Dr.I Triplane with a span of 25 feet
(approx) would have a fuselage length of 20 feet;
actually it was just over 18 feet. At 400 yards
range a machine gunner or a rifleman's 'lead' on
such a target flying at 80 mph would have to be
THREE full fuselage lengths to allow for the
flight time of his bullets. At the 200 yards range
during the chase along the Ridge face, when the
ground speed would have been about 135 mph
(200 feet per second), it would have been
necessary to aim at May in order to hit
Richthofen, and to do that took a lot of courage.
That is why so many shots missed the Triplane.

At 800 yards range the mathematics become
a little more complicated. As we have said earlier,
the second 400 yards of the bullets' passage are at
a slower speed than the first 400. By 800 yards
(half a mile) the speed is down to about 1,000
feet per second, therefore, SEVEN fuselage
lengths as per the basic calculation plus a further
ONE length to compensate for the bullets' progressively decreasing velocity are required.

The machine gunner or rifleman would need
to aim EIGHT fuselage lengths into thin air
ahead of the aeroplane in order to hit it in the
middle. That takes a lot of confidence and
imagination. Additional complications are the
drooping trajectory beyond 400 yards' flight and
the effect (on this day) of a strong wind. The
latter would require one more fuselage length
making a grand total of NINE. To be an anti-
aircraft machine gunner was to be a specialist in
a difficult art.

Like Privates V Emery and J Jeffrey, Sergeant
Popkin of the 24th Machine Gun Company was
classified as a Machine Gunner 1st Class. They all
had knowledge and the experience to perform
accurate deflection shooting. Emery had not
fired but Popkin had, and from the required
direction and distance. He was a good candidate.

CHAPTER SEVENTEEN
Sergeant Popkin – The Fourth Claim

Sergeant Cedric Basset Popkin, Machine Gunner 1st Class, was in charge of four Vickers machine guns located on the top and on the south facing slope of the Morlancourt Ridge, with the Somme canal and river below. He belonged to the 24th Machine Gun Company, 11th Brigade, 4th Australian Division under Brigadier-General James Cannan.

The confusion over the exact position of Private Rupert Weston's Vickers gun when Sergeant Popkin assumed control of it and fired at the red Triplane may again be due to the simultaneous use of different vintages of field maps. Popkin stated in his report that he was somewhere in J.19.d. On the April 1918 map that somewhat imprecise location would place him at least 100 yards south (down the slope) of where he needed to be to have the required field of fire. On an August 1917 map, sub-square J19.d is placed 100 yards north of the April 1918 map position and now has the required field of fire.

Sergeant Popkin fired twice at the Triplane. The first time was as it chased May's Camel along the face [below] of the Morlancourt Ridge over the mud flats. The two aeroplanes had passed Darbyshire's pontoon bridge [off to their left] and were approaching the sharp bend in the river. According to Private Weston, the aircraft were down at tree-top height when Popkin grabbed the machine gun; Weston was then relegated to being second man on his own weapon. Popkin placed the Triplane at about 60 feet [18 metres] above the ground. He allowed the Camel to pass and then fired about 80 rounds at the right-hand side of it from a range of 100-150 yards. Over the trees, the Triplane entered a zone of very choppy air and its bouncing movement in the sky made Popkin believe that he had scored some hits. He was soon dissuaded of this impression for as soon as the Triplane left the trees behind it steadied and continued the chase with an immediate climb up the steep slope of the Ridge as the river bent round to the south. With the Triplane at about 60 feet above the water and Popkin's machine gun at 70 to 130 feet, he would have been firing somewhere between level and downwards.

The Triplane now headed over the Ridge in the direction of the 18-pounder batteries. Popkin turned his gun to the north-west looking up the slope in case the fighter should reappear if it turned round and headed back eastwards. Moments later his readiness was rewarded by the sight of the red plane indeed coming back over the edge of the Ridge, heading south-east towards the brickworks.

After the Triplane had escaped the attentions of Gunners Buie and Evans, Popkin fired his second burst of 80 rounds but nothing available written down by either Popkin or Weston gives us any indication of range. Weston, temporarily degraded to feeding the ammunition belt straight, gave the Triplane's height as 300 feet above the ground, which on the way to Sainte Colette, is already 250 feet above the river, so the Triplane was about 450 feet above them. Popkin, having now traversed the gun towards the north-west, fired upwards and at the right-hand side of the approaching Triplane which was about one third of the way between the 53rd Battery and the place where it came to earth, and was about to cross his line of fire at a right angle. Measurements on a map put the range at 800 to 850 yards.

During Popkin's burst of fire, the distant Triplane's nose lifted up almost vertically and the fighter rolled to the right. This can easily be interpreted as what would happen to a right-handed pilot, hit in the right side; the reaction would be to pull the stick back towards the right shoulder. The Triplane levelled out again and began a steep descent towards Sainte Colette. The few who had seen the action, congratulated the sergeant on his shooting.

In other documentation Popkin states that his gun position was about 1,000 yards south-east of the 53rd Battery [over the Ridge and out of his sight] and his 1918 submission includes: 'The distance from the spot where the plane crashed and my gun was about 600 yards.'

The above two estimated distances meet in the south-west quadrant of map sub-square J.19.d. From the junction, a line drawn 150 yards south-west meets a stretch of the flight paths of

Lieutenant May and von Richthofen as they approached the sharp bend in the river. Although no precise spot can be determined, Popkin's story seems good enough.

Far from Sergeant Popkin's shooting being a case of expert marksmanship, from his own words we can deduce that for the first burst he failed to 'lead' the target sufficiently. For the second burst, which required a lead of eight to nine fuselage lengths, he apparently 'calculated incorrectly again, for if.... if' after he hit the target, it was with only one shot at the edge of the wide spread of the cone of bullets shortly after he began firing.

Three tangential aspects of the event are worth mentioning:

1. The question arises as to why at least one of the other three machine guns of Popkin's detachment did not open fire. The answer is an example of Murphy's Law. Things were quiet that morning. Both sides were 'resting' and preparing for renewed fighting in the near future. Lunch time was about an hour away and someone had decided that fish would be tastier then normal army fare. There was a large, shallow lake beside the canal 500 yards away, and if a hand grenade or two were accidentally dropped into the water and exploded .....!

2. Sergeants in charge of detachments do not have a designated machine gun. When Popkin took over Private Weston's gun and ceased to supervise the others, the odds are that, not having received direct orders, those of their crews who had not gone fishing, just stood about and watched. And it all happened in a few seconds. (Fortunately for the Sergeant's stripes, other reasons were accepted by the Lieutenant for the curious failure.)

3. The approximate map reference positions for Private Weston's Vickers gun given by others (11th Brigade HQ: J.25.a.6.9; Lt Travers: J.25.a.8.9; Lt Fraser: J.25.b.3.7;), when plotted on an April 1918 map, are all in exposed positions spread along the Corbie to Vaux-sur-Somme road which is at the same elevation as the mud flats beside the Canal. Given the sheltered, scrub-covered, higher ground just to the north, such low sitings are illogical; a person would have to try hard to find worse positions. The locations given are obviously a little odd.

Lieutenants Travers and Fraser were competent officers so should not be guilty of such slips. Fraser on one occasion stated that he heard a strong burst of fire coming from the south-east corner of the woods; not from down by the road. The present authors plotted the three strange gun positions on

an August 1917 map and noted their positions on the contour lines. They immediately became sheltered positions in the scrub to the north, especially J.25.b.3.7 given by Fraser, which thereupon fell close to the south-west quadrant of J.19.d on the 1918 map. This is where Popkin himself said he was positioned. (There is no reason to assume that April 1918 maps were distributed to everyone at once, and some of the 11th Brigade may still have been using old maps, which in any event looked very similar to earlier ones.) Add in that there were four machine guns, each some distance from the others, and no one knows beside which of them Popkin was standing when he spoke to the officers who later approximated the NCO's position.

In sum: assuming that the Triplane was not in some strange attitude at the time, Sergeant Popkin's shot would have approached the fuselage of the Triplane at the angles, both vertical and horizontal, from which the fatal one had come. His machine gun was situated in roughly the same plane as the long axis of the German Triplane and the range was within the normal limits for a bullet to be found inside the clothing near the exit wound.

Sgt Cedric Bassett Popkin, 24th MGC.

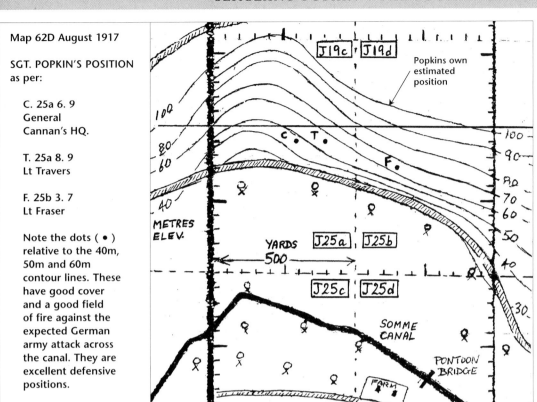

Map 62D August 1917

SGT. POPKIN'S POSITION
as per:

C. 25a 6. 9
General
Cannan's HQ.

T. 25a 8. 9
Lt Travers

F. 25b 3. 7
Lt Fraser

Note the dots (•)
relative to the 40m,
50m and 60m
contour lines. These
have good cover
and a good field
of fire against the
expected German
army attack across
the canal. They are
excellent defensive
positions.

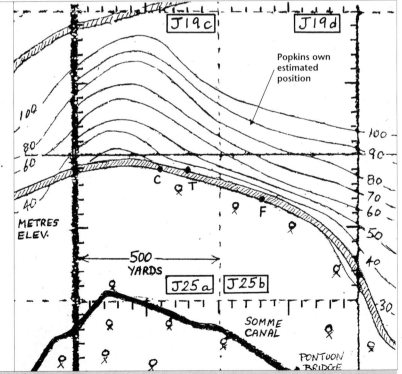

Map 62D April 1918

SGT. POPKIN'S POSITION
as per officers' cited
above and self.

The August 1917
references when
plotted on an April
1918 map are depicted
mainly along the road
at the foot of the slope.
This is 100 yds south
of the true position
(see top map) and
would have no cover
against Germans
advancing across the
river, nor a good field
of fire.
These positions, if
true, would have had
little defensive value.

Two contour maps showing Popkin's position on different issues of the same map.

CHAPTER EIGHTEEN
The Official Report to the Commander-In-Chief
(General Hobbs to General Rawlinson)

Captain Bean was at a disadvantage at the start of his investigation. The science of ballistics was in its infancy and he had not seen any of the three medical reports. He had only the witnesses to go by, and there were hundreds of them.

To begin with, of the one thousand plus soldiers in the area bounded by Vaux-sur-Somme, Corbie and Bonnay, only about ten had seen a second Camel attack the Triplane, and they were mainly from other units which he did not consult. This left him with Gunner George Ridgway, Lieutenant Quinlan and Lieutenant Wood, and if they were correct, the Triplane had not been hit. Basically, he found a thousand men who said that a second Camel had not been involved in the fray, and three who claimed to have seen it.

Many of the thousand had seen other aeroplanes in the distance, but said that they were too far away to have been involved. He did not have the benefit of Sergeant Darbyshire's description of Brown's attack and his observation that the Triplane seemed to run into a brick wall in its flight. Gunner Twycross's evidence on the time of von

SECRET.

REPORT ON THE DEATH OF CAPTAIN BARON VON RICHTHOFEN at 62D. J.19.b.5.2 about 11 am wqst April 1918.

The following report is based on the evidence of eyewitnesses, written down immediately after the events.

Capt. Baron von Richthofen was flying a single seater triplane painted red and reported to be of a new pattern. When first engaged he was pursuing one of our own machines, reported to be a Sopwith Camel, in a W.N.W. direction, flying towards the wood in J.19c. Here, according to a reliable witness, he was fired at by an A.A. gun of the 24th Australian Machine Gun Company. Richthofen's machine seemed to move unsteadily for a moment, but still continued in pursuit of the British plane.

He had now left the Somme valley and come over the high ground North of Corbie. Both machine were flying very low, being not more than 150 feet up. They were coming swiftly towards the A.A. guns of the 53rd Battery, 14th Australian Field Artillery Brigade, situated at I.24.b.9.5 and I.24.b.6.5. respectively. Richthofen was firing into the plane before him but it was difficult for the Lewis gunners to shoot owing to the British plane being in directly in the line of fire. The accordingly waited their time until the British plane had passed. Richthofen's plane was not more than 100 yards from each when they opened fire. The plane was coming frontally towards them so that they were able to open fire directly on to the person of the aviator. Almost immediately the plane turned N.E. being still under fire from the Lewis guns. It was now staggering as though out of control. Further effective bursts were fired: the plane veered to the North and crashed on the plateau near the brickworks near J.19.b.5.2.

The aviator was already dead. There were bullet wounds in the knees, abdomen, and chest. The plane was badly smashed; it was a triplane painted dull red, and was armed with two air-cooled machine guns. It had only been assembled in March 1918.

The British plane was undoubtedly saved by the action of the Lewis gunners. It altered its course and circled back over the spot where the enemy plane had crashed.

The papers of the aviator were then taken to the HQ of the 11th Australian Infantry Brigade. They established his identity as Capt. Baron Mannheim von Richthofen, born 2nd March 1892 in Breslau, province of Silesia, Prussia. The machine was numbered D.R. 425.

Capt. Baron von Richthofen was a great adversary. The German Official wireless for the 21st April 1918, the very day of his death, contains the notice "Capt. Baron von Richthofen, at the head of Pursuit Flight 11, attained his 79th and 80th air victories". It was fitting that he should have fallen, in old Roman fashion, with all his wounds in front".

After the machine crashed, a troupe of German planes flew over

Richthofen's death remained unrevealed to the world until 1996.

Private Emery and Private Jeffrey were keeping low profiles. The battalion officers were trying to learn who had souvenired the Baron's binoculars and luger pistol by means of surprise kit inspections,

_3

2.

and circled above the spot until driven off by the A.A. guns. An Infantry guard was posted over the body and the plane, but they were relieved of their duty shortly after by the German artillery, who placed a ring of shells, bursting with instantaneous fuzes, around the plane.

The Lewis gunners who brought down the plane were: No. 598 Gunner W.J. Evans and No 3801 Gunner R Buie, of the 53rd Battery, 14th Australian Field Artillery Brigade, 5th Australian Divisional Artillery.

----

and the medical reports provides evidence that the tactic of secrecy and closed files was effective. It will be recalled that in the 1930s, 1940s, and 1950s, the surviving pilots of 209 Squadron RAF (those of whom record exists) and all kinds of publications were stating that the content of the Official Report was in favour of Captain Brown.

This Official Report describes von Richthofen's wounds incorrectly, which is proof that the contents of the medical reports were restricted to very senior officers. It seems amazing that having asked Bean to investigate the incident, he at least was not given access to them. One might even assume that Hobbs did not see them or surely he would have felt compelled to have the report altered at least to correct the wounds. The report also repeats the incorrect map reference positions given originally for Gunners Buie and Evans and the Triplane's forced landing site. The correct ones are: Buie – I.24.b.65.36; Evans – I.24.b.74.43, and the Triplane - J.19.b.40.30.

and they did not wish to draw attention to themselves. The missing information held the key to the sequence of the main events which perplexed Captain Bean. As things stood, Bean could not deduce 'x' by relating it to 'y' and 'z'; the latter two were also uncertain in time, place or both.

After much interviewing, discussion and thought, Captain Bean gave his decision. General Hobbs's HQ staff set down the only document which can be described as the Official Report and which is held at the Australian War Memorial in Canberra. It contains a few typing errors.

The Official Report which is undated, was sent to General Sir Henry Rawlinson around the middle of May. It was classified Secret which doubtless avoided a head-on collision with RAF HQ if the contents became widely known. The general lack of knowledge until the 1960s concerning this report

General Hobbs sent a telegram of congratulations to the 53rd Battery. General Salmond countered by sending a telegram of congratulations to 209 Squadron. It can be said that RAF HQ and the Fourth Army HQ agreed to differ.

This, however, was not the end of the matter for Captain C E W Bean continually received statements from people whom he had not interviewed during April 1918 (the German offensive caused much disruption) and he re-examined the whole business after the war.

CHAPTER NINETEEN
Captain Bean Changes his Mind

Between 1930 and 1934, when the Official Histories of the Great War were being written, C E W Bean in Australia and H A Jones in England corresponded on a frequent basis. Extracts from the reports on the first two medical examinations were available and Bean may even have seen a complete copy of the third one.

Bean's support for Gunners Buie and Evans, although expounded by hundred of witnesses, began to wane. The Baron was definitely alive and flying his Triplane after they had ceased firing. The sudden climb in which the Triplane almost turned over was finally explained; it was the convulsive reflex action attendant upon a painful wound. Private Emery stated that this occurred after Buie and Evans had ceased firing, and certainly the position of the Triplane on the way to Sainte Colette would not have allowed Buie or Evans to fire at it frontally, or even semi-frontally. It had already passed overhead, turned to the right and was flying away from them at the time. Emery actually saw and heard more than that, but whether he told Bean would be to speculate. Vincent Emery's complete observations only became public knowledge in 1975, telling them to Australian Historian Geoffrey H Hine, and therefore belong in a later Chapter of this work.

In a letter dated 13 November 1959, to Colonel G W L Nicholson, Director of the Historical Section of the Canadian Army, Bean wrote: [an authors' note at the end explains Bean's numbered references to Nicholson's questions.]

Dear Colonel Nicholson,
Your letter of the 9th October caught me on one foot, as it were – although the trouble is at the other end; I have been overstraining my powers on the eve of my 80th birthday and have been told that the best way to meet this situation is to cut out all writing for a month or two. For that reason, on visiting Canberra for Remembrance Day I took your letter with me and asked the officer in charge of the records at the War Memorial and his chief assistant (Mr Bruce Harding and Miss Vera Blackburn) if they would do their best to find the most important references for which you ask, and have them copied for you. I think the best help I can give is perhaps to tell you, without research, of

the way on which I became specially interested in the death of Richthofen. I think it was on the day after Richthofen's death that I, then the chief Australian official war correspondent in France and the probable future historian of the Australian part in the war, received a request from General Hobbs, then commanding our 5th Division on the Somme, to go up and investigate the shooting down of Richthofen which had been reported in the press and communiqués. I had heard that he had been shot down by an airman of the RAF but General Hobbs said that his men were very incensed at this report as they claimed he had been shot down by the Australians over whom he was flying. My immediate reaction was the thought: 'Why dispute the claim of an airman whose task and risk were immensely greater than that of men shooting from the ground?' However, if I remember rightly, the two Lewis gunners of the 53rd Battery who claimed to have shot Richthofen down were at once sent to me; and after closely questioning them, I had no doubt that their bullets struck Richthofen's plane as it topped the spur south-east of Bonnay and flew low towards them, and that he gave up the chase at that point, and almost immediately crashed. As they, and others, had seen fragments fly from the plane, it seemed probable that they had killed him. When news spread that a British airman had claimed to have done so, it was assumed by those who watched (or like myself had been told of) the fight that the claimant was the man whom Richthofen had been pursuing. All the accounts that came from the ground over which the pursuit took place spoke of two planes only, that of the pursuer grimly firing bursts at the pursued, and that of the pursued, veering from left to right and back, and up and down, in what seemed to be a desperate effort to evade them.

From Vaux-sur-Somme along the Somme Valley (down which the chase had gone very low and thence over the spur between the Somme and the Ancre) it had been watched by hundreds of troops who, drawn by the rattle of machine guns and the whir of the planes ran out of their billets or bivouacs. Among those who did so were several friends of mine; Lieut-Col J L Whitham, a very close friend and a grand soldier 'preux chevalier' as I always felt, Major Blair Wark VC, Brig.Gen. J B

Cannan and others; the one thing that impressed me was that none of them, who described the chase vividly, said anything about a third plane.

It was not until I was writing Vol.V of the Official History in 1934 that I came upon two items of information - I cannot from memory say where - that two Australians had, on the day of Richthofen's death, been watching separately the general dog fight in the air somewhere east of Vaux-sur-Somme and had seen THREE planes, one German and two British, dive out of it into the Somme Valley. Each observer said that one of the British planes turned out of this chase, but the other, with the German on his tail, kept on.

This was the first I had heard of any observer in our area having seen a third plane in the chase, and from then onward my main enquiry into this incident was concentrated on the question whether anyone had seen a third. Neither my letters to those whom I knew to have seen the chase, nor interrogation of them when I met them, brought any other answer but that there were only two in the chase along the valley and up the ridge, almost exactly a mile. Extracts from all the important statements are given in the appendix Vol.V.

A medical officer, General Barber, who had seen Richthofen's wounds, told me that it was out of the question that, with a wound in the neighbourhood of the heart such as the one which killed Richthofen, he could have made the intense attack, for a mile or over from Vaux onwards, that so impressed those who watched it.

That, to my mind, completely disposed of Brown's claim. But the question of who shot him remained open; though many machine and Lewis guns besides those of the 53rd Battery had shot at Richthofen, I was disposed to think that those Lewis gunners had probably done so [shot von Richthofen]; there was no doubt that they (or one of them) hit his plane at close quarters. It was not till I examined the claim of Popkin that I was strongly impressed with HIS claim. Whether I examined him personally or wrote to him I cannot remember though a pencilled note in my papers in Canberra may have been made at an interview. But Lt. Wiltshire (p.696) said that Richthofen had not crashed immediately he was stopped, but turned and began to climb back towards his own lines. It was at this stage that Sgt. Popkin from the Somme valley below, fired at him for the second time with his Vickers machine gun, and he claims to have 'observed at once that his fire took effect' (as mentioned in his report).

As scores of rifle shots as well as those from other Lewis and Vickers guns were aimed at the red plane it is possible that the fatal shot may have been from one of them: I could only conclude with certainty, I think, that Richthofen was shot from the ground; and that I judged that Popkin's claim was the best of those which I heard or read. As to your other questions:

1. I cannot recall having heard that Brown denied having written the article in the *Chicago Tribune*. I wrote to him at least twice - first for confirmation of his name, initials, home town, etc. To which he replied; later I wrote again asking about the difficulties we had found in his narrative; to this I received no reply. I cannot offhand say whether the Tribune and Liberty articles are the same; I will ask Mr. Harding whether we have both articles.

2. As to the statements in Italiaander's book (1)(which I have not seen), and also of Wiltshire, that at the start of the affair Richthofen was chasing two British planes, I cannot judge, except that it seems improbable. All that I know, with certainty, is that from the west of Vaux onwards there were only two planes in the chase, Richthofen's and May's. At the beginning, during the dive there were (on the evidence we have) three. The difference between Ridgway's account and Wiltshire's may, as you suggest have been due to difference between the positions and angles of vision of the observers, or to mistaken memories, though my experience is that, of such events, the memories of most eyewitnesses do not fade for twenty years unless they are blurred by being told and re-told, as often they naturally are.

3. I heard that an officer of the 3rd Squadron AFC had put in a claim but it was not seriously regarded by those to whom I spoke.

4. Brown certainly did not make a second attempt to get Richthofen unless he had already made one attack before our story began; and in the narrative attributed to him in the Chicago Tribune, he says nothing of it. It certainly did not happen after Richthofen first dived on May.

5. As I understand Popkin's action, he fired at Richthofen first from Richthofen's left when the two planes passed at the end of the chase; but when the German turned and began to make for his own area, Popkin was shooting from Richthofen's right; otherwise Richthofen must have swung widely round to the south and the second passing would have been in the rear of Popkin, of which I have never heard any evidence.

6. Mr. Harding tells me that no award was made to an Australian for shooting down Richthofen.

(1) Manfred Freiherr von Richthofen *by Rolf von Italiaander, published in Berlin in 1938.*

7. There were visitors from the RAF. I
will ask Mr.Harding to see if he can
check on those from the 204th Squadron.
     I am most sorry that I could not go
fully into the documents myself; some
urgent work in connection with my
retirement from the chairmanship of
the Australian War Memorial Board and
also from that of the Commonwealth
Archives Committee, and several
consequent functions, brought me
almost to a breakdown and I was told
that a temporary rest was necessary
-though the extreme interest of the
work is a constant temptation to
disregard the advice. Please excuse
the roughness of this typing - I
cannot inflict my handwriting on you.
With every good wish for your work,
both generally and in this matter, of
which I was very glad to learn.

Yours sincerely,
C E W Bean.

Authors' Comments:
Colonel Nicholson had queried Dr Bean MA,
D.Lit., concerning some strange assertions made in
My Fight with Richthofen (of which three slightly
different versions exist) and in a book *Von
Richthofen and the Flying Circus* (Harleyford, 1958).
He was also curious about a few other publications.
Background and/or information on his queries
follows below. It is given in the same order.

1. The question of Brown's authorship of *My Fight
with Richthofen* is covered in Appendix E.
2. The view that von Richthofen was at one time
chasing two British planes could be due to the
deceptive nature of three-dimensional slant views.
There were several other aircraft around in the
background at the time, both British and German,
and one of those could have been mistaken as being
part of the affair. Certainly no expert Fokker
Triplane fighter pilot in his right mind would try to
chase two faster Sopwith Camels; whilst he was
dealing with one Camel, the other would slip
round behind him and ....
3. The officer of 3 Squadron AFC who filed a claim
was Lieutenant Barrow. His claim was withdrawn;
the time of his encounter with Jasta 11 was
too early.
4. In the book *Von Richthofen and the Flying Circus*,
its authors and editor follow the belief that Brown
attacked von Richthofen somewhere between
Sailly-le-Sec and Vaux-sur-Somme. Since nobody
in Vaux or the windmill FOP saw the attack
happen, they believe it must have occurred just after

Sailly-le-Sec. This would have required a gravely
wounded von Richthofen to chase May in a most
expert manner down the river, turning by the
church tower at Vaux, along the ridge front, up the
bluff, over the battery and then TWO MINUTES
after Brown's attack to die from his wound and
crash. That being obviously impossible, the authors,
wanting to show that Brown could have killed the
Baron, suggested there was a case for a second attack
by Brown just about the time that the Triplane flew
over the 53rd Battery on its way to the field at
Sainte Colette. Thus, by a reverse process, they
deduced the place of Brown's attack from the time
it would take von Richthofen to die from such a
wound as he had suffered. The tail is wagging the
dog again.

Unfortunately not one of the approximately
1,000 spectators, from private to general officer, saw
Brown make such an attack which would have
been in their unobstructed view, close by and at low
altitude. The contorted proof of the imaginary
event is that Brown was indeed in the area at the
time which, in the view of the authors of the
Harleyford book, made a second attack possible.
After recovering from his dive and south-west turn,
he had turned right in the vicinity of Corbie, then
headed north towards Bonnay to check that May
was safe before heading back to Bertangles.

The authors of the Harleyford book would have
been extremely glad to have John Coltman's
testimony from Sergeant Gavin Darbyshire, Private
Jack O'Rourke and E E Trinder, for, once Brown's
attack has been positioned correctly, von
Richthofen's remaining flight path becomes short
enough for him to have succumbed to such a
wound within the bounds of possibility.

The positive aspect of the suggested second
attack is that it clearly demonstrates that the
Harleyford book authors were not happy [present
authors' note: and with good reason] with the time
factor relative to the events.
5. An un-named publication discounted Sergeant
Popkin's affirmations that he fired at the left of von
Richthofen's Triplane and that his second burst was
at the right. It claimed both times he fired at the
right. Apparently the good sergeant knew not what
he did.
6. It was only in the imagination of whoever edited
My Fight with Richthofen that two Australian soldiers
received medals.
7. There is a story that on 20 April a pilot (named
Lieutenant J A E R Daley) from 24 Squadron RAF
(SE5s) performed aerobatics over the two gun
batteries. A complaint had been made by the
Officer Commanding and the pilot had been told

to go to the Battery HQ and apologise the next morning. He was there when exciting things were happening and may have also been the source of the legend of the mysterious RAF pilot who 'landed nearby'.

C E W Bean's later discoveries indicated Sergeant Cedric Basset Popkin and eliminated his earlier nominees, Gunners Buie and Evans. In the section entitled *Conclusions* in Appendix 4 to *The AIF in France* (page 700), Bean wrote:

```
It is also clear that Sergeant Popkin's
gun when first fired, and those of the
53rd Battery, cannot have sent the fatal
shot - since it came almost directly from
the right and from below the aviator -
although they may well have caused him to
turn, but that scores of other men were
firing and, when Richthofen banked and
turned back, Sergeant Popkin (who now
opened fire again) was in a position to
fire such a shot as killed Richthofen.
Private R F Watson, who helped Popkin's
gun, wrote, on the day of the event, that
their previous burst did 'some damage',
but that the second burst 'was fatal'.
This was when Popkin himself, according to
his statement made at the time, 'observed at
once that my fire took effect'.
It is just conceivable that Captain Brown,
although above and behind him [1], could
have inflicted such a wound in the region
of the heart, he should have continued for
a mile [2] in his intensely purposeful
flight, closely following the movements of
the fugitive airman and endeavouring to
shoot him. Certainly no one who watched
from the ground the last minute [3] of
that exciting chase with only two 'planes
in the picture will ever believe that
Richthofen was killed by a shot from a
third aeroplane which no one from Vaux
onwards observed.[4]
```

Authors' notes:

[1] Brown's oft-repeated statements that he was above, behind and to the left, had reached Bean in the misleading abbreviated form which omitted the key word left.

[2] The horseshoe path taken by the Baron was indeed about one mile, but the straight line distance from where Brown attacked and the Baron fell is closer to half a mile.

[3] The last minute of the Baron's life is better comprehended if divided into about 30 seconds flying, 15 seconds making an emergency descent and landing, and 15 seconds dying.

[4] Obviously Bean knew nothing of Sergeant Darbyshire's pontoon bridge repair crew which belonged to a British Engineering unit, and

apparently he did not absolutely trust the word of Gunner Ridgway and Lieutenant Wood. There are reasons for this.

Ridgway had been handing around 'copies' of the nameplate from Richthofen's Fokker Dr.I 425/17, and some people had thought that they had received the original one. Unfortunately there were three spelling mistakes in the German, and excepting Fokker, the same words in Dutch are totally different. In addition, the layout resembled a nameplate from a Fokker E.III (a monoplane of 1915 vintage), nothing like that used on a Dr.I.

Lieutenant Wood had written that his platoon was about four miles from the battalion station in Corbie, which was why they had their own field kitchen. The army map, 1917 or 1918, shows the distance to be about 1 to 1½ miles only. On this basis, Wood's testimony has been discredited by many, it being obvious that if he was four miles from Corbie, he was nowhere near Sainte Colette. To verify this, the authors drove along the route which would have been followed to take supplies from Battalion HQ to the platoon near Corbie in the daytime. If a short cut via a cart-track were taken, the distance was 3.8 miles. The all-weather route was 4.2 miles.

Additional support for Sergeant Popkin was yet to surface. Private Bodington of the 10th Australian Field Ambulance revealed many years later that he had been ordered to deliver a dispatch, and was walking along the top of the Ridge with it in his hand when he saw the Triplane coming towards him. He heard a machine gun to his left open fire and saw the Triplane make a sudden steep climb and then nose down. It came to earth near a brick kiln 500 yards away from him. Bodington added that it was the only aeroplane around and that the machine gun, from 24th Machine Gun Company, was the only one he heard firing at it.

C E W Bean, as the Official Australian Historian, may not have researched other units in the area so much as he should have, but his errors of omission were in no way so grave as H A Jones's errors of commission. In letters between Jones and Bean, a strong impression surfaces that Jones (the Official British Historian) appeared to believe that *My Fight with Richthofen* was a true account written by Captain Brown and that he was following its basic line. He discounted all eye-witnesses to the contrary, including statements definitely made by Brown, and produced a seriously flawed work which has been cited by some as proof that the content of *My Fight with Richthofen* is indeed correct, if somewhat exaggerated. Researching in circles is an apt label for the process.

CHAPTER TWENTY
Conclusions

The chain of events which culminated in the death of von Richthofen form a fairly simple story. Whoever in the RAF HQ advised Captain Roy Brown to re-submit his claim on the proper form did so prematurely and then, after the publicity, could not withdraw it. The artificial situation resulted in the instruction to the pilots of 209 Squadron not to talk about the event. The secrecy, aggravated by the files being closed for 50 years, created a vacuum which was filled by rumour, speculation and pure fiction phrased for thrills. Each one fed upon the other until the truth was lost.

Dale Titler, in the foreword to his well-researched book *The Day the Red Baron Died*, puts it so well that the authors can pay him no better compliment than to present his words once more.

> For 52 years sensationalists have filled the undocumented gaps of this day with lurid and dramatic happenings. For all it was worth, they moulded the war drama of a national tragedy and highlighted the mystery and contention. In time, the facts of this gallant nobleman's violent finish became so enmeshed in fiction that the early war records and eyewitness accounts were submerged in a sea of fabrication.

The research conducted by John Coltman, who was killed in action with the RAF in 1942, has filled in one big gap; exactly where Captain Brown attacked the red Triplane. Then Mr A Twycross, by sending the story of his father, Gunner Ernest Twycross, to the Imperial War Museum, whereupon Mr Brad King passed it to the present authors, provided the key to exactly when von Richthofen died, and thus settled the 79 years' old controversy as to whether he was killed in the air during Roy Brown's attack and the Triplane crashed shortly afterwards or whether he died later whilst attempting an emergency landing.

With the new information provided by those mentioned above, tempered by airmanship, military organisation, trained reactions and the modern understanding of ballistics, it now seems possible to connect that fateful day's events together in a logical manner and without significant gaps.

On 21 April 1918 the wind was blowing strongly in the opposite direction to normal. This had a definite effect upon ground speed relative to the previous days and appears to have had a significant role in the events of that morning.

Even though von Richthofen was having trouble with his guns, a novice pilot was a tempting target. To go after him was not a dirty trick; all the aces had begun as novices. Why let him gain experience and possibly become another Albert Ball, James McCudden or Mick Mannock?

Flying west at a ground speed of 135 mph (aeroplane 110 plus wind 25) against the normal 85 mph (with wind speed subtracted), von Richthofen was covering ground 50 mph faster than usual as he chased May. During his dive around or through the low mist, he appears to have made a simple navigation error of the 'time versus distance flown' type, and being too low down for the terrain to look like his mental map of the area, he confused two villages which, although similarly situated on the north bank of the Somme canal, were actually a mile and a half apart.

The obvious landmark which would have revealed his error, the sharp bend from west to south of the canal just before Corbie, was obscured by the trees along the sides of the zig-zags of the waterway. The present authors can attest to this; they did not see it either until it loomed up in front of their aeroplane around what appeared to be just another 'zag'. When the quick kill became hard work, von Richthofen failed to cut his losses and head for home, that was his first wrong decision.

The attack by Captain Brown, which he skilfully countered upon hearing the first shots zip by his Triplane, was a sharp warning, but victory was so close that he, on seeing Brown's Camel banking away towards the south-west at high speed, appears to have decided upon one more try at May. That was his second wrong decision. The Baron saw nothing to tell him his true position, and that the heaviest concentration of anti-aircraft guns in the area was just ahead of him – not two miles away as he thought.

The crucial and unexpected bend in the river suddenly appeared a moment later. Due to the strong tail wind there was only one way out - a steep climb which included a turn of 45°, over a place where the trees were not so tall.

Machine-gun fire from Sergeant Popkin and from Private McDiarmid passed behind him so he would have neither seen the smoke of the tracer nor heard the Rak-ak-ak sounds. As he topped the Ridge, the lower wing and mid-wing of the Triplane would have hidden the camouflaged 18-pounder guns from his view - ironically the very guns he and his men had been sent to the area to help find. He might have seen them if he had banked and looked down, for, from his low height, camouflage netting is not very effective.

Quite unknowingly he followed Lieutenant May's Camel along the west side of the line of guns which was when he began to notice ground fire coming from Buie, Evans and probably Gamble. Although the Triplane's nose was pointing north, the wings were supported by air that was travelling west at 25 mph. The result was the Triplane's track over the ground was close to north-west. The ground machine gunners not only had to lead their target, they also had to aim to the west of it. In addition, the Triplane was flying so low-down that the machine guns had to be traversed and elevated rapidly to follow it. The result was the Triplane presented a complicated deflection shot to machine gunners who had not been trained for such situations. Von Richthofen skilfully avoided their bullets, although some hit his wings and/or interplane struts.

Then he made his third and fatal wrong decision. He started to climb and began following a predictable flight path heading east. He was now flying into the strong wind which greatly reduced his ground speed, for the wind was no longer slowed by the trees and friction with the terrain. Worse still, he was no longer being carried sideways - he was moving in the direction that the nose of the Triplane was pointing. Therefore he became an easy target from the front, from behind and for anyone at the side who was able to calculate the angle of deflection correctly.

Gunner Buie, and possibly Evans also, had emptied their panniers, so until the empty one was taken off and a fresh one locked into place, Buie at least, could not fire again. In any event, as he himself stated afterwards, he thought the Triplane was already finished and he was not even contemplating further firing. Private Emery, up by the brickworks, was biding his time; he was well aware of the danger of firing early, missing, and giving away his position to an enemy pilot who was heading in his direction, sitting behind twin machine guns.

Half a mile south-east of the Triplane's flight path, that is on the right-hand side of its fuselage,

were the soldiers of Lieutenant Wood's platoon who had exchanged tools for rifles and were firing at it. Near them were four Vickers machine guns under Sergeant Popkin, of which only one was manned. The Sergeant opened fire for the second time, having missed with his earlier burst as the Triplane flashed by and below him a couple of minutes earlier. (It is interesting to speculate that if Popkin had shot the Triplane down with his earlier burst, Brown would have had a better claim, having attacked the Triplane just moments beforehand!)

As Private Emery told Geoffrey Hine, it was AFTER he heard the Lewis guns (Buie, Evans and Gamble) stop firing and BEFORE he heard the Vickers gun start, that the Triplane gave indication that its pilot had been hit. He added that there had been a background of rifle fire all the time, and that his first impression was that one of the soldiers in Lieutenant Wood's platoon had scored a hit.

The apparently clear picture becomes blurred when 1,100 feet per second is included; that is the approximate speed of sound in an air temperature of 45° Fahrenheit.

Sergeant Popkin was about 2,100 feet south of Private Emery, therefore Emery would not hear him beginning to fire until two seconds later. Similarly, Emery was about 3,000 feet away from Buie and would not hear him ceasing fire until three seconds after he had actually done so. Add in the wind factor which was carrying the sound away from Emery, and the delay becomes even longer, thus a hit from Popkin's machine gun shortly after he opened fire is definitely possible.

From the foregoing it can be deduced that von Richthofen was alive and well four to seven seconds after Buie and Evans ceased firing. At 85 mph he would be travelling at 130 feet per second, so in that time he would have covered 520 to 910 feet. If von Richthofen is allowed 10 to 15 seconds to descend and touch down, it can be calculated from a map that he was hit somewhere between 900 and 1,200 feet away from the 53rd Battery. This agrees with Gunner Buie's estimate of 300 to 500 yards. The numbers fit together, not precisely, but acceptably. The bounds of probability do not need to be stretched one iota, which contrasts with other hypotheses advanced in the past for which the bounds of 'possibility' not 'probability' were considerably strained.

Who killed the Red Baron?

We have come to the definite conclusion that, despite much of what has been written over the last 80 years, the new evidence available today

113

confirms the elimination by most earlier serious investigators of Captain Brown as being responsible for von Richthofen being shot down.

In the remote possibility that the bullet was not fired from a machine gun, it could only have come from one of the Australian riflemen of Lieutenant Wood's platoon (see table below). They were at the right distance and angle from the Triplane. Some of them came from farming communities back home where they had helped eke out their living by shooting game birds on the wing. Leading a target was second nature to them.

By virtue of the volume of fire per second it is far more likely that the fatal bullet came from a machine gun, and the evidence, as interpreted by the present authors, indicates Sergeant Popkin. His was the only machine gun in action and firing at the right-hand side of the Triplane at that time. This agrees with the findings of Captain Bean and of the late Pasquale Carisella, and it is worth remarking that 'Pat' reached his conclusion by using the evidence available at the time (mid-1960s), most of which he obtained by writing letters to every person involved whose name and address he could find.

The authors find the evidence and probabilites, based on logic, indicate that the honours belong to Sergeant Cedric Bassett Popkin.

	BROWN	BUIE	EVANS	EMERY	PLATOON	POPKIN
Was firing when Baron was struck	NO	NO	NO	NO	YES	YES
Fired at R.H. side of Triplane	NO	possibly	possibly	NO	YES	YES
Fired at an acceptable angle	NO	possibly	possibly	NO	YES	YES
Ammunition included rifle bullets	YES	YES	YES	YES	YES	YES
Range was suited to the wound characteristics	NO	NO	NO	NO	YES	YES

Footnote to the new edition

Some time after this book was originally published, doubts continued over Popkin having fired the fatal shot. Even he himself had had reservations and it has transpired that when firing at the Triplane it had turned right and was flying almost head-on towards him. Popkin was fully aware that a good deal of fire was being directed at the Triplane and it was at 200 feet when it was hit.

The Triplane then headed north and made the forced landing. There is still no doubt that the fatal bullet had to be fired from 5-600 yards away, so there is still the possibility that some unknown soldier had fired at the Triplane yet had no reason to believe he had fired the telling shot. However, there is no definite evidence for this, and Popkin remains the most likely candidate.

Postscript

An interesting statement was made by Roy Brown between 1927 and 1930 at which time he was being badgered by various parties and factions to explain gaps, oxymorons and plain impossibilities in stories on von Richthofen's demise. Some of these had been presented in such a manner as to suggest that they were his own personal memoirs. Brown could not have been very happy for some people were calling him a liar and others a murderer. A few words could have cleared it all up.

Triggered by the furore which resulted from the publication of *The Red Knight of Germany* and *My Fight with Richthofen*, the Australian ex-servicemen's magazine *Reveille* had been featuring letters on the events of 21 April 1918. Apparently, in the hope of straightening things out, the editor wrote to Roy Brown asking what had happened. For certain, without entering the contentious area, Brown could easily have settled the questions as to where and at what height he had attacked von Richthofen. Brown's reply, printed in November 1930, was as follows:

> As far as I am concerned, I knew in my own mind what happened, and the war being over, the job being done, there is nothing to be gained by arguing back and forth as to who did this and who did that. The main point is that, from the stand-point of the troops in the war, we gained our objectives.

An answer that seems to miss the point of the question may do no more than disappoint the recipient, but when the non-answer to *Reveille* is taken together with the earlier non-answer to C E W Bean: 'I cannot comment as I am not a reader of that magazine,' the repeat event and the careful phrasing of both raise suspicion that the evasion is not exactly accidental.

In 1935 Wing Commander H N Wrigley DFC AFC RAAF, in his book *The Battle Below* (The History of 3 AFC Squadron) (published by Errol G Knox, Sydney) and at the time Director of Organisation and Staff Duties with the RAAF, lifted the curtain a little. He revealed that it was not only C E W Bean who had changed his mind after hearing evidence from people who had not been directly involved but who had a very good view of the proceedings. Major D V J Blake and Captain E G Knox MBE (the publisher, and a journalist), who had respectively been the CO and the RO of 3 AFC Squadron, had also changed their minds. The key passage follows:

> Major Blake also states that he made many enquiries from ground eye-witnesses of the combat and crash, including Brigadier-General J H Cannan CB, of the 11th Australian Infantry Brigade, near whose headquarters Richthofen was shot down, and is personally satisfied that Richthofen was brought down by fire from the ground.
>
> Captain Knox, who was also present at the medical examination and some of the subsequent enquiries, supports Major Blake's statements.

The curtain was completely raised and the picture revealed in 1968. Seventy years after the death of Manfred Albrecht von Richthofen, historian Frank McGuire received a letter from Air Vice-Marshal J L Barker CB CBE DFC BA, dated 12 October 1988. When the excerpt which follows is compared with Mellersh's own lecture at the RAF Staff College in 1931, it becomes obvious that Mellersh had an Official Attitude and a Private Opinion. The present authors have Mr McGuire's permission to quote from the letter:

> Nearly 60 years ago [Flight Lieutenant] Mellersh was adjutant of the Oxford University Air Squadron when I went up in 1930 to Brasenose. I was lucky in that I was one of his pupils as he combined the duties of adjutant with that of Chief Flying Instructor - and he sent me on my first solo.
>
> At that time memories of World War 1 [The Great, to those who fought in it] were still fresh - in fact we were equipped with the Bristol Fighter which was such a success at the end of that war.
>
> To those of us who were learning to fly, Richthofen, although a German, was something of a legend, and all I can recall is that Mellersh was convinced that the Red Baron met his end as the result of ground fire - and none of the flight claimed otherwise.

A close look at many of the post-war statements made by 209 Squadron officers reveals that they are mainly in the third person and contain statements such as: 'The RAF recognised...', or 'The doctors said ... '. 'The opinion at RAF HQ ...'; 'Brown was given the credit', and so on. These cannot be described as definite personal opinions. They bring to mind the tradition that officers of the armed forces, when told not to talk, did not talk. When told what to say, they said it, and they took their secrets with them to the grave.

Wilfred May's letter to Donald Naughton in which he professed lack of knowledge of the true direction of von Richthofen's wound, may have been part of the same code of honour to which Roy Brown can be seen to have adhered, at great personal inconvenience, for the rest of his life. For what he had to put up with later on, he really earned the Distinguished Service Order that he was denied in 1918.

Lieutenant F J W Mellersh RNAS.

APPENDIX A: CABLE'S ACCOUNT

On 25 May 1918 an account of the end of the Red Devil was published in the London (England) *Graphic*. It was accompanied by the painting of the air fight by Joseph Simpson. Boyd Cable was named as the contributor. A careful reading will reveal that it is obviously an honest attempt at a true rendering and appears to be based upon the account of a 209 Squadron member. In its simplicity, it is far closer to the truth than later more detailed efforts by others.

Unfortunately Cable gave no idea of the elapsed time between the events which he described; this opened a door to much invention. His story may be said to be a skeleton to which others have added flesh, created sometimes from out of thin air, and which have transformed what was quite close to the truth, into virtual fiction.

Cable's account contains one major error and three minor variations from the truth; three of which were to appear again and again; sometimes expanded, sometimes paraphrased, as later writers added 'interest' to the basic story. The major error is treated in Item 4 below. All-in-all, however, it was a good effort.

The Red Baron, with his famous circus, discovered two of our artillery observing machines, and with a few followers attacked; the greater part of the 'circus' drawing off to allow the Baron to go in and down the two. They put up a fight, and, while the Baron manoeuvred for position, a number of our fighting scout machines appeared and attacked the 'circus'. The Baron joined the mêlée, which, scattering into groups, developed into what our men call a 'dog fight'. In the course of this, the Baron dropped on the tail of a fighting scout, which dived with the Baron in close pursuit. Another of our scouts, seeing this, dived after the German, opening fire on him. All three machines came near enough to be engaged by infantry machine gun fire, and the Baron was seen to swerve, continue his dive headlong and crash in our lines. His body and the famous blood-red Fokker triplane were afterwards brought in by the infantry, and the Baron was buried with full military honours. He was hit by one bullet, and the position of the wound showed clearly that he had been killed by the pilot who dived down after him.

Author's Notes:

1. The attack on the two RE8s was not made by von Richthofen alone. He was accompanied by Leutnant Hans Weiss. Subsequent elabortions have not copied Cable's count; they seem to have leaned the other way by increasing the number of Triplanes to three or even four.

It should be carefully noted that Cable's story does not have Captain Brown diving to the rescue of the RE8s. It states correctly that Brown engaged the rest of JGI and that von Richthofen then desisted from attacking the RE8s and rejoined JGI.

2. Cable suggests that Lieutenants Banks and Barrow, the observers in the two RE8s, were reporting the fall of artillery fire. That was not so. They were taking photographs of the German troops and supply concentrations in the Le Hamel area.

3. Cable gives the impression that the machine-gun fire from the infantry occurred at the same time as the second fighting scouts attacked the triplanes (near the bottom of the valley). That was not so. There may have been some rifle fire, but the first machine gunner definitely known at that time to have fired at the Triplane was Sergeant Popkin as it approached the crest of the ridge after climbing up from the valley.

4. Cable shows knowledge of the single bullet but gives its path through von Richthofen's body as being the reverse of what is known to be true. The wording looks rather like a paraphrase of what is said to have been the opinion of the group of 209 Squadron pilots who, on 2 May 1918, studied the evidence and beliefs, both right and wrong, available to them.

Conclusions

Cable's 1918 story appears to have been the basis for an anonymous account of the same events published in Canada in 1925. Unfortunately, some of the additions, which considerably distorted the story, had little or no basis in fact. (see Appendix B)

Two famous paintings are worth commenting on. They were both painted shortly after the event and were not influenced by later fanciful writings. Although the background of the Simpson painting (referred to above) is incorrect (it depicts the encounter as being at high altitude), the position of Brown's Camel relative to von Richthofen's Triplane should be carefully noted. Brown is shown attacking from the left.

The other 1918 painting, this time by Geoffrey Watson, is worthy of study as well. The background too is incorrect but the attack direction is correct - from the left - as per Brown's statements.

From 1927 onwards the direction of Roy Brown's attack, as shown in sketches, drawings and paintings, will be found to be from the right. (see also Appendix D)

NB. Boyd Cable was the pseudonym of Ernest Andrew Ewert OBE, from west London, who wrote several books for John Murray & Co. Ewart was an observer with the RFC and saw service with squadrons at the front for over a year. His stories were fictional but based on facts gleaned while on active service. He ended the war as an acting Lieutenant-Colonel.

The two 1918 paintings of the fight, one by Joseph Simpson (right), the other by Geoffrey Watson.

APPENDIX B: ANONYMOUS ACCOUNT

On 2 December 1925 the Canadian newspaper the *Ottawa Citizen* published what it termed: 'A full account of the fight' given, it claimed, by an officer who had been engaged in the air battle over Cerisy and Sailly-Laurette on 21 April 1918. The officer was not named.

Some of the phrasing of that *Anonymous Account* will look quite familiar to a reader once he has digested the contents of the *Summary* (Appendix C), provided (it is claimed) by the Air Ministry in London to the author Floyd Gibbons (but see our misgiving in that appendix).

If, after studying the transcript (below) of the Anonymous Account, the reader peruses *My Fight with Richthofen*, (Appendix E), further similarities will be noticed.

The Anonymous Account was as follows – verbatim:

> 'Fifteen of our planes were patrolling along the lines,' he said. 'Captain Brown was leading his squadron [1] of five machines parallel with the second squadron, and some distance above the third and leading squadron.
>
> 'We had not gone far when we saw below us two or three RE8s out on artillery observation, and attacking them were several German triplanes [2]. At that time we were at an altitude of some fifteen thousand feet, and the enemy planes were flying quite low [3].
>
> 'Captain Brown, without hesitation, dived, the others following. Within a few minutes we were in the middle of a "dog fight". We discovered we were attacking 22 [4] enemy machines. Fortunately the speed of the onslaught threw the Germans off their guard, and the old REs were able to get away undamaged [5].
>
> 'Captain Brown, as leader of the squadron, was keeping an eye on the entire fight. He had one pilot, Captain "Wop" May of Edmonton, who had never before taken part in an air battle [6] and quite naturally he paid particular care to the new man. Captain May dived with the rest, engaged with a German, and after bringing him down [7], made towards our own lines in accordance with instructions.
>
> No sooner had he become detached from the others than Richthofen made after him and opened up heavy fire [8]. Fortunately Captain Brown had been watching this turn of events and he immediately followed after Richthofen. His first bullets ripped through the fuselage of the enemy plane [9]. We [10] saw him elevate his fire slightly [11]. Richthofen collapsed in his seat and the plane plunged to the ground [12].

GOT EIGHT ENEMY PLANES

> 'When the battle was over, we discovered that we had accounted for eight enemy planes, and we had received no damage at all [13].
>
> 'Richthofen,' continued the airman, 'was usually successful because he invariably followed any plane which became detached from the fight. I question whether he ever realised that he in turn, was being followed. He was killed instantaneously by the first burst of bullets and his machine was riddled [14].

Authors' Notes

1. The flights are called squadrons; an error repeated in the *Summary*. The writer obviously was not a RAF pilot.

2. The RE8s and Fokker Triplanes which were out of sight over Le Hamel, not below Brown's Camels near Cerisy, have been inserted. These appear again in the *Summary*.

3. The genuine RE8s and Triplanes over Le Hamel were not 'quite low', they were at 7,500 feet. That altitude is given in the Combats in the Air Report written jointly by the two RE8 crews.

4. 22 German machines are said to have been present. How anyone could have counted them is not explained, and the same number is cited in the *Summary*. The figure is about double the actual number.

5. The genuine RE8s carried on with their photography in peace and neither crew made any reference to Camels being present.

6. This was not the first time that May had been in combat; actually it was his second combat and third flight over the lines. Also his rank is shown incorrectly, although he became a captain later in 1918.

7. May is incorrectly said to have shot down a Triplane. This is repeated in the *Summary* which then adds – 'flames' – to the fiction. The only Triplane lost over the Somme on that day was Richthofen's 425/17.

8. The heavy fire is pure invention. The aces on both sides only fired a few shots at a time in short bursts they were so close that they knew they couldn't miss.

9. 11. 12. The bullets through the fuselage, Brown elevating his fire, and the Triplane plunging to the ground all reappear in *My Fight with Richthofen* in a more elaborate manner. In some of the published versions, Richthofen collapses in his seat as well. The text is still recognisable as having originated in the *Anonymous Account* and having been 'laundered' on its way through the *Summary* and *The Red Knight of Germany*.

10. 'We' suggests that two, or more, Sopwith Camel pilots were flying within 50 yards of Captain Brown when he fired on the Triplane. To see such minute detail, 'they' would have to be extremely close to him yet nobody saw them. This positively identifies the 'story' as a fabrication.

13. Eight enemy planes shot down is again pure invention. Only von Richthofen's Triplane was lost although another may have been forced to land.

14. 'Riddled with bullets' is more invention. The people who examined the Triplane 425/17 after the forced landing were amazed to find how undamaged from gunfire it was. Private Craven, who souvenired a piece of fabric with a bullet hole in it, was said to have been lucky. There was only one bullet hole in the fuselage; Captain R Ross, Lieutenant W J Warneford and 1AM A A Boxall-Chapman, all testified to that effect.

The Anonymous Account may have been the source of a

fictitious story published on 26 February 1930 in the *Herald*, a Melbourne, Australia newspaper, under the name of Lieutenant L A Mellor of 209 Squadron RFC [sic]. Like the writer of the *Anonymous Account* he claimed to have been flying close to Brown when the latter attacked the Red Baron. Unfortunately C E W Bean could not find a Lieutenant L A Mellor in the RAF or AFC lists of officers. The present authors have made a similar search with the same result. The 209 Squadron Record Book does not mention him as having flown on 21 April 1918, nor is his name listed in the Squadron pilot roster.

APPENDIX C: SUMMARY
(FOR FLOYD GIBBONS)

In the Public Record Office, the following document which is transcribed verbatim, is to be found under AIR 1/2397/262/2:

MATERIAL ON BROWN FOR GIBBONS' RICHTHOFEN STORY

Captain Baron von Richthofen's career was ended by a British pilot who was unaware of the identity of his victim until after the fight which wrote a large page in the history of the World War.

Captain A. Roy Brown of the Royal Air Force had been engaged in active service along the British front for fifteen months prior to the engagement on April 21, 1918. This had been punctuated only by a month's leave to visit Canada and his nervous system had become so disorganised that it affected his stomach and for the last month of that time his diet consisted of brandy and milk.

Confined to his bed, he nevertheless arose and led his two patrols daily into the enemy's territory. The British held a momentary supremacy in the air and this very favourable condition added the greatest hazard to flying – the necessity of making all engagements over foreign territory. A new and more serious factor likewise had appeared – the Richthofen Circus.

This aggregation of gaily decorated Fokker triplanes, superior to anything the Allies possessed, had appeared in this sector three weeks previously. With them they had brought new tactics consisting principally of flying in Squadron formation. Whereas contact with the enemy previously had been in flights of five planes each, the British now worked in squadrons of various numbers, dependent upon last minute developments.

Captain Brown commanded a flight of Sopwith Camels in Squadron 209, stationed at Bertangles, four miles from Amiens. The squadron was commanded by Major Butler, holder of the Distinguished Service Order.

Captain Brown had been awarded the Distinguished Service Cross in a career which had included the dropping of about 15 enemy planes, although he is not certain of the official total.

During the time that Richthofen's Circus had opposed Squadron 209, the latter had come in daily contact with it, without marked results. Without realising which plane belonged to the German flier who had nearly eighty Allied planes to his credit, the British aviators each day had their skirmishes with the aggregation, and Captain Brown formed an unusual attachment with one which remained as a vivid memory after the war.

He had singled out a Fokker triplane with a pale green fuselage and lavender wings and each day had his private duel without either himself or his German opponent ever gaining the advantage. For all he knew at the time, this might have been Richthofen, but this belief also was shared by each of his compatriots who were conducting their own private affairs.

On April 21, with the memory of these occurrences of the past few days in mind, Squadron 209 (sic) set out for the regular morning patrol at 10.30 a.m. The Squadron consisted of three flights of five planes each. The first flight flew in a V-shaped formation, close together, with Major Butler leading, two planes slightly behind him and at each side and two others still farther apart and above behind them.

Flanking the leading flight on the right, in the same formation, was Captain Brown's flight, he being second in command. A similar flight was to the left of the Major's detail.

The patrol first took a methodical path up and down the lines where (sic) here ran north and south and where, below, the Australian Colonials were facing the Germans. Back and forth they flew, gradually gaining altitude as they flew in wide arcs until the squadron was at 15,000 feet. The visibility was fair with a few clouds but when the squadron reached this altitude, flying over the lines, Captain Brown noticed the Squadron Commander Butler and his flight were not in evidence. Thereupon, Captain Brown assumed command of the two remaining squadrons [sic], signalling for the other to take position behind and above his own. With this formation made, he headed east in search of enemy planes and to do whatever reconnaissance was possible. This latter was secondary, however, to the main purpose of the Camel pilots to find and destroy whatever enemy planes might be sighted.

The captain, his attention attracted by a burst of fire from his own anti-aircraft guns, looked over the side of his plane and far below sighted three Fokker triplanes attacking two R.E.8 type British planes over the German lines. The R.E.8s were slow, cumbersome planes sent up only for the purpose of spotting Allied artillery fire and quite unable to cope with the expert German pilots in their new equipment.

A kick on the rudder turned Captain Brown's Camel on its side and the sight that met his eyes sent a tremor down his spine. A whole swarm of German aircraft had appeared, as if from nowhere, and, while neither of the observation planes had gone down, he realised it to be but a matter of seconds until they were both over-powered by virtue of numbers alone.

But while he watched the fight more than two miles below – he estimated the engagement to be at 3,000 feet altitude – his mind, trained to the mathematical formula of flying formations, reviewed the situation.

His first responsibility was to get enemy planes, but equally important was the requirement that he exercise every precaution to get his men back safely. Up to this time both records were clear for he had got more than his share of planes and he had never lost a man in the enemy's territory.

The question was whether he should exercise prudence and permit the sacrifice of the two planes already involved below or whether he should make the heroic effect of endeavouring to save them. And then a third element entered into his reasoning – plain, cold fear.

His own craft were outnumbered two to one, he knew, and by the bright colourings he knew the German planes to be members of the Circus which had made its reputation even before he had set foot on French soil. As a matter of fact, he later found his machines outnumbered three to one.

Never before had he encountered so many of the Circus members at once and, as patrol leader, he would be the first on into the mêlée, probably arriving thousands of feet ahead of his support. He also knew with certainty that among the nine other planes there might be at least one who would falter.

Possibly the fear of fear itself was what prompted his decision. In any case, he knew it was not reason.

He waggled the wings of his plane, the signal for the others to follow him, and within a fraction of [a] second after the stream of thought had begun to pour through his mind, he pushed forward on the stick, stood the plane on its nose, and dived straight for the combat with 'the gun wide open', his plane going with the combined speed of the motor and the acceleration of gravity.

Seven of his planes followed. Two faltered. They returned home safely but their pilots' stories were not those of the eight heroes of 209.

There is no opportunity to give many orders to a fleet of roaring airplanes but every man with one hand on the control stick and another on his machine gun trigger knew what he was supposed to do.

Each was to distract as many of the enemy as possible and permit the escape of the R.E.8s who still feebly held their own by the grace of their skill and luck. That duty finished, each British plane was to get home as best it could – but get home! Pilots had been lost in wholesale lots and each was considered an individual asset and necessity of the army.

Among those seven pilots following Brown toward the ground with every strut and spar of their Camels straining at the excessive speed was one boy who that morning had gone out for his baptism of fire. He was Lieutenant May, R.A.F. who survived the war and returned to his home in Melbourne, Australia.

He was operating under special orders. These were that in case of an engagement he should not try to join the general fighting but pick out a single plane, put it down if he could – if not, play with it until he could break away – and then head for home. Pilots on their maiden flights had the habit of trying to do too much and too many had been lost.

A few thousand feet above the Germans the falling phalanx pulled into a circling glide to size up their opponents. Still the lone R.E.8s held their own. But more of the Circus had appeared and now there were 22 planes bearing the black cross.

Into the mêlée plunged the eight Camels with motors wide open, guns roaring and every man for himself.

There was no regular order of battle – only more than thirty planes rolling, diving, turning, circling, banking, and firing bursts of machine gun bullets each time an opponent passed before the sights of their guns. Plainly perceptible from the ground, the Australians and the Germans who looked aloft could hardly distinguish their own planes in the dog fight but they looked on a battle royal such as had seldom occurred over the lines prior to that time.

Three times two planes got on Brown's tail, the one direction which renders a single pilot helpless. Most of the German planes were of the Fokker triplane type, but here and there zoomed an Albatross [sic].

Brown estimated that the fight must have lasted ten minutes, an unholy eternity to a fighter in the air, flying automatically and concentrating on the double problem of putting his own bullets where they will count and at the same time protecting himself and his plane from two or three opponents equally intent upon doing the same thing.

Brown's men were fighting the same odds, aided occasionally by him when he was not in momentary danger.

Somewhere in the 'dog-fight' was Richthofen – fighting with the cunning and skill and disregard of danger which had caused the German high command to print his exploits in a book and circulate them in the army as a shining example of the spirit of His Majesty's Army.

His plane was one of those gaily decorated craft which made the fight a rainbow, streaked here and there with the cerise of the Red Nosed Camels, the distinctive mark of Brown's squadron.

The R.E.8s both had retreated to safety and the Camels now were trying to extricate themselves. A hurried count assured Brown that all still were in action when Lieutenant May broke from the engagement.

Acting under his orders, he had sent a plane hurtling down in flames and then he followed his other orders to return home. Bertangles was to the north-west of the fight and the planes had dropped to about 1,000 feet during the action. Brown saw May leave while he was engaging two of the Fokkers and then turned his attention to his other planes, planning to stay with them unless May got into trouble. May did.

When perhaps a quarter of a mile away a bright red plane swooped down upon him and May, without ammunition, was helpless.

He did every stunt he had been taught on the training field to distract his pursuer. Pulling up sharply he would go into an Immelmann turn, looping until flat on his back, then side-slipping over into normal position headed in the opposite direction, flying a zig-zag course, making short bursts of speed – always followed by the scarlet plane which spat fire at him that he was helpless to return.

Brown decided that May needed aide worse than the seasoned pilots and darted out and down upon the red plane.

When he overtook the craft manoeuvring after May the three combatants were not more than 200 feet above the ground, directly over the Australian first line trenches. Brown could see the infantrymen looking up at him and the machine gunners spraying lead in the vicinity of the red plane.

His dive took him directly above and to the rear of the German plane and he opened fire with his last drum of ammunition.

Interspersed with the bullets were tracers, small shells which left a trail of smoke at every tenth shot. The first tracers went through the red plane's tail.

A slight pull on the stick, a fractional elevation of the Camel's nose, and Brown's tracer showed a line of fire approaching the cockpit. The pilot had not noticed him.

As the gun stopped, empty, the German plane wavered and fell to the ground between the first line support trenches of the Australian infantry.

Richthofen was down! But Brown was unaware of the magnitude of his victory.

Brown managed to get back with only two cylinders of his machine working. The Camel otherwise was a sorry sight with twisted wires and punctured wings and fuselage where many German bullets had come dangerously near to him. Every one of his men came in – one by one – each in as bad a condition. One had suffered a slight wound. But the day had been fruitful.

When the reports had been read they read:

```
Lieutenant Mackenzie - Fokker triplane out
of control.
Lieutenant May - Fokker triplane destroyed
and himself wounded in arm.
Lieutenant Taylor - Albatross shot down
in flames.
```

There was no unit added to Captain Brown's score. The infantry claimed the prize for their machine gunners and he had hardly landed before word was spread that Richthofen was dead.

Brown was in a state of intense nervous excitement, his mental powers and physical condition almost overcome by the strain of the engagement in a weakened condition. But he asked Lieutenant Colonel Cairnes, Wing Commander of the sector, to aid him in making an investigation.

With Cairnes he went to the support trenches where he saw the plane, lying as it had crashed, under fire from the German trenches.

With the aid of infantrymen, Brown brought in Richthofen's body.

A post-mortem confirmed the fact that Brown had 'got' Richthofen. One bullet hole only was found in the body – the missile had entered the left shoulder, gone through the heart and emerged from the right side; making it apparent that the fatal shot had been fired from above and not from beneath.

Immediately after the post-mortem the day following the fight, Richthofen was laid in state – and Brown went on another patrol.

He does not remember returning – or anything, for that matter, for the next few weeks.

He landed his Camel safely, collapsed and was carried to the hospital near Amiens, listed as a critical case suffering from stomach trouble, accentuated by nervous strain. For three weeks he was delirious.

While Richthofen was buried by the Allies with full military honours, plans were being made to transport Brown to England.

After six weeks he was pronounced sufficiently recovered to assume duty as a combat instructor in England and a bar was added to his Distinguished Service Cross by the Prince of Wales. But fate had ruled that for Captain Brown the war was ended.

In spite of a slight attack of influenza, he took up a plane for practice and when at about 300 feet his comrades saw the machine plunge nose downward to the ground with the engine going full speed. Brown had fainted in the air.

They actually lifted the engine off his neck and he first was pronounced dead. Then a trace of life was found and the physicians set about mending twenty-two fractures in his skull.

Today, at 33 years of age, Captain Brown is actively engaged in business, has a wife and three children and is contemplating the not-far-distant date when his nervousness resulting from his experiences will have abated sufficiently for him to trust himself to drive a motor car.

Authors' Comments on a Selection of Major Points

Once having read the above account, one is immediately amazed at how such a dramatized document came to be written in the first place by a staff member of the Air Ministry Historical Section. It is certainly not a product of someone in the 1920s working in a government department, and it certainly would not have passed inspection by the senior 'winged-collared' clerk. For one thing it is not a historical document. The style closely resembles the work of a pulp-fiction writer. While it obviously has some accurate facts, the writer is clearly not really au fait with the subject matter and seems to make a number of assumptions. In fact, it almost seems as if Gibbons himself wrote it from a number of notes that may have been merely given to him by Air Ministry, as there are too many 'Americanisms' in the phraseology although except 'airplane' the spelling is English, not American. It was then typed by an English person.

Richthofen's aeroplanes were not the only ones which were highly decorated so one cannot assume they were up against JGI as opposed to any other German flying unit. Also, saying that the Circus was operating before Brown himself landed on French soil is wrong. Brown was in France in April 1917 and JGI – the Circus – was not formed until June.

In the opening stage of the air fight, the writer initially makes the point that Brown had only seven other Camels with him in the attack, then goes on to say there was 'a fleet of roaring aeroplanes' then a 'falling phalanx' of aircraft. Why he imagines Brown to have been 'arriving several thousands of feet ahead of his support' ie: the other Camels, is not known, but it makes Brown look an idiot – or the others reluctant participants. Furthermore, the phrase: 'every man with one hand on the control stick and another on his machine-gun trigger' (twice he assumes the Camel to have only one gun) indicates that the writer had no idea whatsoever how a fighter pilot controls his aeroplane, British, French or German, ancient or modern.

The mystery is how such a document came to be in an Air Ministry file, but it did, and over the years has assumed the mantle of an 'official' document. A simple explanation is that Gibbons sent the Air Ministry a copy of his typed-up notes, which were duly filed and later became a PRO document when records were transferred into the public domain.

Carrying on from this to specifics. On page 2 paragraph four of the document, it is stated:

'The first flight flew in a V-shaped formation, close together, with Major Butler leading.'

'Major Butler' is not a slip of the pen. The error is continued on page 3 which begins as follows:

'.... but when the squadron reached this altitude, flying over the lines, Captain Brown noticed that Squadron Commander Butler and his flight were not in evidence. Thereupon Captain Brown assumed command of the remaining two squadrons. [sic]

Unfortunately for the writer, 209 Squadron's Record Book shows that Major Butler did not fly on this day, in fact there is no record that he flew at any time that month. The RAF actively discouraged Squadron COs from flying combat; for trained and experienced administrators who could also command men were hard to find. The CO who flew when his work permitted tended to be so out of practice at the quick responses and distant vision required that he often became a liability. Von Richthofen's 79th victim, Major R Raymond-Barker MC is a case in point. A senior flight

commander was normally appointed and he led the squadron on patrol or into battle. In the case of 209 Squadron, this was Captain Stearne T Edwards, who was on leave in England during April. The applicable pages of 209's Record Book are to be found in PRO file AIR 1-1858/204/214/8.

The final word 'squadrons' could be a slip of the pen for 'flights'. It could also have been 'inherited' from the *Anonymous Account*. Either way it shows a lack of familiarity with aerial formations on the part of the person who prepared the *Summary*. Similarly his comment that May could, if engaged, try to put down (a strange phrase) an enemy plane if he could, if not, *play with it until he could break away*. And this is the same author who is telling us about the deadly nature of the Richthofen Circus, but that May can 'play' with one of them until he finds himself in trouble. Good chance! On page 3, paragraph two, it is stated:

The Captain, his attention attracted by a burst of fire from his own anti-aircraft guns, looked over the side of his plane and far below sighted three Fokker triplanes attacking two R.E.8 type British planes over the German lines. The R.E.8s were slow cumbersome planes sent up only for the purpose of spotting allied artillery fire and quite unable to cope with the expert German pilots in their new equipment.

The following comments apply to the above excerpt which develops on pages 4 and 5 into how 209 Squadron Camels dived steeply and succeeded in rescuing the RE8s.
1. On 21 April, the pilots of 209 and the crews of 3 AFC's RE8s, to a man, did not report any contact, indeed the latter vehemently denied it when the subject was broached after the war. 209 and 3 AFC documents show that the rescue of an RE8 by Captain Brown's flight occurred the following day, the 22nd.
2. The task of the two RE8s is again described as artillery spotting. This error may again have been 'inherited' from the *Anonymous Account* or from *Cable's Account*. The writer is also over sensitive to the plight of the RE8 machines. While they were not on a par with German scouts, they could still handle themselves and often got out of trouble. As we know the two 3 AFC machines escaped Richthofen and Weiss shortly before the main air fight began, whereas the summary has the RE8s surviving the onslaught of several Circus pilots for some minutes, while Brown manoeuvres and then attacks.
3. The reference to 'German pilots in their new equipment' is a dangling phrase. No equipment change is mentioned anywhere before or afterwards in the *Summary*. The 'dangle' suggests that the phrase was 'lifted' in its entirety from some other work where it fitted in properly. Fokker Dr.I triplanes were far from being 'new equipment'; they had been in service on and off for six months and were now becoming obsolete. They had some advantages over Allied fighter types, not the least of which was their turning ability,

but experienced Camel and SE5 pilots could generally cope with the Triplane. The Fokker DVII biplanes destined to replace most front-line German fighters, Triplanes and Albatros Scouts by the end of the war, were already being delivered to the aircraft parks for issue to Jagdstaffeln at the beginning of May. Richthofen himself was looking forward to flying one over the front.

On page 5 paragraph two, it is stated that after the war Lieutenant May returned to his home in Melbourne, Australia. He would have a long journey for nothing and a disappointing welcome upon arrival. He lived in Edmonton, Alberta, Canada.

On page 5 paragraph five it is stated:

> Into the mêlée plunged the eight Camels with motors wide open, guns roaring and every man for himself.

The pilots of 209 Squadron were anything but a disorganised mob. Until 1 April it had been 9 Naval Squadron and in the RNAS discipline was spelt with a capital 'D'. The tactics described above for attacking three enemy aeroplanes would be the perfect recipe for mid-air collision, that is given the remote chance that the wings of the Camels stayed attached to the fuselages and their rotary engines did not disintegrate in flames. With only 50 second's worth of ammunition on board expert pilots only fired their guns after careful aiming; normally at close range. Any flight leader responsible for such a shambles would have had an unforgettable interview with his CO upon returning to base.

On page 7, paragraph five it is stated:

> He (Brown) opened fire with his last drum of ammunition.

Brown's machine gun was belt fed. And nowhere is there any mention of him being down to his last rounds in any event. Just as there is no report of his aircraft suffering the heavy damage supposedly found upon his return to Bertangles.

On page 8 paragraph two it is affirmed that Lieutenant May's Combats in the Air report indicates the following:

> Lieutenant May - Fokker destroyed and himself wounded in [the] arm.

1. May's report claimed nothing of the sort, only that 'he (the enemy aeroplane) went over and dived down. I was unable to observe the result.' The report was annotated 'Indecisive' by Major Butler.

2. Lieutenant Mackenzie was wounded, not May.

Conclusion

The person who provided the information for Floyd Gibbons had not read the sealed files and had little, if any, personal knowledge of the events which he described. His use of the words 'drop' and 'dropped' for shooting down hostile aircraft are curious and not normally used then or now. The information appears to have been derived from an anonymous fictitious account of the air battle published around 1925 together with garbled third or fourth-hand stories interspersed with guesses, not to mention a penchant for the dramatic.

APPENDIX D: FLOYD GIBBONS IS MISLED

In the mid-1920s the author Floyd Gibbons began research for what became a famous book on the life of Manfred von Richthofen. His meticulous research in Germany produced *The Red Knight of Germany* which is possibly the best biography of the life of the Baron from the day he was born until the day before he was killed in action. At that point the confusion began.

Floyd Gibbons was faced with some strange stories. One was that the British had placed a bounty on the Baron's head and that when he made a forced landing due to engine failure, two Canadian soldiers, whose persons and regiment were named, had murdered him to collect it. It is fortunate that names were specified as it became easy to prove that no such named soldiers existed. It was also discovered that the regiments were not stationed in the area either. Despite the proven fabrication, the story was resurrected in the early 1940s as a new discovery.

Another story which was quite widely believed, is related by the Baron's mother in her book *Mein Kreigstagebuch* (My War Diary), published in 1937. The tale runs as follows:

> In the 4th May 1917 edition of the newspaper *Vossische Zeitung* it is reported that the British have formed a squadron of volunteer fighter pilots whose purpose is to destroy the most successful German fighter pilot, Rittmeister Freiherr von Richthofen. The flier who succeeds in downing or capturing him will receive the Victoria Cross, a promotion, the gift of a personal aeroplane, 5,000 pounds sterling and a special prize from the manufacturer of the aeroplane which he used on the occasion. It is also said that a cine-camera operator will fly with that squadron to film the entire event for the British Army film archives.
>
> The newspaper suggested the addition of some observation balloons to provide an aerial grandstand and commented that the Richthofen Fighter Wing would ensure that the performance took place in a most interesting manner. (1)

Her son also read the article and commented: 'This is a great honour for me, but I must honestly say that I am rather embarrassed about it.' He added that he wondered what would happen if his first victim in such an air battle were to be the aeroplane which carried the cine-camera.

To anyone with even a little common sense and even a little knowledge of British military decorations, the mention of a Victoria Cross immediately indicates a fabricated story. The VC is awarded not so much for an achievement as for courage against overwhelming odds shown on a single occasion or a succession of actions above and beyond the call of duty. A surprisingly high proportion is conferred posthumously.

There were also stories which involved enemy aircraft. One described how the Baron had been shot down by two enemy aeroplanes piloted by Canadians which sneaked up behind him. In another story, one pilot cowardly shot him down as he was gliding in to land inside enemy territory after suffering an engine failure. There were others of this nature, most of which involved 'Canadians' and 'engine failures'.

The following report published in a German newspaper eight days after the Baron's death gave contrary information:

> *Berlin Tageblatt (evening edition)*
> *Monday 29th April 1918. Volume 47, No.217*
> *The Death of Baron von Richthofen*

A German war correspondent has recently spread around a story that Freiherr von Richthofen did not fall in combat but that after having landed he was killed by Australian soldiers. This report is false, for English statements and German observations confirm each other with regard to the circumstances of the death of Baron von Richthofen. These show that there can be no doubt that Richthofen was hit by a bullet from a ground-based machine gun whilst he was pursuing an enemy aeroplane at a very low altitude.

On Thursday, 2nd May, 1918, a grand ceremony in memory of Baron von Richthofen will be held in the Old Garrison Evangelical Lutheran Church (Garnisonkirche) in Berlin. (1)

In an attempt to learn the truth Floyd Gibbons went to England and asked the Air Ministry for information from the records concerning the events of 21 April. He found that the records were sealed until 1969 under the 'fifty year delay rule' and than an exception would not be made for him. The sealing had considerable justification for the files, which the present authors have examined, include personal character evaluations, fitness for promotion assessments, and recommendations for transfer to less exciting duties. Many of them concerned war veterans who were still living. Sadly, also included amongst the files were letters of condolence from commanding officers to the family of a son who was missing, had been killed, or had died of wounds in hospital. If he had been trapped in a flaming aircraft at 10,000 feet or burned to death in a landing accident, it was never revealed to the family. The saddest letters of all are the replies from grieving mothers or father, praying for some glimmer of hope that a son may be a prisoner, and some of which refer to the inclusion of a cheque to cover their dead son's mess bill and/or address to where his belongings should be sent.

The Air Ministry offered to arrange for someone to study the records and to provide Gibbons with the information requested. (see Appendix C) A typed form is to be found in the Public Record Office, Kew, London, England where it has been filed together with a *Resumé* of an interview with Captain Brown, without

(1) Translation by Dr Diane M Bennett.

date or place specified, but said in the index of files to have taken place ten years after the death of the Baron. However, the final sentence of the *Resumé* indirectly dates the interview evenly with the *Summary*. This reduces the ten years to about eight. The *Resumé* and the *Summary* are to be found in File Air I - 2397/262/2.

The record of the interview is entitled *Resumé of the Military Career of Captain A Roy Brown*. In the *Resumé* part, which in the main is perfectly accurate, there are some strange slips in familiarity with the Naval side of the British armed forces. It may be said, with a fair degree of certainty, that Roy Brown did not proof-read it. Indeed, from what can be reasonably ascertained today (1997), he was in Canada at that time. The first 'slip' instanced below suggests that the 'interviewer' was an American who was unfamiliar with British terminology. Below is the interview with 'slips' noted in square brackets [ ].

A Roy Brown, living in Toronto, joined the Royal Navy as a Flight Sub-Lieutenant September 1, 1915. At this time only civilian [trained] flyers were accepted and previously he had gone to Dayton, Ohio, to study aviation at the Wright Flying School; this at his own risk and expense. [A couple of strange statements here, in that the vast majority of men joining up would of course be civilians, and the inference is that had he trained as a pilot directly and not at Dayton, he would have encountered no 'risks'. He would also have been made a Probationary Flight Sub-Lieutenant upon joining up, which is why, in the following paragraph mention is now made of his commissioning, for the Probationary rank did not hold a commission.]

After being accepted at Montreal, and commissioned, Brown sailed for England from New York in December of the same year.

While in training for combat at Chingford, England, Brown crashed and broke a bone in his spine which kept him confined in a hospital until January of 1917.

Then, as a Sub-Lieutenant of the Royal Navy, he was assigned to land duty in France with Squadron 9 of the naval aviation corps. [this should have been, of course, the Royal Naval Air Service.] *His unit patrolled the Belgian coast, escorted bombing raids, engaged in photographic and reconnaissance work, and offensive flights over the German lines as far south as the British area extended.* [As a scouting squadron 9 Naval Squadron's duties, flying Sopwith Triplanes and then Camels, would ordinarily not include photographic and recce work, although they would have escorted two-seater aircraft that were engaged in such activities.]

From January 1917 to April 1, 1918, this work continued with Brown chalking up a large number of planes to his credit. He believes his official record is 15 German planes, but in company with many other pilots he did not report his victories, leaving that to other observers due to the habit, he said, of many aviators discrediting their work by telling too many tall stories. [This seems to be something of a myth that was created post-war, whereby many

high scoring pilots were supposed not to have made claims against enemy aircraft. Brown's combat reports exist and as it was a positive requirement that pilots complete or at least dictate them, this at first glance appears to be something of a post-war journalistic statement in order not to show Brown, or anyone else, as a glorified scalp hunter. In fact Brown's combat record indicates claims for three German aircraft destroyed and another six 'out of control' (ie not seen to crash), between 17 July 1917 and 12 April 1918.]

However, his work was recognised by the award of the Distinguished Service Cross and promotion to the full rank of Flight Lieutenant, Royal Navy, which ranked an army captain. [In fact it only ranked as a Full Lieutenant., one up from Second Lieutenant, which was the Flight Sub-Lieutenant rank equivalent.]

When the naval fliers were consolidated with the Royal Flying Corps, into the Royal Air Forces [sic], operating independently of either army or navy, Brown became a Flight Commander, with the rank of Captain [and now equivalent to an army Captain, not to be confused with a naval Captain which is the equivalent of an army Colonel. 9 Naval Squadron RNAS then became 209 Squadron RAF.]

He remembers few details of this period and has practically no records so refused to talk of his services. His succeeding history is recorded in the story of his victory over Richthofen. [This might well be pure modesty on his part, which is not unknown among airmen of any war, but especially Brown who was being constantly asked about his career following the Richthofen fight.]

An interesting point is that when the RFC and RNAS merged, former RNAS personnel were not required to purchase new uniforms, for the RAF did not have one. Like most RFC pilots joining or transferring from army regiments, it was far more expedient and cost effective to continue using their regiment uniforms over the left breast pockets of which they would have their wings or half-wings sewn. Only direct entrants would need to have the well-known 'maternity' jackets of the RFC.

Many former RNAS men would, as a matter of pride, make sure they continued to wear their dark blue naval uniforms, some right up till the Armistice, and RAF uniforms, per se, were not available until well after the war. It is worth noting that a careful examination of several photographs of Brown reveals that his jacket sleeves have rings of a naval lieutenant around the cuffs. The point is made because of the assumed identity of the visiting pilot who was seen at the von Richthofen crash site.

In the Public Records Office, the *Summary* (also undated) is entitled *Material on Brown for Gibbons' Richthofen Story*. A complete and verbatim transcript is to be found in Appendix C.

A point by point critique of the contents of the Material on Brown presented in the *Summary* would be to give it more attention than it deserves. Appendix C contains a selection taken from the major errors which should suffice to prove that document is seriously flawed.

Gibbons also received at least two more documents:

1. A transcript, with one omission and a few inconsequential changes of arrangement, of the second Combats in the Air report written by Captain Brown and dated 21 April 1918. The omission, which was the description of the armament fitted to Captain Brown's Camel, was to cause embarrassment for Gibbons when the first edition of his book was published.

2. Some information assembled from the first two medical examinations which stated that there had been only one bullet, defined its path as being from right to left and affirmed that it could only have been fired from the air.

The *Summary* gave the direction of Brown's attack as from above and behind. The *Anonymous Account* did not mention it. In the serialized version (about 25 parts) published in *Liberty* magazine starting around June 1927, Gibbons used the *Summary's* version of Brown's dive on von Richthofen but corrected the machine-gun error. (The *Summary* described Lewis guns whereas Brown's Camel had Vickers.)

It was not the only time Gibbons took the preferred route, nor was he above 'correcting' documents to substantiate his conclusions. Take for instance his account of von Richthofen's combat of 29 April 1917. It was unfortunate that the Baron did not record the type of machine he shot down (victory 52) only that he had been in combat with Nieuports, Spads and Triplanes. As, presumably, he could find no Triplane loss but had a very fine Nieuport pilot (Captain F L Barwell) being shot down that day, he 'corrected' the translation of von Richthofen's combat report to read: 'Plane: Nieuport one-seater, no details, as plane burned', adding the - 'Nieuport one-seater..' in front of Richthofen's: 'No details....'

He then went on to ignore Richthofen's comment about shooting the British aircraft down after a short time, knowing full well that the report on Barwell's loss, showed the combat had lasted half an hour. He even ignored the fact that the German Nachrichtenblatt clearly identified the victory as a Sopwith Driedekker, for a Sopwith Triplane it indeed was, from 8 Naval Squadron. Bearing this sort of alteration in mind, one has to be very careful about other things Gibbons may have recorded as being 'official'. In other words, while Gibbons was occasionally misled, he also misled his readers.

Gibbons' next step has served to bedevil researchers for the next 60 years. The medical information regarding the direction of the bullet (right to left) was in conflict with the *Summary* which stated left to right. Gibbons did not know that Captain Brown, who surely was aware of his own actions, had stated that he had been on the left hand side of the Triplane when he opened fire. Gibbons therefore chose to prefer the medical examination version, which was not unreasonable under the circumstances.

In the book form, first published in November 1927, in order to match Brown's attack to the true direction of the wound, he added, not as an opinion, but as a statement of fact, the word 'right'. He wrote as follows:

But Brown had arrived at the end of his dive. He came out of it slightly above and to the right of the darting Fokker.

He watched the tracer bullets going to the red Triplane from the right side. They hit the tail first. A slight pull on the stick – a fractional elevation of the Camel's nose, and the Canadian's line of fire started to tuck a seam up the body of the Fokker.

Brown saw his tracers penetrate the side of the Fokker's cockpit.

It is worth noting that the two phrases: 'A slight pull on the stick – a fractional elevation of the Camel's nose...' are taken word for word from the *Summary*. They will re-appear, paraphrased, in *My Fight with Richthofen* (see Appendix E), viz.: 'Very gently I pulled on the stick. The nose of the Camel rose ever so slightly. The stream of bullets tore along the body of the all-red tripe.'

The 'slight elevation of fire' business actually originated from the *Anonymous Account*, which tells the reader:

'His first bullets ripped through the fuselage of the enemy plane. We saw him elevate his fire slightly.'

If the *Anonymous Account*, the *Summary*, *The Red Knight of Germany*, and *My Fight with Richthofen*, are carefully compared in that order, it will be seen that in many areas each one is an amplified re-write of its predecessor. Even Quentin Reynolds, author of *They Fought for the Sky* (Cassell & Co, 1958 – and incidentally the book credited with starting the whole new wave of post-WW2 interest in WW1) was taken in. Basically speaking, the fact that the two major works of the late 1920s are in agreement on many points which were later disputed by Titler and Carisella, means nothing historically. If a dozen writers state that Wilfred May came from Melbourne, Australia, it proves nothing if each one has used the same flawed source.

And of course, journalistic licence only adds to the confusion: eg: '...watched the tracer bullets going to the red Triplane ...' '... line of fire started to tuck a seam up the body of the Fokker.' '.. saw his tracers penetrate the side of the .. cockpit.' This is what the layman 'sees' in his mind's eye, the dramatic, rather than the historic. Hollywood's air aces always stitch a close line of bullet holes in the target, so this is what must occur in real life!

The Aftermath

Gibbons' work, *The Red Knight of Germany*, has been published in more than twenty editions over the years and was serialised again, this time in the *Chicago Tribune*. The flawed information was continually recycled.

In different editions of the serialisation and/or the book, some of the errors instanced above were corrected. The case of Gibbons not having information or proper knowledge on the type of armament fitted to

Captain Brown's Sopwith Camel caused him much grief. The *Liberty* serialized version said: '.. his last belt of ammunition was in place.' This suggested it was something Brown had fitted prior to his last attack. Unfortunately the Vickers machine-gun belts on a Sopwith Camel could only be changed on the ground, and even worse, two men were required to perform the operation. The book form circumvented the belt problem by going back to the *Summary* and stating: '.. his last drum of ammunition was in place' and thereby unwittingly introduced further error. Drums were fitted on Lewis guns, not Vickers.

A similar case occurred when Gibbons tried to correct the erroneous information that Captain Brown organised the removal of von Richthofen's body from the red Triplane. Gibbons nominated Lieutenant Mellersh in Brown's place, which was also incorrect. He was right in so far as it was an airman, but it was actually Lieutenant Warneford of 3 AFC Squadron.

It appears that rather than consult the Air Ministry in London, Gibbons would have done much better to have travelled to Canada and to have interviewed Roy Brown, always assuming he had not already tried and been rebuffed. Incidentally, Roy is his correct name, not Royal as has sometimes been stated.

In short, Floyd Gibbons honest, best efforts were seriously flawed due to no fault of his own. Who, in his situation, would entertain doubts as to the veracity and completeness of information provided by the Air Ministry. It would never have crossed his mind that it

had been selected so as to provide a specific conclusion and that any evidence to the contrary had been downplayed or totally omitted.

There is also some irony too that Gibbons, as well as adding a few 'facts' to fit his researches, sometimes missed an important point. When he was writing his book he enquired of Air Ministry about a certain Sergeant McCudden, and was he the man known later as Captain James McCudden VC? They confirmed this to be so and in hindsight it appears that Gibbons had stumbled upon the possibility that Sergeant McCudden had possibly been the Baron's opponent on 27 December 1916. With the limited information available to Gibbons in the 1920s he could not take the premise further and so missed the vital clues that showed that McCudden was indeed his 15th 'victory', although in this particular case it was one that got away.

Gibbons' legacy to mankind is that from 1928 onwards most drawings and paintings show Brown attacking from the right, and this has become the popular belief or misconception. Other artists have placed all three aircraft in a line astern chase situation along the Somme canal, May-von Richthofen-Brown, which is equally incorrect.

For historical purposes both the *Summary* and the chapters in *The Red Knight of Germany* which cover the death of the Baron have no value whatsoever. They may be said to contribute negatively to a proper understanding of what happened on those two fateful days in April 1918.

APPENDIX E: *MY FIGHT WITH RICHTHOFEN*

In 1927 the US magazine *Liberty* began publishing articles on the air fighting during the First World War. A short story, developed from an interview with Captain Brown on his career in the RNAS and RAF, was published in the edition dated 6 November 1927 and was later serialised in several newspapers.

Upon transcribing his notes, the copywriter converted serious facts into a thrilling story for boys by 'jazzing up' what he had been told and by including additional information drawn from material found in previously published stories. The *Anonymous Account* was one of them as was an early version of Gibbons' *Red Knight of Germany* whose serialisation had just ended in the magazine, so it comes as no surprise that 22 German aircraft are again mentioned. To do the copywriter justice, he, doubtless, was doing his best to make the story interesting by filling in details which Roy Brown had apparently omitted. It is quite probable that the copywriter was merely composing an entertaining story and that it never crossed his mind that his efforts might be taken to represent history or that some of his additions might be seriously flawed. Indeed, some of his effort found its way into the British Official History of the Great War which was being written around this time. Information on the end of the Red Devil was scarce and *Liberty* seemed to have what was needed.

By a 'tail wagging the dog' process, the items 'borrowed' from *My Fight with Richthofen*, and now wearing the clothes of the Official History, have been presented by some as proof that the former represents the truth, the whole truth and nothing but the truth. Such had happened once before. Sir Arthur Conan Doyle took the findings of the abandoned sailing ship *Mary Celeste* (the correct name) as the idea for a thrilling story. He named his ship *Marie Celeste* and added many mysterious items such as a ticking clock, warm food found on the table and the Long Boat still present. Sir Arthur was most surprised when his artistry was taken to be the latest information and the official history in a shipping company was 'corrected' to suit.

Although the title block did not specifically so state, its wording encouraged the reader to believe that Captain Brown had written or at least dictated every word of the story. However, the contents clearly indicate that this was not so. The obvious give-away is the citing of RAF 209 Squadron as existing on 21 March 1918. To have served in 9 Naval Squadron was considered to be a distinction and Captain Brown would not have forgotten the date, 1 April 1918, when the military world around him changed.

Whoever made the final draught was not an aircraft pilot, was unfamiliar with rotary engines and combat instructions and did not know how the most famous Allied and German wartime airmen had been killed. Even worse, he had no idea of the true condition of the pilot's seat from von Richthofen's Triplane which was Captain Brown's personal trophy of the event, and had

been in his personal possession for over one year before he donated it to the Canadian Military Institute's private museum. In short, *My Fight with Richthofen* parallels the tale of the *Marie Celeste* in that more people appear to be familiar with the fiction than the facts.

It would seem that Captain Brown, who had accepted payment for his story, which was published on 26 November 1927, had not been given the right of approval over the final text. This placed him in a difficult position when what had been published as 'his version of events' was challenged by people who had also participated. When the Official Australian Historian asked him for his personal comments on the story, Brown declined the invitation on the ground that he was not a reader of *Liberty* magazine. The careful wording of his reply, which evades the issue, tells quite a lot. Being short of money, having signed a receipt and with two more stories to be published (*Dirty Work at the Cross-roads*, 24 December 1927 and *Nighthawks* the following week) by the same magazine, he would hardly wish to antagonise his benefactor.

In 1971 the Editor of *Liberty* responded in print to a request for clarification on the authorship. In Volume 1, No.3, he offered the following statement. The operative words are 'probably', 'won't rule out' and 'not unusual'. To anyone who reads it carefully, the meaning, written between the lines, is quite clear.

Roy Brown was paid for the article and probably contributed all or most of the facts. We won't rule out the possibility that the piece was ghost-written but this is not unusual in any national magazine.

As tacitly admitted by the 1971 Editor, the article is a mixture of fact and fiction. Historically speaking, it is extremely dangerous as there is more than enough fact and detail to make the whole story seem to be genuine to anyone unfamiliar with the items, situations and events described.

The most unfortunate part of all is that some recent scholarly works have, in complete innocence, quoted items from earlier well-known works which had in turn derived them from the flawed parts of *My Fight with Richthofen*. In modern parlance one can say that certain events or descriptions have been 'laundered' until their true origin has been lost and they have become accepted truth. They continue to appear again and again, even in major newspapers, when certain anniversaries come around.

A small selection of easily provable deviations from the truth follows below. The page references are for the reprint in *Liberty*, Autumn 1971, Volume 1, No.2.

1. The seat, page 55, middle left.
   Starting at the elevator, bullets had ripped their way along the fuselage: bullets fired from above and behind. They had travelled right along to the cockpit. There were holes in the cockpit. Blood spattered the seat. There was a hole in it.

Apart from blood on the seat, the entire statement is untrue. The seat was officially given to Captain Brown as his personal souvenir (he had actually requested the engine) and he was well aware that there was no hole in it that could have been made by a 0.303" bullet, or indeed any bullet, and that it was on display in Toronto. There is ample photographic documentation and testimony from 3 Squadron AFC personnel, including two officers, Lieutenant W J Warneford and Captain R Ross, on the absence of bullet holes in the area specified. Although there is no confirmation that Brown looked at the dismantled Triplane when it arrived at Poulainville, it is highly unlikely that he failed to do so.

Brown would also have known that having attacked towards the left-hand side of the Triplane as he intercepted its line of flight, his fire would not have 'stitched' its way up from the tail to cockpit, the way a layman would describe an assumed attack from the more usual astern (six o'clock) position.

It has been postulated by historian Frank McGuire that when Brown discovered that the text to be published was not quite what he had in mind and that *Liberty* would accept no changes, he caused the display location of the seat to be added so that anyone who cared to look at it would learn that the article had been 'edited'.

2. The Crash Site, page 55, upper left.

We (Col. Cairnes and Capt. Brown) walked towards the place where the red Triplane lay. It was possibly a mile and a half away (from the battery). A road ran part of the distance. Then we entered the reserve trenches. And shortly we saw the machine. It lay on high ground, between the trenches, in what was once a cultivated field. Sticking to the trenches we got as close to it as we could, but it was still possibly 100 yards away.

The road did NOT stop short of the crash site. The reserve trenches were NOT on the route from the battery to the crash site. The Triplane was NOT in between the trenches on the high ground; it was about 800 yards south-east of them and on the opposite side of the road. No-one at the crash site has ever mentioned seeing Cairnes or Brown there.

Captain Brown knew full well where the crash site was located. The copywriter appears to have composed his location from descriptions given in the *Summary* and in the *Red Knight of Germany*.

3. Von Richthofen's Body, page 54, middle left.

Cairns (mis-spelled all through the article) asked the whereabouts of the body, and was told that it had been turned over to the Royal Air Force. We learned later this was done only after a verbal dog fight. The Aussies had not wanted to part with it.

Captain Brown was well aware that 3 AFC at Poulainville had jurisdiction and that all the examinations and official procedures including the burial had been conducted under its CO, Major D V J Blake.

The paragraph on page 54 which follows the one transcribed above contradicts it in that according to the copywriter, Brown then proceeds to examine the body that is not there. Brown was well aware when he first saw the body; it was at Poulainville that evening. He so stated in a letter to his father.

The entire episode, as presented by the copywriter, is pure invention.

4. Deaths of the Aces, page 42, top right.

The greatest of them – Boelcke, Ball, Guynemer, McCudden, died like the poorest dub when an enemy pilot spewed a straight burst at the right moment.

Only Guynemer was shot down, and there is a question as to whether by plane or by ground fire. The other three were killed in flying accidents which were used in Advanced Flying Schools as examples not to be copied, Boelcke collided in air combat, Ball became disoriented in cloud, and McCudden, suffering engine failure, turned back rather than make a forced landing straight ahead. Brown, who served as an instructor, was certainly aware of the truth and would not have subscribed to such nonsense.

5. Engine Trouble, page 52, top right.

[After shooting down von Richthofen] I turned towards Bertangles …. Only three cylinders were hitting [firing]. The propeller was scarcely turning over. But I made the 'drome.

No aeroplane pilot would have written that! However, it is an improvement on the *Summary* which allowed Brown only two cylinders out of the nine.

An aeroplane with a rotary engine in that condition would be likely to catch fire in short time. Unburned petrol would be issuing from the six spinning exhaust ports, collecting inside the cowling and then washing along the bottom of the fuselage just waiting for a spark. The loss of power would be far too great for the Camel to maintain height and the vibration from the unbalanced forces would cause rapid failure of the engine support frame.

A pilot of the calibre and experience of Roy Brown would instinctively have switched OFF his engine and made a precautionary landing. Even over enemy territory, no pilot who valued his skin would have done otherwise. The story is probably a gross exaggeration by the copywriter of some lesser difficulty described by Brown, although nowhere else is there a mention of a problem with his engine.

6. Decorations, page 56, top right.

I was given neither decoration nor award, although two Australian Tommies were credited with receiving Distinguished Conduct Medals for their unsuccessful shooting from the trenches.

The entire statement is untrue. Lieutenant May is on record as being amazed when he read it. It would appear to be a dramatised distortion of Brown's disappointment that the recommendation that he be awarded the

Distinguished Service Order (DSO) was not approved. That would not be shabby treatment; the DSO is but one step below the Victoria Cross and requires great bravery in action on the occasion for which it is awarded.

Instead, later in the year, at a ceremony conducted by the Prince of Wales, he was awarded a Bar to his Distinguished Service Cross. This decoration was more applicable to the circumstances. The complete recommendation is to be found in Appendix J.

No Australian received a medal of any kind whatsoever.

It may come as a surprise to the reader to learn that the well-known story of von Richthofen looking round to see who was firing at him originated in *My Fight with Richthofen* on page 52, bottom left. To look round is the reaction of a novice and it was in such a way that a surprisingly high number of newly graduated pilots met their death, for, whilst they were looking round (instead of getting out of the line of fire), their attacker – most likely with the sun behind him – was correcting his aim.

If a novice pilot survived long enough to conquer that fatal, although natural, reaction, he had a chance to see the end of the war. The reader may recall that on the silver screen the hero pilot always hears shots, looks round puzzled, (probably curses: swine! if he is British; schweinhund! if German) and is then killed from behind (accompanied by a small trickle of blood from one corner of his mouth). An excellent book: *No Parachute*, by the late AVM Arthur Gould Lee MC (Jarrolds 1968), contains a good description of how by bitter experience he learned how not to look round if attacked and that it was by the grace of the enemy's poor marksmanship that he reached that level of expertise.

Von Richthofen was not a novice; it was well-known by the British aces who tangled with him that at the first sign or sound of a shot he took sharp evasive action. He only survived in front-line duty for eighteen months by being quick. Gould Lee commented that he could never hold von Richthofen in a good position long enough to take aim and then fire. With that in mind, *My Fight with Richthofen*, in sentences too close to the *Summary* for co-incidence, asks its readers to believe that despite the loud Rak-ak-ak noise of bullets striking his tail, von Richthofen calmly flew straight ahead and allowed Brown to correct his aim. That he then continued to fly straight ahead whilst hearing Brown's bullets stitching their way up the fuselage to the cockpit and that his only defensive manoeuvre was to look round. The mind boggles at the ineptitude. It is fortunate that many photographs of that part of the fuselage (despite the ravages of looters and souvenir hunters) and tail/elevators still exist to counter the slur on the Baron's intelligence and proficiency.

The 'looked round' story is obviously an addition which the copywriter thought applicable to the circumstances and tacked onto the scenario 'lifted' from the *Summary*. The authors have been surprised at the number of people who have heard that *My Fight with Richthofen* is seriously flawed and yet have firmly

believed, until advised of the origin of the tale, that von Richthofen did indeed look round when he saw tracer coming his way.

Dirty Work at the Cross-roads (*Liberty*, 24 December 1927).

Reference was made earlier to Roy Brown's second contribution to the magazine. Basically it follows the same pattern as the first one; Brown's story has been heavily edited to heighten suspense and to create thrills. The description of how to dive a Sopwith Camel has no relation with reality. Once again truth has been converted into a load of old rabbit:

> *Down went the stick. And down went the nose of the Camel, plumb vertical, engine full out. That was one wild dive! In eight seconds we dropped 8,000 feet.*

Pilots were taught NEVER to dive a Camel vertically. It tended, against the pilot's wishes, to go 'over vertical' and to progress into an inverted dive from which recovery in one piece was extremely difficult. The lack of knowledge of the copywriter who 'enhanced' Brown's account is indisputably revealed by a simple conversion into Miles Per Hour of the stated descent rate of 1,000 feet per second.

Every pilot knows that Miles Per Hour, divided by two, gives Yards Per Second fairly closely. 1,000 feet is equal to 333.3 yards, therefore, the descent given by the copywriter would be approximately 667 mph. (The calculated answer is actually 682 mph.) This is more than three times the speed at which a Camel's fuselage would leave the wings behind, and is faster than every jetliner in service in 1997 except for Concorde.

Let the Reader be the Judge

The reader, who by now should be aware of the relative positions of the three aeroplanes, is invited to decide which is true; Lieutenant May's written assertion that he did not see Brown attack von Richthofen, or the following statement in *My Fight with Richthofen* on page 52, middle left:

Then he (May) heard my guns. He flashed a look. 'Thank God, its Brownie.'

Conclusion

Rather than supporting Captain Brown as having shot down von Richthofen, the heavy editing of his story has destroyed his credibility by using obvious falsehoods to present his case.

APPENDIX F: EVEN OFFICIAL HISTORIAN TAKEN IN
British Official History of the Great War • The War in the Air

The RAF Official History of the Great War (World War 1) contains the following description of the death of Rittmeister Freiherr Manfred von Richthofen. It was written, after considerable debate and argument, by the RAF Official Historian, H A Jones, in 1932. The significance of the date is that it was compiled three years after the publication of Gibbons' *The Red Knight of Germany* and *My Fight with Richthofen* (Appendix E). A comparison of those two stories with the Official History (below) reveals a further step in the progress of what began as an *Anonymous Account* (Appendix B). There is a marked similarity to the process by which the sailing ship *Mary Celeste* became the *Marie Celeste*.

At this moment he [von Richthofen] was seen by Captain Brown who had eluded converging attacks by two Fokkers and was climbing rapidly again to rejoin the other 'Camels' in the main fight. At first Captain Brown thought that Second Lieutenant May (with whom he had been at school in Edmonton, Alberta) was beyond danger, but almost at once he noticed the triplane diving on the tail of the 'Camel'. Soon the 'Camel' was twisting and zigzagging with Richthofen closely following every movement until the moment should arrive when he could, as he had so often done before, begin and end the fight with a short burst of bullets fired from decisive range. Captain Brown was not aware of the identity of the Fokker pilot, but that Second Lieutenant May was in jeopardy was obvious enough, and the Flight-Commander thereupon dived steeply to his subordinate's help. By this time the aeroplanes were near the Australian front-line trenches. [1] Brown came out of his dive above and to the right [2] of Richthofen who, his eyes fixed on the elusive 'Camel' ahead of him, was oblivious of the danger which threatened. The German leader was caught in a position from which few pilots, no matter how skilled or confident, could expect to escape. As a burst of fire came from the twin machine-guns of the 'Camel', Richthofen turned in his cockpit. [3] It seemed to Captain Brown that he then crumpled [4], and the Fokker zigzagged to a rough landing two miles inside the British lines ......

Authors' notes. The items 1-4 are explained below. The tail is doing more than wagging the dog; it is positively shaking it.

[1] Taken from the *Summary*. In truth, the aeroplanes had already crossed the Australian front lines and were almost two miles deep into Allied territory.
[2] Taken from *The Red Knight of Germany*. Brown stated many times in Canada that he was behind, above and to the left of the Triplane.
[3] Taken from *My Fight with Richthofen*. An ace pilot on either side would 'break' first and then look round.
[4] Taken from the *Anonymous Account*. Those who saw it happen said that von Richthofen stiffened and his head fell to one side, or that he seemed to shrug, but this action was some time after Brown's attack, and after Richthofen had survived the machine guns of the 53rd Battery and was heading for home.

A continuation of the Official History, in a possible oblique reference to the arguments with C E W Bean, states:

The official decision was that Richthofen was killed by a bullet from the machine guns of Captain A R Brown.

Re-examination of all evidence, official and un-official tends to confirm this decision in the field,....... It is impossible to see how any of the bullets fired from specified machine-guns on the ground could have entered the German Pilot's body from the right-hand side.

The reference to a 'decision in the field' which is earlier called 'the official decision' is puzzling. Neither the discussion on the evening of 21 April nor the meeting held on 2 May were official in nature. (See Chapter 15) The British Fourth Army Official Enquiry, of which a complete record exists, decided that Gunners Buie and Evans had been responsible.

Even more puzzling is the disqualification of Buie, Evans and Popkin due to the allegation [incorrect] that they could not possibly have fired at the right-hand side of the Triplane. That argument apparently does not apply to Captain Brown who could not have done so either.

The argument that the RAF official History confirms the truth of *My Flight with Richthofen* has no validity whatsoever; the former being largely derived from the latter.

APPENDIX G: Lt BANKS' ACCOUNT
(Written in 1962)

Many stories have been told regarding Baron von Richthofen's last fight and his final defeat on the 21st April 1918. These accounts have mostly been compiled by persons other than combatants. They all differ so fundamentally it is safe to say they cannot all be true.

My story of Baron von Richthofen's last battle has never been told publicly though I have had many requests to publish it. I could see no benefit by being involved in this ever-green controversy.

I believe the four Australian airmen from No.3 AFC, Lieutenants Garrett and Barrow in Number 1 machine, with Lieutenants Simpson and Banks in Number 2 machine, who fought von Richthofen that day, shot down the red triplane and drove down another triplane damaged. My story is supported by many precise and indisputable facts as set out in this document.

For some days before April 21, 1918, the Australians were warned that the Germans had massed their strongest air squadrons opposite our front with the intention of driving the British from the air in this sector.

About 10 am on the 21st, two RE8 machines from 3 Squadron AFC flown by the above officers set out on a mission to photograph the corps front, a routine performance every few weeks. The flight arrived in position about 10.20 and commenced photography with Number 2 machine (Simpson and Banks) towards the Germans and Number 1 machine (Garrett and Barrow) on the Australian side flying North.

Some six photographs had been taken by each machine when we saw a close formation of about eight triplanes heading directly towards us. The observers, Barrow and Banks, signalled each other and manned their Lewis guns for an attack. As the Germans drew close two triplanes swept away from the formation as shown in diagram 'X' on page 136 and one attacked one of our planes. The leader was a red Triplane.

Both of our gunners were experienced at this type of fighting and the pilots knew their battle tactics. Each time a triplane tried to manoeuvre on to the tail of an RE8 our pilot turned his machine around and the procedures started all over again. Our machines kept together and protected each other.

This fight lasted about six to eight minutes while von Richthofen and his mate were always under fire. The fight was at short range and the airmen could see one another clearly.

Suddenly the red triplane turned over and fell away rapidly. Barrow and Banks then concentrated their fire on the remaining triplane. He took a bad battering and after splinters were seen to fly from his wings pulled out of the fight and dived for home.

This fight occurred a few minutes before the recorded time when von Richthofen crashed and was precisely above the pin-point on the military map where his plane landed. The mosaic diagram of photographs prepared in the mapping section of the Squadron clearly shows a gap in the sequence around the crash point. With the combat finished the two RE8 machines continued their photographic programme.

This was a wild day for Lieutenant Simpson and Banks. About half an hour later they were again confronted by a formation of some twelve Albatros planes flying at 7,000 feet. As this 'armada' approached Simpson and Banks, now separated from the other plane, assumed the big formation was a squadron of our own machines and flew over to take a photograph.

Their amazement was complete when suddenly they could see a mass of Maltese crosses and wildly gesticulating German airmen in the cockpits. Fight was out of the question as their ammunition was almost exhausted. Simpson put the RE8 into a steep dive and passed through the Germans so closely that their faces were clearly visible. The long dive continued for about 6,000 feet while the whole German formation broke and followed like hornets. The Australian machine was riddled and broken control wires streamed out behind but at 200 feet Simpson pulled out and hedge-hopped home.

The reports of these adventures were written and recorded by our four officers in the Squadron headquarters before it became known that von Richthofen had been shot down. The four officers were overwhelmed with congratulations by the commanding officer and staff officers of the Wing.

A party was sent from the Squadron to collect the body of the German airman and the remains of his plane. Both were placed under guard in one of our squadron hangers for a post mortem to determine the fatal wound. About 20 officers attended the final examination when Richthofen's uniform was carefully cut from his body. The fatal bullet entered about 3 inches below and behind the right armpit. It pierced his lungs and emerged from the left chest about 4 inches below and in front of the left armpit. It was formally decided that this bullet was fired in aerial combat and could not have been fired from the ground as had been rumoured.

Von Richthofen's pockets contained miscellaneous items including 5,000 French francs, letters and articles which might serve him in case of his capture. Many of the articles were commandeered by the officers present. While this court was in session souvenir hunters were busy stripping the triplane. My share was a piece of red fabric, a length of driving chain and a wire strainer. Over the years the red fabric has shrunk considerably and now measures only four inches by two.

A full military funeral was accorded our late enemy. His coffin was placed on a gun carriage and drawn to the military cemetery near Bertangles. Four Australian Flying Officers including myself were the pall-bearers into the graveyard. The ceremony was most imposing and a mark of respect for a tough fighter. The cross [on the grave] was cut from the four-bladed propeller of an RE8.

After the burial a request was received from the German Flying Corps seeking permission to drop a wreath on the grave. I understand that this was given and a wreath dropped, but I did not witness the event.

Authors' Note

A German account of the fight with the RE8s published on 23 April 1918 in the *Tägliche Rundschau* by war correspondent W Scheuermann, names the five pilots in the flight led by von Richthofen whilst Leutnant Richard Wenzl, in his book *Richthofen Flieger* places Leutnant Weiss as leader of the second flight. He was accompanied by Wenzl and two other un-named pilots. On this basis it might appear that one of the un-named pilots was Lieutenant Banks's adversary, not von Richthofen. Banks may have failed to notice that the Triplane attacking him carried a pilot's personal identification insignia or colour in addition to the red

fabric. However, this is conjecture and it should be remembered that it was usual for the leader always to attack first; ie: Richthofen in this case. Richthofen and Weiss being leaders of both flights of Triplanes, were most likely to have been the attackers.

It was the German tactic that the leader would always attack first, supported and protected by his men. It is this tactic that is often overlooked and ignored by those who wish to denigrate Richthofen's prowess by saying he always picked out a victim to attack whilst others covered him. That is exactly right and proved its worth, not only with Jasta 11 and JGI but with every other Jasta, whose Staffelführer or flight leader made the initial attack. Only after this did the others break off to engage other aircraft as the dog fight developed. This was nothing peculiar to the Germans, the RFC and RAF used much the same tactics after 1916, the leader generally controlling his pilots up to the initial clash and signalling the attack. Of course, there would always be the hot-head who would break off and attack on his own.

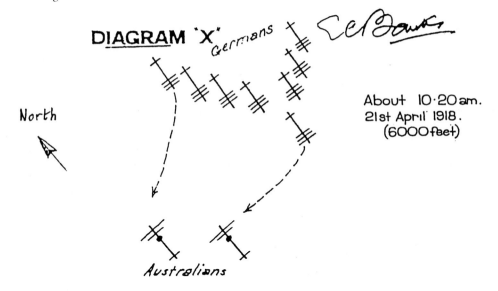

APPENDIX H: THE EFFECTS OF VON RICHTHOFEN'S WOUND PATH

The authors of this book gave the Graham/Downs and the Sinclair/Nixon post mortem reports to a highly experienced pathologist who lives in Grimsby, Ontario, Canada. He studied them for some time, discussed them with colleagues and gave the following opinion in non-medical terms which is reproduced below with his kind permission:

There is a noticeable difference in the degree of medical detail documented in the first two post-mortem examinations.

Without the precise descriptions of the location of the entry wound and of the exit wound given by Colonels Sinclair and Nixon, I could not have determined either of the two possible paths of the bullet. The ribs slope downwards and by themselves are imprecise reference points. The Colonels, by stating that the entry wound was just ahead of where the ninth rib crosses the posterior axillary line, have pin-pointed its position. Similarly, the male nipple, in the vertical plane it is normally on the fifth rib. However, in the horizontal plane its position varies widely from man to man.

The entry and exit wounds as described would place the path of the bullet through the vital organs of the thorax. The bullet most likely punctured the aorta if it passed posteriorly [dog-legged via the spine] or the heart if it passed anteriorly [straight through]. If we also take into account that the bullet was tumbling as it passed through the body, the injuries would indeed be devastating. The expected result would be massive internal and external haemorrhage.

Regardless of whether this injury caused immediate death or not, it would certainly cause immediate severe functional impairment. It is extremely unlikely for an aircraft pilot with such an injury to retain the ability to control an aircraft in the skilful fashion described by witnesses on the ground.

In summary, the severity of MvR's injury would be expected to cause profound functional impairment especially including the co-ordination of the eyes with the hands, and death within a matter or seconds, not minutes.

Dr. José Segura MDCM (McGill)
Pathologist.

Doctor Segura then mentioned a point that had just occurred to him. The type of wound suffered by von Richthofen would most likely result in an immediate spasm of muscular contraction. Such spasms have been mentioned by Lothar von Richthofen (Manfred's brother – 40 victories in WW1 – who survived the war but died in a crash in 1922), by Arthur Gould Lee MC, (later Air Vice-Marshal) and others. This agrees with Private Wormald's statement: 'When the Baron was hit, the Triplane began to climb steeply,' and with Sergeant Darbyshire's: 'The Triplane seemed to run into a brick wall.'

Von Richthofen's reaction to pull back on the stick, and probably move it to the right also – the roll to the right as observed – would logically have been the same at whatever map location the bullet struck him. However, according to Brown, von Richthofen's response to his burst of fire ('He went down vertical') was the exact opposite of the expected initial effect of such a wound. This is a statement of profound significance because it confirms medically that von Richthofen's fatal wound was not acquired above the mud flats down in the valley beside the southern face of the Ridge. This realization had apparently occurred 40 years ago to the authors of *Von Richthofen and the Flying Circus* (Harleyford) who found that it could only be explained, within the knowledge available at that time, if Captain Brown had made a second and un-noticed attack upon the Triplane about 20 seconds before it made its rapid descent. They therefore posited that such an attack had taken place about 300 feet overhead and in front of a good 500 soldiers, none of whom noticed it.

Until Doctor Segura referred the present authors to Doctor David L King, the fact that a 0.303" British Army rifle bullet tumbles during a long passage through tissue had not been appreciated by them. This

characteristic of a Spitzer-shaped bullet was confirmed by ballistics expert Peter Franks. In the light of this information, which was new to them (and one suspects by many others before us – NF/AB), the authors looked back into medical opinions gathered many years earlier by Frank McGuire and Pasquale Carisella. They agree in principle that the wound was severe, that there would be a strong reaction in the nervous system of the body and that the wound would prove mortal in one minute or less. One of the surgeons said that probable cause of death would have been a massive loss of blood.

In short, the medical evidence as interpreted by Doctor Segura agrees with the testimony gathered by John Coltman.

A Different Opinion

In the 1980s two or three American doctors and/or surgeons attempted to analyse the effects of such a wound as that suffered by the Baron. They 'proved' that he could have lived for two or three minutes and have guided an aeroplane through intricate manoeuvres during that time before suddenly collapsing. One even stated that people shot in such a manner had been known to survive. That misleads by placing 'possibility' ahead of 'probability', and not taking the type of bullet into consideration.

Unfortunately, in the USA and Canada, many seem to have to accepted the 'possibility' as being what happened in the Baron's case. A few years ago, the theme was re-cycled in a presentation and an article which required Brown to have attacked von Richthofen from the right near Sailly-le-Sec. When all three inputs to an evaluation are incorrect, the answer hardly merits confidence.

Unlike the commonly cited excerpts, the *complete* report by these doctors clearly states that their opinion was based upon a shot inflicted on a deer by a bullet from an American deer hunting 0.3" 30/30 cartridge. Whether the bullet passed through the heart from front to back or from side to side was not specified. The effect of the 30/30 is so different from a British Army standard 0.303" rifle bullet as to make any comparison meaningless.

A 0.303" bullet would not have made a hole through von Richthofen's heart, it would have torn a huge channel through it, whilst, with deflection off the spinal column, it would have carved a chunk out of the aorta and the oesophagus. The final result of either path, when created by a tumbling 0.303" bullet, would have been the same, therefore to argue which one was followed is a wasted exercise. Also, due to the distance travelled through the tissues of the Baron's body, the exit wound would have had the same appearance in either case; namely the typical shape caused by a 0.303" bullet travelling somewhere between side-first and base-first.

APPENDIX I: MACHINE-GUN STOPPAGES AND TYPES OF 0.303" AMMUNITION

Sir Hiram Maxim's belt-fed machine gun was adopted by several countries, each of which made redesigns to suit circumstances and requirements. However, the basic principle remained the same.

In England, the Maxim gun developed into the Vickers water-cooled machine gun and used the same size Spitzer-type 0.303" (7.69 mm) ammunition as the Lee-Enfield infantry rifle. The bullets (projectiles) were identical.

The Maxim gun, as redesigned in Germany, used the standard German army infantry ammunition, the Spitzer-type Mauser 7.92 mm x 57 cartridge. A lightweight air-cooled version was adopted for use on aircraft and was known as the LMG 08/15, which stood for air-cooled machine gun, type 8, designed in 1915. It was manufactured, principally in the town of Spandau, just to the west of Berlin, by several companies and various different names, however, all parts were fully interchangeable. Apart from the synchronising mechanism and the barrel, the infantry and the aerial versions used identical parts in the feeding, loading and firing systems.

The German and the British machine guns, being the same basic design, responded almost identically to defective ammunition, to wear and tear and to the failure of component parts.

Cartridges were fed, loaded, locked in place, fired

and extracted somewhere between eight to ten times per second, and the lock had to withstand pressure between 45,000 and 55,000 pounds per square inch. The duty cycle of the complicated mechanism was quite heavy, and the moving parts and springs were prone to high rates of wear. In aerial use, the close-tolerance parts were subjected to the extreme cold of high altitude flying in winter; an environment for which the original design was not intended.

It was not uncommon for a fighter pilot, who had finally caught up with a high flying two-seater or airship, to have his machine guns fire just one round and then refuse to reload. The hump on the Sopwith Camel was actually a chamber which directed hot air from the engine onto the breech end of the guns to prevent that from happening.

The crank handles (or cocking handle/lever), which came in various shapes and sizes to suit aircraft types, made one backwards and forwards movement through an arc of about 110 degrees for each round fired. A jam would cause the handle to cease motion in one of four positions. The position in which the handle stopped was a reliable indicator of the basic type of jam which had occurred. Each position was known by a number, and machine-gun jams were described, for example, as 'a number two stoppage'.

A number 1 or 4 stoppage could be cleared in the

MAXIM-TYPE MACHINE-GUN STOPPAGE POSITIONS

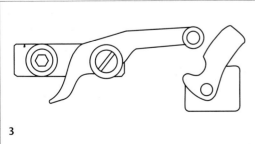

1

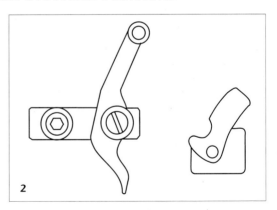

2

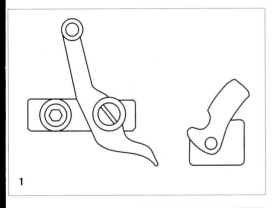

3

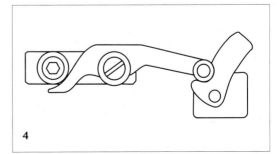

4

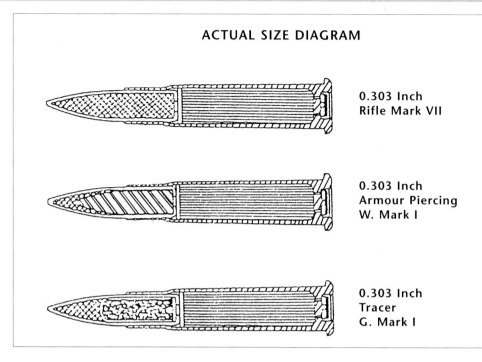

ACTUAL SIZE DIAGRAM

0.303 Inch
Rifle Mark VII

0.303 Inch
Armour Piercing
W. Mark I

0.303 Inch
Tracer
G. Mark I

air. The pilot would extract the defective cartridge by pulling the crank handle back to the far stop and then releasing it. The spring return would feed the next cartridge into the firing chamber.

A number 2 stoppage caused by a tight cartridge case could often be cleared in the air. A small hammer, sometimes a wooden mallet, (secured by a strap) was carried in the cockpit, and the pilot would apply it vigorously to the crank arm to force it forwards to position 4. The expression: 'the pilot hammered his machine gun', means exactly that; not as portrayed in the movies as beating on the breech with clenched fists.

A number 2 stoppage, caused by the previous cartridge case having separated during extraction, would have the new cartridge telescoped into the broken piece. The crank arm, when hammered, would not move. To clear such a jam was a major operation that could only be performed on the ground.

A number 3 stoppage was generally impossible to clear in the air. Both a number 2 and number 3 stoppage could be caused by the pilot himself, usually a novice who had indulged in over-long bursts of fire. This overheated the breech mechanism thus destroying the lubricant and causing the delicate parts to seize.

A component failure, frozen moisture, dirt and/or congealed lubricant could also cause any one of the four types of stoppages.

Vickers Machine-Gun Stoppage Positions

With the constant improvement in rifle design, muzzle velocities began to exceed 2,000 feet per minute. The result was that the soft round-nosed lead bullets such as the British Mark VI then used would disintegrate inside the human body causing really complicated wounds. Fragments of lead were spread over a large body area to no purpose.

The 1907 Hague Convention produced an agreement between the major European powers that lead bullets would have a pointed nose and that the lead would be fully encased in a hard metal jacket. The result is known as a Spitzer-shape (or type) bullet.

The aerodynamic Spitzer shape, when spun by a rifled barrel, was stable in flight and had excellent accuracy.

The British version, the Mark VII cartridge when fired from a 0.303" rifled barrel, as in Lee-Enfield army rifles or in Vickers and Lewis machine guns, had a nominal muzzle velocity of 2,440 feet per second (1,664 mph) and was spun by the rifling at about 175,800 rpm. In flight the speed and rpm would gradually decrease, but even after having travelled half a mile the bullets were still supersonic. Bullets which passed close by could be heard quite clearly.

Unfortunately at ranges over 300 yards the lighter weight tracer bullet did not conform exactly to the trajectory of the rifle bullet; it lost height rapidly. Pilots who lifted the nose of their fighter to correct their aim, often achieved exactly the opposite of their intent.

In daytime, tracer ammunition could only be seen from directly behind the gun which had fired it for the trace was actually a bright pinpoint of light from inside the bullet. Stories which make reference to 'seeing flaming tracers' are pure journalistic invention.

APPENDIX J: RECOMMENDATION RESULTING IN THE AWARD OF A BAR TO BROWN'S DSC

Less than one week after the death of von Richthofen, Major Butler began efforts to obtain an award for Captain Brown. His initial attempt to obtain the Distinguished Service Order was unsuccessful as this high award requires great bravery in heavy fighting or an above average period in action or command producing material results. A suitable award for having shot down Germany's greatest ace was thought to be a Bar to his Distinguished Service Cross. Had the event not been so close to the formation of the RAF it may well have produced not a Bar to the DSC but the new RAF equivalent to the Navy's DSC or the Army's MC, the Distinguished Flying Cross.

Butler's recommendation was submitted as follows:

Commanding Officer,
22nd Wing,
Royal Air Force

I wish to recommend the under mentioned Officer for immediate award for marked skill and gallantry in aerial fighting during the present operations, particularly on the occasions mentioned below.

Captain A. R. Brown, D.S.C.

April 21st. 'Dived on formation of 15 to 20 Albatros Scouts D5's and Fokker Triplanes, two of which got on my tail and I came out. Went back again and dived on pure red Triplane which was firing on Lieut. May. I got a long burst into him and he went down vertical and was observed to crash by Lieut. Mellersh and Lieut. May.' Engagement took place over Vaux-sur-Somme at about 11 a.m. Note. This machine crashed in our lines and pilot was subsequently identified as Captain Baron Richthofen.

April 12th. 'Dived on two Fokker Triplanes over Warfusee-Abancourt followed by Lt's Mellersh, Mackenzie and Lomas. Lt. Mackenzie dived on one Triplane and fired about 100 rounds. E.A. went down vertical and Lt. Mackenzie lost sight of him. I observed it going down but could not watch him right down. Capt. Brown & Lt. Mellersh dived on the other Triplane. Each fired about 200 rounds. E.A. then went down vertical and we followed him down. Lt. Mackenzie & Capt. Brown observed burst of flame come out of him then. Followed him down to 500 feet when he came out of dive. Capt. Brown and Lt. Mellersh opened fire again. E.A. carried on gliding and looked as if pilot was landing or was dead and machine gliding automatically.' Note. Confirmed in R.A.F. Communiqué No.2. April 12th 1 brought down and 1 driven down out of control.

March 22nd. 'Dived from 15,000 feet on 7 E.A. two-seaters. At first dived on one after another keeping E.A. from getting above us. Picked one and fired about 100 rounds into him at fairly close range. He did climbing left hand turns right in front of me while I was firing then went into vertical dive and I lost him under left wing.' Engagement occurred N.E. of Forêt d'Houthulst whilst escorting a French Caudron. Confirmed by pilot of Caudron (as per RNAS Communiqué No 18) to have crashed.

February 2nd. 'I dived on 2 Albatros two-seaters over Forêt d'Houthulst and opened fire on one getting in about 100 rounds when the other two-seater began to get above me. I turned on him and fired about 350 rounds. Both E.A. disappeared in the mist after I had turned to dive again.'

This Officer was awarded the D.S.C., in October 1917, whilst with this Squadron.

C H Butler, Major
Commanding 209 Squadron R.A.F.

In the Field.
April 26th 1918.

The award of a Bar was announced in 22 Wing Routine Order No.552 dated 11 May 1918. The presentation was made in Toronto on 4 November 1919 by the Prince of Wales. The citation was as follows:

Announcement of award of 'Bar to the Distinguished Service Cross to Lieut. (Hon. Capt.) Arthur Roy Brown, D.S.C., R.A.F'; in *London Gazette*, Fourth Supplement to 18 June 1918, published 21 June:

For conspicuous gallantry and devotion to duty. On 21st April, 1918, while leading a patrol of six scouts he attacked a formation of 20 hostile scouts. He personally engaged two Fokker triplanes, which he drove off; then seeing that one of our machines was being attacked and apparently hard pressed, he dived on the hostile scout, firing the while. This scout, a Fokker triplane nose-dived to the ground. Since the award of the Distinguished Service Cross he has destroyed several other enemy aircraft and has shown great dash and enterprise in attacking enemy troops from low altitude despite heavy anti-aircraft fire.

APPENDIX K: LATER CLAIMS TO FAME

1. Sergeant Alfred George Franklyn

Around 1929 English newspapers carried a report that the real victor over the Red Devil might have been Sergeant A G Franklyn who had been in charge of Section 110, 'F'; Anti-Aircraft Battery of the Royal Garrison Artillery. The Battery was composed of a number of 13-18 pounder guns mounted on lorries and they took up position on the road where needed. These were 18 pounder guns modified to fire 13 pound AA shells.

The former Sergeant stated that his battery had shot down a German aeroplane on 21 April 1918 and that it had crashed 200 yards from the battery's position. He further claimed that the pilot had been von Richthofen who had been chasing TWO Sopwith Camels at the time, and that the pilot of one later came to the battery to thank him.

Careful examination of Franklyn's written claim reveals that the position which he gave for his lorries on 21 April agrees with his description of the area; he was somewhere on the Corbie road about half a mile east of Bonnay (on one occasion he gave his position as 880 yards, and on another 800 yards). The ground between the lorries and a high ridge in front of them was occupied by Australian field batteries. A line drawn on a map certainly places a road as described, but it is the road from Corbie to Mericourt L'abbé, not that from Corbie to Bray.

Upon checking exactly what Franklyn wrote, the simple words 'Corbie road' will be found. These words were later clarified by others; they became the 'Corbie-Bray road'. This so-called clarification, which was not of the sergeant's doing, moved his lorries from the east side of the Morlancourt Ridge (the Ancre River side) to the west (Somme River) side. Taking the closest point of the Corbie to Bray road to the location described by Franklyn, the unnecessary literary help moved the lorries a minimum of 600 yards south-east from where he had placed them. If we take 200 yards from the crash site as a bench mark, and interpret it as favourably as possible, the lorries will have been moved by almost one mile and into clear German view. It will be recalled that the Corbie to Bray road was considered to be dangerous in daylight and that vehicular traffic either moved along it at night or very rapidly.

The War Diary of the 4th AA Defences records 'F' Battery as having shot down a German aeroplane on 22 April. Franklyn's claim is not helped by another witness, Lieutenant P Hutton, who claims that the two aeroplanes were DeHavilland DH5s. These machines had a very distinctive back-stagger of their top wing but unfortunately, the DH5 was no longer in service in France in April 1918.

Franklyn sent a detailed hand-written account of the action to John Coltman in which he stated that the reports that von Richthofen was flying a Fokker Triplane were untrue! According to him he had been flying an Albatros biplane. The plain truth is that during a long battle there are no weekend breaks to separate the days and they soon tended to blend together. For one person to recall exactly when something happened, albeit only about ten days earlier, he would often have to ask somebody else or to consult the War Diary. 'F' Battery definitely shot down a German aeroplane which crashed nearby, but one day later than the Richthofen affair.

2. Corporal William C Gamble

In June 1984, in Volume 55, No.2 of the *Journal of the Royal Historical Society* of Victoria, Australia, there appeared an article by Ronald East, on the autobiography, itself unpublished, written in 1978 by former Corporal Gamble who had served with the 25th Machine Gun Company in WW1.

Gamble described how he saw three Triplanes flying between Le Hamel and Villers-Bretonneux. One of them separated from the other two and dived down to attack a British aeroplane which had been flying too low down for Gamble to see. A standard story of von Richthofen chasing May up the cliff and over to the north-east towards the 55th and 53rd Batteries then follows. Gamble did not see Brown attack the Triplane, that would have been hidden from him by the terrain.

Gamble and his crew opened fire on the red Triplane after it levelled off over the crest and headed north. He supplied two sketches, one horizontal and the other vertical, which Ronald East included in the article. They depict the trajectory of his shots. Aiming in front of the fuselage, he fired a whole pannier of 47 rounds upwards and semi-frontally at the left-hand side of the Triplane. The Triplane turned right – north-east – and he remarked to his crew: 'Well, at least we saved our chap's life.' He marvelled that an aeroplane could pass through so many bullets without the pilot being injured, although from later information received, he came to believe that he had hit him. Shortly afterwards, the other two German aeroplanes came within range and he opened fire on them too, but without any observed results.

With the German attack expected any day, before he could report the event to his officer, his gun team was moved down to the low ground between Le Hamel and Corbie. On the 24th he was caught in a barrage of poison gas shells, and then wounded in the head the next day, eventually losing an eye. He never did file a claim.

Corporal Gamble obviously fired at the von Richthofen Triplane and may even have put a few shots through some fabric, but his sketches show clearly that he could not have inflicted the right-to-left wound.

3. Private Ernest Boore

The London *Daily Express*, 20 March 1995, published a

story sub-titled Foot Soldier Grabbed Rifle to Shoot Down German Ace, says family. Private Boore's grandson said: 'I can remember Grandad holding up his trigger finger and telling me, "That's the finger that shot down the Red Baron."'

Ernie's close friend Bill Carless, who was still alive at the time, clarified that Ernie had tears in his eyes as he explained how he had seen the Red Baron firing at this Canadian. Ernie, who had no weapon at the time, snatched a rifle from a New Zealander, pointed it and hit the Baron with a single shot.

The Daily Express consulted the RAF Museum, Hendon, London, where they were told that Ernie's story was possible. It agreed with Professor Nixon's medical report. The Museum also confirmed [the obvious], that Captain Brown's squadron had forced [sic] von Richthofen down so low that he could have been hit by a shot from the ground.

If Private Boore formed part of Lieutenant Wood's platoon or was somewhere near it, the story is possible. The only error present is in the clarification provided by an official at Hendon, viz: the reason why the Baron was flying so low down.

Unfortunately the reporter who wrote the story, did not mention where Private Boore was standing at the time which makes it impossible to evaluate his claim until such information is discovered or provided.

4. Private Theodore Henzell

A newspaper clipping with the page heading missing but known to be from Brisbane, around 1986, presented the claim of a pensioner who, in 1918, was serving in the Australian 3rd Trench Mortar Battery. Due to illness, he was on light duties and was serving as a batman to a lieutenant (unidentified) who was stationed in Vaux-sur-Somme.

Private Henzell said that on 21 April, at Vaux, he watched a German aeroplane shoot down two British observation balloons. The aeroplane changed direction and was heading directly towards him. With his .303 rifle and standing slightly to the left of the flight path, he fired one shot at it from about 80 yards range. The German aeroplane, which he defined as a Fokker, nosed downwards and crashed about 1,000 yards away near some British trenches. He claimed that the angle of his shot agreed with the results of: '... years of painstaking research .... into the medical records which showed that he [von R] had been killed by a bullet which entered his chest on the left side, piercing his heart and exited behind the right shoulder.' Unfortunately the only painful thing for Private Henzell is that the true original medical records state no such thing, although some edited combinations of the First and the Second Reports do.

The Baron, who regarded a live, effective pilot as more valuable to Germany that a dead hero, would never go near an observation balloon, and in his earlier career was fortunate enough never to be ordered to do so. There is no evidence that he ever even contemplated such a move in his entire combat career. Very wise.

5. Trooper William Howell

In 1969, the Melbourne newspaper, The Age, published the story of a member of the Australian Light Horse, Trooper W Howell. He stated that he had fired his .303 rifle at the Triplane that was flying at a height equivalent to about 'three gum trees'. The Australian eucalyptus (or gum) tree grows quite tall, so the height at which he placed the Triplane is quite possible as von Richthofen was climbing, heading east after surviving the shots fired by Buie, Evans - and Gamble. Howell was supposed to be quite good at deflection shooting and allowing for the wind.

Unfortunately the reporter who wrote this story did not mention where Howell was standing either, which also makes it impossible to evaluate his claim until such information can be found.

The above stories are just a few of the many which have appeared over the years in various forms. Most have some basis of truth, but the only thing that brings them together is the fact that all eventually become part of the Richthofen legend. Author Norman Franks remembers vividly looking at a display of WW1 model aeroplanes some years ago outside a shop window in Twickenham, Middlesex.

An elderly gentleman came along and stopped, looking keenly at a large model of the Baron's red Fokker Triplane. He was obviously eager to relate some tale about it as he turned first to the left and then to the right to see if anyone was in earshot. Finally looking behind him, he saw Franks. Without hesitation the man said: 'I saw him come down, you know.' Franks looked interested. 'Yes, he was quite near me and he climbed out of his cockpit, gave his iron cross to one Tommy and his scarf to another, then they took him away to prison camp.' A companion standing next to Franks, as the old gentleman walked away, the smile of recollection on his face, enquired why Franks did not chase after him and ask him more about it. The reader can imagine what Franks said in response!

The thing is, the old gentleman believed unquestioningly that the German pilot was Baron von Richthofen. He had obviously witnessed something similar while in France and over the intervening years he had associated this with Richthofen because that became a well known event. Or was he just shooting a line…?

INDEX OF NAMES